THE

LIBERAL SOUL

THE
LIBERAL SOUL

APPLYING THE GOSPEL OF JESUS CHRIST IN POLITICS

Richard Davis

Salt Lake City, 2014
Greg Kofford Books

Greg Kofford Books
P.O. Box 1362
Draper, UT 84020
www. koffordbooks.com

Also available in ebook.

2018   17   16   15   14   5   4   3   2   1

Library of Congress Cataloging-in-Publication Data

Davis, Richard, 1955- author.
  The liberal soul : applying the gospel of Jesus Christ in politics / Richard Davis.
      pages cm
  Includes index.
  ISBN 978-1-58958-583-6 (pbk.)
  1. Liberalism--Religious aspects--Church of Jesus Christ of Latter-day Saints.
2. Liberalism--Religious aspects--Mormon Church. 3. Mormons--Political
activity. 4. Religion and politics. 5. Christianity and politics. I. Title.
  BX8643.P6D38 2014
  261.70973--dc23
                        2014015451

The liberal soul shall be made fat:
and he that watereth shall be
watered also himself. —Proverbs 11:25

Dedicated to those I have known
who model characteristics of the liberal soul

TABLE OF CONTENTS

INTRODUCTION

I remember sitting in a priesthood meeting one Sunday in a ward in up-state New York when the instructor asked the class whether we thought being members of the Church had made us more liberal or more conservative. It was a provocative question, and probably one that would never be included in an actual Church manual. Nevertheless, the question and the answers have remained with me many years later.

It wasn't that the answers of several other class members surprised me. They all said that Church membership had made them more conservative. Their argument was that the Church had taught them to be more cautious with their money than they might otherwise be. They also reflected that they were more likely to oppose the social trends of the day, a position that like-wise made them more conservative, particularly compared with many who were not LDS.

I had never thought about this question before, and my answer surprised me. I said I thought I was probably more liberal than I would have been without the gospel. Because of the tenets of the gospel, I was more likely to view others as my brothers and sisters—fellow children of God—and not just people, and I was more willing to give my money and other resources to serve them. I'm not sure how much I would do that were it not for the gospel of Jesus Christ.

Liberal or Conservative?

As a student of politics, I understand that these ideological terms of "liberal" and "conservative" are so vague that they seem to have lost any inherent meanings. Traditional conservatism, New Right conservatism, neo-conservative, compassionate conservative—these have become muddled in most people's minds. Yet regardless of the adjective attached, most Latter-day Saints today, at least in the United States and Canada, consider themselves conservatives. By contrast, the term "liberal" is a largely pejorative description in the minds of many Latter-day Saints. Many Latter-day Saints would say it is an ideology no active Latter-day Saint would share.

The answers of the other brethren in the priesthood class then were predictable. In fact, given the general perception about liberals within the Church, I would not have expected them to answer otherwise. Admitting that one is "liberal" and a Latter-day Saint is not common. This is not true only in the Church. For much of American society generally, "liberal" has lost much of its favorable connotation. More people in the United States today consider themselves conservative than liberal.

That has not always been the case. In 1946, when Americans were asked whether they would want to belong to a liberal party or a conservative one, 57 percent chose the liberal option. In 1965, another survey found that as many people called themselves liberal as called themselves conservative.[1] However, since the 1970s and 1980s, conservatism has become a more popular ideological label and liberal a less popular one. According to a 2011 survey, 41 percent of Americans self-identified as conservative while only 21 percent viewed themselves as liberals.[2]

That tendency toward conservatism among the general public today in the United States is even stronger among Latter-day Saints. For Latter-day Saints, the gap between the percent who consider themselves conservative versus those who are liberal is much larger. A Pew Research Center study of Mormons in the United States found that 60 percent of Latter-day Saints self-identified as conservatives while only 10 percent considered themselves liberals.[3]

The term "liberal" has become a shunned appellation among Latter-day Saints because it has acquired such a negative connotation. Given how derisively the term "liberal" has been used by many Latter-day Saint writers, politicians, and even some Church leaders, it would be surprising if Latter-day Saints did not have a negative impression of "liberal." Indeed, one apostle attempted to write liberals out of the Church. While serving as president of the Quorum

---

1. Gallup Poll (AIPO), January 1946, retrieved from the iPOLL Databank, The Roper Center for Public Opinion Research, University of Connecticut, http://www.ropercenter.uconn.edu.erl.lib.byu.edu/data_access/ipoll/ipoll.html (accessed May 14, 2012); and Survey Research Service Amalgam, June 1965, retrieved from the iPOLL Databank, The Roper Center for Public Opinion Research, University of Connecticut, http://www.ropercenter.uconn.edu.erl.lib.byu.edu/data_access/ipoll/ipoll.html (accessed May 14, 2012).

2. Lydia Saad, "U.S. Political Ideology Stable with Conservatives Leading," Gallup.com, http://www.gallup.com/poll/148745/Political-Ideology-Stable-Conservatives-Leading.aspx (accessed August 1, 2011).

3. "A Portrait of Mormons in the U.S." The Pew Forum on Religion and Public Life, July 24, 2009, http://pewforum.org/Christian/Mormon/A-Portrait-of-Mormons-in-the-US.aspx (accessed January 8, 2013).

of the Twelve, President Ezra Taft Benson remarked that it was incompatible to be a liberal Democrat and a good Latter-day Saint.[4] Even though LDS Public Affairs issued a statement at the time explaining that President Benson was speaking for himself and not the Church, as evidenced by the number of times I have heard this remark repeated (almost always without the term "liberal") President Benson's remark, or their version of it, seems to have stuck in Church members' minds much more than the disclaimer.

Where did this antipathy toward liberals come from? How did Latter-day Saints—both among the membership and the leadership—become suspicious and hostile toward liberals and conclude that ideological conservatives were closer to the gospel of Jesus Christ? Why have these ideological terms become so tightly bound in the minds of Latter-day Saints with wrong (liberals) and right (conservatives)?

Most likely, the antipathy toward the term comes because of its current association with two concepts. One is the idea of the welfare state. Liberals are viewed as those who believe in the use of a welfare state to aid the poor and needy. "Welfare state liberalism" is a negative term in the writings of some Church members who view social welfare liberalism as equivalent to communism. This concern was a recurring theme in the work of LDS writers such as Cleon Skousen, Duane Crowther, Elder H. Verlan Andersen, and, of course, President Benson. Rarely has there been a defense of the welfare state in the rhetoric of Latter-day Saint writings about politics.

The other concept, and one that is probably of greater concern for Latter-day Saints today, is the association with cultural liberalism. The Equal Rights Amendment (ERA), abortion, gay rights, and gay marriage are all issues that have sparked cultural wars in the United States. However, cultural liberalism actually originated with the 1960s movements advocating free love, recreational drug use, and a set of U.S. Supreme Court decisions that limited censorship of free speech and resulted in increased permissiveness in media such as newspapers, radio, and television.

Individual Church leaders decried the societal changes occurring in the 1960s and early 1970s as contrary to common decency and as assaults on marriage and the family. The Church as an organization became involved in these culture wars when taking institutional stances through First Presidency statements opposing the legalization of abortion, the ERA, and state sanctioning of same-sex marriage. Repeated conference talks and articles in Church

---

4. John Dart, "Mormon Leader's Life 'A Miracle,' Benson Says: Kimball Eulogized by Likely Sucessor," *Los Angeles Times*, November 10, 1985, http://articles.latimes.com/1985-11-10/news/mn-3360_1_spencer-w-kimball (accessed January 8, 2013).

publications urged Church members to act to save the family by taking public policy positions in conjunction with those advocated by the Church.[5]

In addition, the Church itself joined lobbying efforts by other organizations such as the U.S. Conference of Catholic Bishops, the Family Research Council, and the National Organization for Marriage. Those efforts were publicized broadly to members, who were encouraged to become involved in fights to stop the ERA and same-sex marriage. Proposition 8 in California in 2008 became the most publicized electoral battleground between opponents of same-sex marriage, which was banned through that initiative, and proponents of equality of marriage opportunities for both heterosexual and homosexual couples.

Those who took the opposite position from the Church were viewed as liberals on these issues. The term became synonymous with moral permissiveness, a disregard for traditional values, and a willingness to destroy marriage and the family in order to uphold personal choice and acceptance of various lifestyles. Church members were warned not to adopt such beliefs.

The Church's involvement in the culture wars softened somewhat after the California Proposition 8 vote. However, even before Proposition 8, the Church sought to convey the message that it was not homophobic. In a 2004 interview, President Gordon B. Hinckley said the Church was pro-family, not anti-gay.[6] Immediately after the vote, the Church Public Affairs Department issued a statement that it "does not object to rights for same-sex couples regarding hospitalization and medical care, fair housing and employment rights, or probate rights, so long as these do not infringe on the integrity of the traditional family or the constitutional rights of churches."[7]

A year after that vote, which Prop 8 supporters narrowly won, the Church voiced support for local non-discrimination ordinances in Utah protecting the right of gays to be protected in housing and employment. Public support

---

5. See, for example, Spencer W. Kimball, "God Will Not Be Mocked," *Ensign*, November 1974, 4–9; Boyd K. Packer, "The Equal Rights Amendment," *Ensign*, March 1977, 6–9 ; Russell M. Nelson, "Reverence for Life," *Ensign*, May 1985, 11–14; Boyd K. Packer, "Covenants," *Ensign*, November 1990, 84–86 ; and Russell M. Nelson, "Abortion: An Assault on the Defenseless," *Ensign*, October 2008, 32–37.

6. "A Conversation with Gordon B. Hinckley, President of the Church of Jesus Christ of Latter Day [sic] Saints," CNN.com Transcripts, December 26, 2004, http://transcripts.cnn.com/TRANSCRIPTS/0412/26/lkl.01.html (accessed January 8, 2013).

7. "Church Responds to Same-Sex Marriage Votes," Church of Jesus Christ of Latter-day Saints Newsroom, November 5, 2008, http://www.mormonnewsroom.org/ldsnewsroom/eng/news-releases-stories/church-responds-to-same-sex-marriage-votes (accessed January 8, 2013).

for those ordinances in Utah skyrocketed after the Church announcement.[8] Despite the weakening of the association of gay rights with Church opposition, the association with liberalism is still viewed negatively. One piece of evidence is the 2011 survey noted above showing that relatively few Latter-day Saints are willing to call themselves liberals.

Remarkably, the "liberal" problem, as perceived by a majority of Latter-day Saints, is of recent vintage. A change has occurred in the past forty years that has given "liberal" a negative connotation. This change is linked to political rhetoric decrying the welfare state and condemning cultural liberalism that has emanated from Republican Party candidates, but also from presidents such as Ronald Reagan and George W. Bush. Latter-day Saints have reflected national trends. However, those trends have been greatly magnified by some Church leaders' writings and statements, as noted above, as well as by the official Church role in political lobbying related to these issues.

Prior to the culture wars of the 1970s, there did not seem to be a deep-seated hostility by most Latter-day Saints toward the term "liberal." For example, even though liberalism was associated with the Democratic Party, Latter-day Saints were willing to vote for Democrats. Utah voted consistently Democratic from 1932 to 1948 and Democratic presidential candidate Lyndon Johnson won the state of Utah in the 1964 presidential election against Republican Barry Goldwater, who should have been a popular winner given his arch-conservative ideology. Democrats such as Frank Moss, Wayne Owens, and David King represented Utah in Congress during the 1950s through the early 1970s. Democrats Calvin Rampton and Scott Matheson served as governor for twelve and eight years respectively from the 1960s through the 1980s, and the majority control of the Utah State Legislature seesawed between the two parties during the 1960s and early 1970s.

The more recent antipathy toward being "liberal" and the embrace of ideological conservatism does not have scriptural origins. For example, the word "conservative" is never used in the Book of Mormon, Doctrine and Covenants, or Pearl of Great Price. Nor does it appear anywhere in the King James Version of the Bible.

The term "liberal" does appear several times in the scriptures, and not in the negative way that characterizes some current writings and speeches. Obviously those mentions do not refer specifically to contemporary political ideologies or issues. But they do illuminate a certain approach to each other in society that historically has been part of the gospel of Jesus Christ. And

8. Rosemary Winters, "'Dramatic Jump' with Utahns for Gay Rights," *Salt Lake Tribune*, January 29, 2010, at http://www.sltrib.com/news/ci_14297021 (accessed December 13, 2013).

that has applicability for Latter-day Saints today who contemplate how their political views should correspond to the gospel of Jesus Christ. Let's see how "liberal" is treated in the scriptures to help us understand the lack of roots of this antipathy in canonized scripture.

In the Old Testament, Isaiah describes the day when justice will be meted out: "The vile person shall be no more called liberal, nor the churl [miser] said to be bountiful." In contrast, the liberal will be rewarded for righteous acts: "The liberal deviseth liberal things; and by liberal things shall he stand" (Isa. 32:5, 8).

In the New Testament, "liberal" is an adjective to describe how Heavenly Father treats His children. In the Epistle of James, we are told that when His children ask of Him, God "giveth liberally to all men" (James 1:5). Interestingly, while "liberal" is often a pejorative in our society today, including among Church members, in this verse it is applied to describe Him in whose image we all were made.

It also is used positively in the Book of Mormon. There, too, the term "liberal" is a synonym for generosity, inclusiveness, selflessness, and openness toward others. In Alma, the term is used to describe how everyone was included in the gospel: "Now, I would that ye should understand that the word of God was liberal unto all, that none were deprived of the privilege of assembling themselves together to hear the word of God" (Alma 6:5). Also, in Alma, the saints of that day were described as generous in their treatment of the poor and needy:

> And thus, in their prosperous circumstances, they did not send away any who were naked, or that were hungry, or that were sick, or that had not been nourished; and they did not set their hearts upon riches; therefore they were *liberal* to all, both bond and free, both male and female, whether out of the church or in the church, having no respect to persons as to those who stood in need. (Alma 1:30; emphasis mine)

This scriptural usage of "liberal" says less about the ancient origins of the term than it does about language in the sixteenth through the early nineteenth centuries. For example, other versions of the Bible written during other time periods use other terms. The Douay version of 1899 and the Wycliff Bible of the fourteenth century refer to "the soul which blesseth" instead of the adjective "liberal." The New International Version, published in 1973, refers to "the generous person." Similarly, the Book of Mormon's usage of "liberal" would have been related to its common usage in early nineteenth-century English and its frequent reference in the most common English version of the Bible of the day—the King James Version, as just discussed.

The term "liberal" would not have had political connotations in the early 1800s because the concept of liberalism as a political ideology emerged later in the nineteenth century. For example, Noah Webster's 1828 dictionary defined "liberal" as "generous, ample, large," as well as "free, open, candid." A liberal education was one that was broad.[9] However, by the 1913 version, "liberal" had been expanded to include political references such as "one who favors greater freedom in political or religious matters; an opponent of the established systems; a reformer; in English politics, a member of the Liberal party.[10] And today's Merriam-Webster dictionary highlights the political implications when the first definition of "liberal" is "believing that government should be active in supporting social and political change: relating to or supporting political liberalism."[11]

The scriptural usage of "liberal" is not ideological as much as it is descriptive of certain personal characteristics of generosity, magnanimity, and charity. It is the more modern usage that has acquired political overtones, particularly negative ones. Let's discuss how "liberal" has morphed from a term connected to positive personal characteristics to one evoking apostasy or adherence to political views seen by many Latter-day Saints as antithetical to Church teachings and doctrines.

Church leaders have used the term "liberal" in an affirmative sense and not just a negative one. These uses take "liberal" to mean open, accepting, and broad-minded. For example, Elder L. Tom Perry once explained that service in the Church had given him "a much more liberal, well-rounded education than a college degree could possibly bestow."[12] Joseph Smith once wrote that he had "the most liberal sentiments, and feelings of charity toward all sects, parties, and denominations."[13] He also associated the term "liberal" with the attributes of God, once declaring that "Our Heavenly Father is more liberal in His views, and boundless in His mercies and blessings, than we are ready to believe or receive."[14] President James E. Faust once offered this

9. Webster's Dictionary 1828 – Online Edition, *American Dictionary of the English Language*, http://webstersdictionary1828.com/ (accessed February 27, 2014).

10. Webster's 1913 Dictionary, http://www.webster-dictionary.org/definition/liberal (accessed February 27, 2014).

11. Merriam-Webster Dictionary, *s.v.* "liberal," at http://www.merriam-webster.com/dictionary/liberal (accessed April 3, 2014).

12. L. Tom Perry, "Nauvoo—A Demonstration of Faith," *Ensign*, May 1980, http://lds.org/ensign/1980/05/nauvoo-a-demonstration-of-faith (accessed January 8, 2013).

13. Joseph Smith, Letter to Isaac Galland, March 22, 1839, *Times and Seasons*, February 1840, 55–56.

14. Joseph Fielding Smith, ed., *Teachings of the Prophet Joseph Smith* (Salt Lake City: Deseret Book, 1977 printing), 241.

self-description: "I am a conservative on fiscal and property matters, and I am liberal in terms of human values and human rights."[15]

Members also have been urged to be liberal in their giving to the poor. This usage often has been narrowly focused on fast offerings, but it also has the broader application of caring for the poor. President Thomas S. Monson repeated an admonition by President Joseph F. Smith that members should provide, if possible, "a liberal donation to be so reserved and donated to the poor."[16] And Presiding Bishop H. David Burton urged members to be "liberal in our contributions for the care of those who suffer."[17]

Clearly, there have been negative uses as well. Occasionally, these examples have referred to Christian churches that Church leaders suggest do not teach traditional Christian doctrines. But the term "liberal" also has been used in a political sense to describe those who are not supportive of the government's military policies, particularly in time of war. In a general conference talk given not long after the Vietnam War, Elder Vaughn J. Featherstone related Captain Moroni's prayer for liberty and then added: "What a contrast to the attitude of some of our liberals."[18]

Sometimes these references have been applied to those who are not faithful members of the Church, who are sometimes termed "liberal Mormons." President Harold B. Lee defined a "liberal Mormon" as "one who does not have a testimony."[19] Elder Russell M. Nelson lumped "liberal" in with others who are labeled by Church members as sinful: "People tend to become what is expected of them. Labels convey those expectations. . . . Yet, in spite of the obvious dangers, we are prone to label one another. 'Smoker,' 'drinker,' 'inactive,' 'liberal,' 'unorthodox' are but a few terms applied, as though we cannot separate the doer from the deed."[20] This usage does not refer to generosity as much as it does an alleged laxity or permissiveness in living the doctrines of the Church.

---

15. Peggy Fletcher Stack, "Faust Pulled for Democrats," *Salt Lake Tribune*, August 12, 2007, http://www.sltrib.com/news/ci_6605032 (accessed January 8, 2013).

16. Thomas S. Monson, "Goal beyond Victory," October 1988, http://www.lds.org/general-conference/1988/10/goal-beyond-victory (accessed January 1, 2013).

17. H. David Burton, "Go, and Do Thou Likewise," *Ensign*, May 1997, http://lds.org/ensign/1997/05/go-and-do-thou-likewise (accessed January 8, 2013).

18. Vaughn J. Featherstone, "But Watchman, What of the Night?" *Ensign*, November 1975, http://lds.org/ensign/1975/11/but-watchman-what-of-the-night (accessed January 8, 2013).

19. Harold. B. Lee, "The Iron Rod," *Ensign*, June 1971, http://lds.org/ensign/1971/06/the-iron-rod (accessed January 8, 2013).

20. Russell M. Nelson, "Love Thy Neighbor," *Ensign*, January 1987, http://lds.org/ensign/1987/01/love-thy-neighbor (accessed January 8, 2013).

The word "liberal" is full of contradictory meanings in current LDS usage. On one hand, it has become a pejorative term when used to describe one who is permissive and not fully living specific commandments such as the Word of Wisdom. On the other hand, it is a positive term when applied to those who reach out to others and are willing to be generous with their own resources.

The term "conservative" does not have as many meanings or negative associations in the minds of Latter-day Saints. Typically, it is used to describe modesty in dress and grooming. For example, missionaries are urged to dress conservatively. Or it refers to someone who is not extravagant in his or her lifestyle. It also can mean one who favors preserving sacred and important things, as in the responsibility to "hold fast that which is good" (1 Thess. 5:21).

Yet in reality, it does have negative connotations. It can mean one who is slow to act. Elder Loren C. Dunn of the Seventy once observed that his views about missionary work were "very conservative" until President Spencer W. Kimball urged the Church to "lengthen our stride."[21] Sometimes it is used to describe those who are opposed to change and even reactionary in seeking to turn back progress. Latter-day Saints who resist shifts in Church policy, such as the ordination of blacks to the priesthood or support for laws that prohibit discrimination against gays, are examples of conservatives unwilling to change. "Conservative" can be negative as well, although the term is rarely used as such in LDS culture.

Both "liberal" and "conservative" as terms have their favorable and unfavorable applications. Yet, the approaches of both are important in how a society functions. A society that cherishes one at the expense of the other and rewards association with one while denigrating the other loses essential societal character traits of service, mercy, and magnanimity.

This is problematic for any society, but particularly so for a Zion society seeking to follow the example of the Savior. Without a personal liberalism that enriches and enlivens the soul, discipleship is impossible. How can a society give liberally or "be liberal to all," as Heavenly Father is, if it so uniformly rejects liberalism? How can such a society manifest discipleship to Christ?

It would seem that Church members, particularly in the United States, are at that point now where the "liberal" side, in a political sense, is out of favor. The term "conservative" has been used so approvingly (and "liberal" so unfavorably) that LDS society has lost an appreciation for the liberal traits every society sorely needs to function adequately. Within LDS culture, Church members have heard so much about conservatism that liberality in compassion for the poor too often has been trumped by fiscal conservatism. Similarly,

---

21. Loren C. Dunn, "Receiving a Prophet," April 1983, http://www.lds.org/general-conference/1983/04/receiving-a-prophet (accessed January 8, 2013).

tolerance, acceptance, and broad-mindedness have become unpopular traits compared with conservatism and therefore are not emphasized.

Perhaps worst of all, optimism about the future, typically associated with progressivism, has been replaced by fear, dread, and suspicion. Church members worry about how evil the world will become rather than looking at what progress has been made in various ways—economic, social, and even religious. Instead of appreciating how these advances have contributed to the growth of the Church and improved the lives of humans generally, they concentrate on the negative and their own perception of the inevitable gloom and doom coming in the future.

This emphasis on conservatism has placed Church members out of balance. The positive traits associated with liberalism—compassion, mercy, faith, tolerance, generosity— all should be more positively portrayed as a part of LDS culture. The purpose of this book is to help restore the role of liberalism as essential to the Church member who seeks to become a disciple of Christ.

The Liberal Soul

One of my favorite scriptures is Proverbs 11:25 because it describes the "liberal soul." I love that term. That type of person, Proverbs says, is one who "shall be made fat; and he that watereth shall be watered also himself."

"Liberal" in the sense of this verse may be viewed in narrow terms, such as providing material needs for others. Indeed, that is an important part of being a "liberal soul." And the promise is that such persons will not suffer for their liberality; rather, the Lord will take care of them. Moreover, their giving will provide them with abundance, not the scarcity that we assume will follow from giving away what we have to others.

But I believe that this term also has a broader meaning in this scripture. Does it also mean liberality in terms of the treatment of others beyond temporal matters? Elder Alexander B. Morrison may have described it when he wrote that generosity, particularly to others who hate us, "is one of the most demanding requirements of Christian discipleship. . . . But hard though the commandment is, Jesus still requires such generosity of spirit as part of our service to Him."[22]

This kind of generosity is something other than just the bestowal of material things. It is an attitude toward other people, particularly those who are different or even hostile. Of course, we all know that such a situation is when the real test of generosity of spirit comes. It doesn't come when others praise

---

22. Alexander B. Morrison, "No More Strangers," *Ensign*, September 2000, http://www.lds.org/ensign/2000/09/no-more-strangers (accessed January 8, 2013).

us, easily share our values and views, or treat us well. It comes when they don't do any of those things.

The liberal soul is a magnanimous person—one who does good. The liberal soul is a person who thinks more about giving than receiving. I perceive the liberal soul as having an expansive view of the world and those who are in it. The liberal soul looks with mercy and compassion on others and seeks the creation of a society where everyone is treated as the daughter or son of God he or she really is.

We all know those who fit this characterization of the liberal soul. They are the people in our lives who are generous to others—both in terms of their time and resources. They are simply willing to share and urge others to do the same.

Their generosity of spirit extends to all. They cherish others. And because they do, they are willing to accept others, regardless of circumstances or sins. These are people who love others, seek to be inclusive rather than exclusive, and, therefore, are willing to do what they can to improve the lives of others. They see the world around them, and the future before them, in positive rather than negative terms.

The Liberal Soul, Society, and Government

I see the liberal soul as someone who considers the importance of the individual, the society, and government simultaneously rather than as separate, and typically conflicting, entities. The liberal soul views them as intertwined. The individual gives to the society in which he or she lives and is rewarded, in turn, in ways that help the individual. The society helps protect the individual and in turn is supported by the individual. The government is society's mechanism for carrying out those functions—serving and protecting the individual—through programs designed to educate citizens, offer economic opportunities, and provide temporal essentials in time of need.

The liberal soul understands the tendencies of human nature. The "natural man" that King Benjamin talks about is an "enemy to God." He or she must put off that natural man and, instead, take on the traits of a saint (Mosiah 3:19). The process of transforming from the natural man to the saint is one that we each experience if we desire to be a disciple of Christ.

This process is not one that we must experience alone. Rather, we have aids all around us. These include prayer and its accompanying personal inspiration, the scriptures that contain inspiring messages for our lives, the support of our family, and the organization of the Church with prophetic revelation and an infrastructure to help guide and direct individuals.

But must those means of assistance end there? Is it possible that society itself can aid individuals in seeing and realizing their God-given potential? Is it out of the question for the broader society in which we live to help us all to live full lives on earth and better ourselves together for celestial glory?

In the Church, we sometimes talk about a Zion society. But it is presented in one of two contexts: either as something in the distant scriptural past or as a community of the far-off future when the Savior reigns personally on the earth. It is a remote concept that we do not really believe can exist today. In fact, often Church members say it is an unrealistic concept because of the increasing wickedness of the current world.

However, early Church leaders believed they could create a Zion society on earth. Revelations to Joseph Smith on the United Order and the law of consecration were intended to begin the process of forming a Zion society. Brigham Young followed upon those earlier models when the Saints first came to Utah in the mid-1840s by also seeking to create Zion in the Rocky Mountains.

Early Church leaders did not think that a Zion society was so far away. They believed they could institute it here and now. Perhaps they were right. Maybe a Zion society is not so remote or distant as we may think. Perhaps it is attainable in this life and at this time. It may not be a perfect society or one where everyone is LDS. It may not be a society where every policy is to our liking or every governmental action is in accordance with our views. But is it not possible to form a society that is at least closer to the ideal we wish to achieve? Should we not work to bring about such a society?

What kind of society would it be? Could it be one where each individual is perceived as a child of God with divine lineage and attributes, but who is placed on this earth in a setting that challenges that divinity? Could it be a society that recognizes that natural man will sin, but neither condemns nor neglects that individual? Instead, the society assists that individual in achieving the goal of becoming Christ-like and eventually returning to Heavenly Father.

Such a society cherishes the goal of helping each individual fulfill his or her own purpose. It seeks to provide opportunity for growth—both temporal and spiritual. It desires to preserve the good in the status quo while making progress toward improvement.

However, the government of that society would need to structure the laws of the society to accomplish those ends. These include regulations that help individuals resist the temptations of the natural man. For example, such laws would prevent excessive selfishness that results in a class-based society where the most vulnerable—the poor, the aged, the young, the invalid—are neglected or abused and where attitudes of entitlement to riches are fostered. Other laws would punish individuals and organizations for abusing others and acting without regard for the well-being of others.

These laws are not designed to enhance governmental power but to help stimulate positive behavior in the individual and help each citizen of the society avoid the temptations of the natural man. They include, for example, a tax system that rewards individuals for giving to charitable causes, or laws that prevent the misuse of the environment in ways that benefit the individual in the short term despite long-term societal loss.

The liberal soul would want such a society to exist. But it is difficult to achieve such a society when the attitudes of those who should promote it are negative. As long as Latter-day Saints believe such a society cannot happen and should not happen today, then its achievement is difficult.

But who says it cannot and should not happen? Unfortunately, some LDS writers and speakers have been the promulgators of such a view. These pessimists fall in two broad, but different categories. One category consists of libertarians who see government as playing little role in assisting individuals economically. Beyond the protection of private property, the libertarian opposes society's role in anything. The basic premise is that everyone is "on their own." Society and its arm, government, should intervene as little as possible in the lives of individuals.[23]

The second group consists of the economic conservatives who concentrate on society and government's economic role. Bluntly, they argue that government should "get off our backs." The government should not regulate economic relationships, even though such interactions are the most susceptible to the natural man's tendencies and the consequences of deregulation lead to some of the most rampant abuses of fellow beings. The economic conservative typically is unconcerned about society's role beyond economics, while the libertarian opposes a government role in almost any area of life.

Both of these groups oppose government role as if government is the enemy, incapable of performing a positive role in society. Neither of these camps views society, through government, as having a role of helping lift people. Instead, government is primarily an oppressive medium. Neither understands the value of government as a tool to deal with social problems such as teen pregnancy, urban decay, and safe neighborhoods that plague many people and limit individuals' abilities to develop and improve.

Due to the influence of economic conservatives and libertarians in the Church, particularly in prominent positions, many Latter-day Saints also have no understanding of what society can achieve, through government and other means, to create the kind of society that all Latter-day Saints would like

---

23. It is important to note that Church leaders and members who have promoted economic libertarianism typically do not apply that libertarianism to social issues such as pornography, abortion, or same-sex marriage.

to live in. For example, prominent LDS politicians like Mitt Romney and Orrin Hatch have equated economic conservatism with gospel principles as if to suggest that there is no other way to view the relationship between the gospel and politics.

The Purpose of This Book

This book is a call to Latter-day Saints to become "liberal souls" and to apply that term to the various facets of our lives—personal relations, group interaction, and societal/governmental role. It is an articulation of an approach to government and politics that appreciates that society and government, along with the individual, play a part in the process of attaining the Zion society we desire. Indeed, the current focus on the individual or the local community that dominates LDS political writing, offers only part of the solution for bringing about that society. And through the disparagement of society and its governing role, the current approach actually makes the realization of such a society a more remote, rather than a more immediate, prospect.

The term "liberal" in the phrase "liberal soul," in this sense, goes beyond welfare state liberalism or cultural liberalism. Rather, it describes those who follow Jesus Christ in his love and acceptance of others, specifically in his care for the poor and the needy, his concern for the most vulnerable in society, and his compassion toward all. And it suggests a holistic approach to the application of this attitude.

That holistic method consists of three levels. These levels can be demonstrated by looking at the Savior's three types of audiences during his mortal ministry. First, he directed his teaching one-on-one. For example, he taught the woman at the well, the woman taken in adultery, and Peter when he told him to feed his sheep. But he also spoke to groups at various times—his disciples, those standing around at the temple or in the street, and large crowds gathered on hillsides or coasts to hear the gospel. Then, at times, he addressed society in general. For example, he spoke to all of the inhabitants of Jerusalem when he said "O Jerusalem, Jerusalem . . . how often would I have gathered thy children together . . . and ye would not" (Matt. 23:37). Before his crucifixion, he spoke generally when he told the daughters of Jerusalem not to weep for him "but weep for yourselves, and for your children" (Luke 23:28).

Similarly, our application of the gospel generally occurs at three levels. One is the individual level. This could include individual acts of kindness that brighten someone's day, such as a word of praise, a kind statement, an act of service, etc. It is taking personal responsibility for caring for and helping others, particularly those in need. One example for Latter-day Saints is home teaching or visiting teaching. The Church generally can promote the program as a way for members to help each other, but home teaching works when each individual feels a sense of duty to carry out his assignment and develop love for those he serves.

A second is a set of "liberal souls" who combine efforts in a group or organization to take collective action for good. At this level, people work together with others to achieve the work that an individual liberal soul cannot do alone. Obviously, the Church is an example of just such an organization. A Church welfare assignment or collective action by a ward council to reactivate a less active family is something a group can do together. Much of our service comes in this way as we participate with others to complete acts of service carried out by a group.

A third level is a society. That is where a whole society makes decisions regarding how it applies the gospel to all within the society. The society determines whether some of the resources of individuals will be collected and dedicated to the lifting up of the whole society. The means by which the society accomplishes this goal is public policy set by the society's government. Through government, the society makes rules and initiates a set of policies that creates a culture of order, as well as benefits the individuals by helping them achieve their God-given potential.

LDS Church members have been urged to care for the poor and needy. Yet due to the popularity of some personal writings and statements by a few Church leaders and members who have been the most vocal on politics, many Latter-day Saints view the command to help the poor as applicable only through individual or group actions. They have been taught that society as a whole cannot act through its government to fulfill these objectives.

Additionally, many Latter-day Saints, like many people of all faiths, may conclude that there is not much they can do on the societal level. Many people throw up their hands in despair at national policy or even the decisions of local communities. They believe they cannot make a difference. So why try? For them, the focus on the individual or the group is pragmatic. These are levels at which they believe they can make a difference. Changing society, however, is a hopeless task.

But the cynic is wrong. Societal change is not only possible but happens all the time. Societal attitudes are rarely static things that never change. It is public opinion that shapes society and society's government, particularly in a democratic society. And public opinion is, at root, individual opinion that is expressed. When Latter-day Saints choose not to express their opinions, then societal views are determined by others. By extension, when Latter-day Saints do not vote, speak up at government meetings, or express views in other forums, then others will shape public opinion.

Recent examples of ordinary individuals, not necessarily high public officials, affecting society and government are legion. Rosa Parks refused to give up her seat on a bus and sparked a boycott by African Americans that helped spur the civil rights movement. Candy Lightner decided to form Mothers Against Drunk Driving (MADD) and publicized society's lethal leniency toward drunk drivers. And one man, almost singlehandedly, added a new amendment to the U.S. Constitution. Gregory Watson, a Texas college student, devoted years of his life to getting states to ratify the Twenty-seventh Amendment to the U.S. Constitution, which prohibited a member of Congress from voting to increase his or her own salary.

But one of the largest barriers to Latter-day Saints' involvement with government is the view that society has no business improving the lives of its citizens through government. It is a perspective on government that has become popular with economic conservatives and it has become almost a mantra that government cannot solve problems and therefore should not try. For some Latter-day Saints, this way of seeing government is associated with LDS Church policy. Statements by some Church leaders, particularly President Benson, are used to demonstrate that this approach is not just one approach but the only valid way of understanding politics and the gospel.

However, this approach is not hand in glove with the gospel of Jesus Christ or LDS Church policy, as some of these advocates claim. It does not enjoy a monopoly of truth and is not endorsed by the Church. It carries within it the seeds of failure because it is unwilling to adopt the holistic approach to society and government that is essential to resolve problems—both individual as well as societal.

Nevertheless, the discussion has become increasing unbalanced in recent years about the relationship between the gospel of Jesus Christ and the role of government in a society. In essence, only one side has really been represented in LDS culture. Books, articles, speeches, and conferences tout the economic conservative and even libertarian approach to government and seek to convince Latter-day Saints that is the "true" way.

This book refutes that notion and suggests that government already is, and theologically can be, one of a set of approaches to implementing these attributes of a "liberal soul." It seeks to address the imbalance in LDS discussion of the role of government in relation to Latter-day Saints. It does not claim a monopoly. No effort is made to write out of the Church those who hold differing views.

Rather, this book offers something lacking in LDS culture. That is the presentation of a different way for Latter-day Saints to examine the question of how to be faithful disciples of Christ and good citizens. It shows government's role as the manifestation of the "liberal soul" rather than as a negative force characterized in the libertarianism advocated by some LDS speakers and writers. It also takes a different approach from the less radical but still traditional economic conservative attitudes of well-known politicians such as Orrin Hatch or Mitt Romney.

This book suggests that a Latter-day Saint can approach economic policy, war, the environment, and social issues with the perspective that society is basically good and not evil, that tolerance and forbearance are desirable qualities not bad ones, and that government can and does play a positive role as a vehicle of society in improving the lives of citizens. It describes how Latter-day Saints can apply the gospel of Jesus Christ to our roles at each of these three levels—individual, group, and society—rather than assuming that the societal level violates the principles of the gospel. The result is that Latter-day Saints can help bring about a Zion society—one in which all benefit, in which the most vulnerable are aided and not ignored, in which inclusion is the rule and not the exception, and in which suspicion and fear are replaced by love and acceptance.

I do not assert that this is the one and only way to apply the gospel of Jesus Christ in politics. Again, the objective is not to establish a new religious-political nexus monopoly. Even that very assumption is offensive to the notion of the liberal soul. However, this is a perspective that may bring us closer to a society where the gospel will flourish and will help create the kind of community, society, nation, and world in which we would all prefer to live.

CHAPTER 1

GOVERNMENT
IS ORDAINED OF GOD

"We believe that governments were instituted of God for the benefit of man." This statement in Doctrine and Covenants 134:1 would seem clear to Latter-day Saints: God created government and did so to benefit His children. The divine intent of government is to enhance the lives of the governed. Elder Steven Snow of the Seventy expressed this belief in the role of government when he commended those "who, regardless of their political persuasion, work within our local, state, and national governments to improve our lives."[1]

Indeed, that is the intent of government—to better our lives. It is an intent that is even incorporated verbally into societal documents—constitutions—creating governments in the first place. For example, the preamble to the U.S. Constitution declares that the purpose of the United States is to "establish Justice, insure domestic Tranquility, provide for the common defence, promote the general welfare, and secure the Blessings of Liberty to ourselves and our Posterity." Similarly, the Philippines Constitution asks for the aid of Almighty God in creating a government that will help "build a just and humane society." The Constitution of India seeks to "secure to all its citizens" certain rights including justice, liberty, equality, and fraternity.

Of course, these are words. The real test comes in deeds. Admittedly, governments do not always live up to these written ideals. There are plenty of examples—both historical and contemporary—of evil leaders running governments to enrich themselves at the expense of citizens or to gratify their pride and lust. Nevertheless, as the Doctrine and Covenants asserts, there is a positive role for government. Even libertarians, who are often critical of governmental role, will admit that government has some good qualities for people because it offers peace and security for citizens, and some economic conservatives acknowledge that government can take positive action to preserve capitalism in times of economic crisis.

---

1. Steven E. Snow, "Service," *Ensign*, November 2007, 103.

In the eighteenth century, political thinkers such as Thomas Hobbes and John Locke elaborated on the benefits of government in raising people out of a primitive state where law did not exist and personal security was tenuous.[2] They argued that the societal order brought about by a government's imposition of respect for property rights allows individuals to live their lives without constant fear of attack from others. Without it, society would devolve into anarchy.

The value of government is not restricted to law and order, security, and protection for property. It also creates the concept of community. Through government, we are better able to think about public good and not merely our own personal gain. We are better able to move beyond ourselves and our self-centered interests.

That natural tendency to be concerned only with self-interest is easy to adopt, particularly when we live active lives dominated by our own situations and problems. It is a tendency of the "natural man" to be selfish and to care only for what we believe directly affects us or a small group of our family and friends. On the other hand, government enables us to further broaden our perspective of life and our relationships with others, particularly those whom we do not know personally. It helps us think about others beyond the scope of our family, friends, and immediate neighbors. This effect is particularly true of democratic government where the people are sovereign and make collective decisions. Using that power, we contemplate the good of the whole and not just ourselves. We understand that our happiness is tied together with the happiness of others and that their ambitions affect our own. All of us are interrelated by the fact that we occupy the same space (neighborhood, community, nation, world) at the same time and must work together to solve problems that affect us all.

This broader perspective is not only essential in a democracy, but also is critical to the functioning of the society the Lord admonishes us to build—a Zion society. That kind of society is not one of individuals living separately; it must be achieved collectively. No one can do it alone, nor can we do it only in small groups isolated from each other. We cannot form our own enclaves and separate ourselves from the world. Such an isolationist approach may have worked in an earlier day, but our world today is much too small. No longer can Latter-day Saints move to a desert place far away from others. Even early Latter-day Saint pioneers settling in Utah, who migrated at least in part

---

2. Thomas Hobbes, *Leviathan or the Matter, Forme, and Power of a Common Wealth Ecclesiasticall and Civil* (London: Andrew Crooke, 1651), Internet Archive, at https://archive.org/details/hobbessleviathan00hobbuoft (accessed March 12, 2014); and John Locke, *Two Treatises of Government* (London: Awnsham Churchill, 1689), Internet Archive, at https://archive.org/details/twotreatisesofg00lockuoft (accessed March 12, 2014).

because of their shared desire to geographically isolate themselves, eventually needed to forge relationships with the larger society as transportation and communication developments steadily reduced the distance between Utah and the rest of the United States.

Both as part of our responsibility to create a truly democratic society and to build a Zion one, we need to think beyond ourselves and consider the good of the larger community. Fortunately, the very nature of democratic government helps us do that. For example, the act of voting is a recognition that we are part of something larger—a society where decisions must be made by all of us together. Through voting, each of us has a responsibility to participate in making policy that affects us all. When each of us casts a vote for president, we not only consider whether one candidate is closer to our political views than the other candidates, but we also ponder which candidate would be best for the nation. Who would best build the economy? Who would do the best job of guiding the nation through foreign policy crises? Who would be a wise steward of our natural resources? Through voting, we are concerned about the nation as a whole and not just ourselves. Through that simple act, democratic government has begun to transform us into public beings rather than just private ones.

As public beings we take a wider view of our actions, as well as the actions of others. We consider whether our individual actions have broader implications. We care about society generally and not just our own individual lives.

For example, it is easy to consider littering as a private act. Let's say that I do not want to carry around a gum or candy wrapper when I am done with it. Since I do not see a trash can nearby, I simply throw it on the ground. A law is passed to prevent littering. As a private individual, I might resent that law because it inconveniences me. However, the law (and often the public education campaign that accompanies it) makes me think about the consequences of littering as affecting the society as a whole. Someone else must clean up after me. That person must be paid to do so, which means tax dollars pay for the consequence of many private, selfish acts. Also, until that wrapper is picked up, I have affected the aesthetic beauty of some place—a roadside, a park, or a playground. That beauty is there to be enjoyed by the public, including me, but my private, selfish act has diminished it.

The difference between the two beings—the private and the public—is stark. The private individual may litter selfishly. The public being considers others and not just self. Government, through law, has played a role in changing a potentially self-centered individual into a citizen of society who feels a sense of responsibility to others.

Government, however, does more than just lead us to think like public beings. It can provide a vehicle for us to help one another and the opportunity for all citizens to enjoy full and productive lives. Through societal efforts, and government's role in achieving those aims, we can help families grow and flourish by creating safe and secure communities, gaining temporal assistance for those in need, and helping our children acquire necessary educational skills.

Of course, government already does that in many ways. Most people rarely think when they get up in the morning that they will have much interaction with government in the course of a day. To the extent they do, it may be a hope that they do not get caught speeding or have to spend any time at the motor vehicle department renewing their car or driver's license. Of course, people think more about government at tax time, again usually without fond thoughts.

Although they might not realize it, the fact that they had a peaceful sleep the night before is partly due to government. It means their nation was at peace. Bombs did not rain down on their house. Invading armies did not roll tanks down their streets. They were protected by government. They were also protected by police who patrolled their neighborhood for burglars, gangs, or even wayward youth wandering the streets. When their teenage son or daughter appears at their front door late in the night, often a police officer is standing next to them, making sure they got home safely. This may not be the most welcome sight for a parent, but it could be worse. Again, government is there.

Government is also there for the "what ifs." What if a neighbor's kid had played with matches in his backyard? It would have been government (in the form of the fire department) who would have come to put out the fire and save the neighborhood, including our own house, from being reduced to ashes. What if there was a natural disaster in the night—a hurricane or tornado? Government would have provided the civil defense signal to warn the community of the impending disaster—and that civil defense team would have received their information from a government agency responsible for tracking the weather.

Our hypothetical citizens may have also slept well because their house did not fall apart. This was partly because local housing ordinances mandate that builders follow certain prescribed codes in building homes. Local and state ordinances (which some economic conservatives may cite as examples of overregulation) protect citizens from the possibility of an unscrupulous builder willing to cut corners to make a larger profit. That is government, again, protecting our average citizen.

When an average citizen gets up in the morning and sends the children off to school, he does not think much about who educates his children and how they do so at a fraction of the cost the citizen would have to pay to have them instructed at a private school. Nor does he think about who or what built and maintains public universities for his children to attend, nor the federal grants and loans that help his children as young adults pay for that higher education.

When our typical citizen drives to work or takes public transportation, again there is little thought about who built the roads she is driving on and who maintains them, or who provided the funding for the subway, train, or bus system. Our citizen does not consider that, while she is away, someone hires and pays the police officer who patrols her neighborhood. Nor does she think about who provides the pension check and the medical care for her elderly parents or grandparents.

That is a small sample of the day-to-day involvement of government for our average citizen. The fact that this citizen goes about his or her daily activities without having to think much about government's role is not an indication that government is not there. On the contrary, it is an indication that government is playing its role so efficiently that the citizen can worry about other concerns.

Isn't Government Bad?

The very fact that government's delivery of services typically goes unnoticed by the average citizen is a testament to its usual efficiency. Obviously, there are times when Social Security checks are lost, firefighting units arrive too late, or police officers make false arrests. Government, like any other entity in a human world, is far from perfect. However, that is not the same as saying it is inherently bad or even usually incompetent.

Anti-government sentiment is not a recent phenomenon. Americans have historically been distrustful of governmental role. The frontier mentality and a history of rebellion against the existing government, such as in the Revolutionary War and the Civil War, have characterized Americans' approach to government. However, cynicism about government and the rhetoric expressing that cynicism has heightened in recent years. Talk show hosts on radio and television routinely criticize government's role as being inherently bad or grossly incompetent. Even politicians attack government. In his inaugural address in 1981, President Ronald Reagan claimed that "government is not the solution to our problem; government is the problem."[3] More recently, a prominent conser-

---

3. Ronald Reagan, "Inaugural Address," January 20, 1981, The American Presidency Project, http://www.presidency.ucsb.edu/ws/index.php?pid=43130#axzz1uxZ01pbV (accessed January 16, 2013).

vative activist announced that his goal is to shrink government to the size that he can "drag it into the bathroom and drown it in the bathtub."[4]

These statements may well have had an effect on Americans' attitudes about government. Trust in government has reached alarming lows. While two-thirds of Americans in 1974 said they had at least a "fair" amount of confidence in people who hold or run for political office, by 2010 that figure had fallen to 45 percent. In 2011 only 43 percent believed the federal government could handle domestic problems—as opposed to three-fourths of Americans who had confidence the federal government could solve such problems in 1972. Perhaps even more disturbing is a recent survey showing that half of Americans felt that the federal government posed an "immediate threat to the rights and freedoms of ordinary citizens"—compared with only 30 percent who felt that way just ten years ago.[5] This decline in trust is not limited only to the federal government. State governments are also losing public support. Through the 1970s to the late 1990s, about two-thirds of Americans said they had at least a "fair" amount of trust in their state government; by 2009, that figure had dropped to only half.[6]

In light of the Doctrine and Covenants declaration that government is designed to benefit man, this denigration of government itself is disturbing. It is one thing to find fault with a current administration or its policies. Americans often find themselves at odds with a current president or the controlling political party. Given the democratic alternation of power that generally characterizes American government—a Democratic president serves for a term or two and then a Republican does—it is no surprise that many Americans will disagree with how the government is run at any given time. It is another thing to malign and mistrust government itself.

A One-Sided Political Discussion

Unfortunately, some Latter-day Saint authors, politicians, and other commentators have joined that condemnation of government. Using the term "the proper role of government," they accuse the federal government of robbing

---

4. Drake Bennett, "Grover Norquist, the Enforcer," *Business Week*, May 26, 2011, http://www.businessweek.com/magazine/content/11_23/b4231006685629.htm (accessed January 16, 2013).

5. Lydia Saad, "Americans Express Historic Negativity toward U.S. Government," Gallup Poll, September 26, 2011, http://www.gallup.com/poll/149678/Americans-Express-Historic-Negativity-Toward-Government.aspx (accessed January 16, 2013).

6. Jeffrey M. Jones, "In U.S., Trust in State Government Sinks to New Low," Gallup Poll, September 10, 2009, http://www.gallup.com/poll/122915/Trust-State-Government-Sinks-New-Low.aspx (accessed January 16, 2013).

Americans of their liberties through taxation, business regulation, environmental protection, and so on. The welfare state, public education, a central banking system, and other features of today's government, they argue, take the government beyond the bounds the Lord has set through the U.S. Constitution. Of course, the limits they describe are not found in scripture nor are they in the U.S. Constitution, but they are quick to interpret certain scriptural passages to suggest the federal government has become an evil entity.

For example, they might point to the Book of Mormon's account of Riplakish imposing heavy taxes on the people (Ether 10:5) and infer that the Book of Mormon opposes the tax rates imposed by current governments. They might also point to King Noah taxing his people one-fifth of their possessions (Mosiah 11:13). Of course, "heavy" is a relative and unspecific term, and there is an important distinction between a coercive tax imposed by a dictator and a tax that people place on themselves through either a direct popular vote or through their democratically elected representatives.

Specific scriptural support for this lambasting of government, or even their idea of proper role of government today, is lacking. One reason is that democracy as a governmental system was not present through most of the historical periods when the scriptures were written. Ancient prophets lived under monarchies that were actual dictatorships—not the democratic societies that prevail in most of the industrialized world today. Therefore, little was said about democratic government one way or the other in scriptural accounts.

Despite the lack of scriptural commentary on contemporary governments, these appeals to the Book of Mormon are intended to imply that particular political views enjoy divine sanction rather than being merely one way Church members could approach politics. This is often done by quoting particular Church leaders, many of whom were not always careful about distinguishing their personal political views from official Church positions. Because of these quotations and cherry-picked passages of scripture, it is easy for some members to conclude that there is only one right way for Latter-day Saints to perceive government.

As a result, the popular political message to Latter-day Saints is that, when a government regulates the economy, protects consumers, enacts labor laws, and engages in other actions for the benefit of individual citizens, it is violating the divine intent of governments. For example, Social Security, Medicare, Medicaid, and other government programs are portrayed as sinful government overreaching rather than expressions of a society's attempts to use government "for the benefit of man" to help keep people alive and healthy, provide the elderly with some income when they can no longer work, and assist the poor.

For many years, LDS discourse has featured a certain perspective on the relationship between the gospel and politics. LDS commentators who are economically conservative or even libertarian feel comfortable writing and speaking out in expressing their political views. Indeed, those views have been trumpeted broadly through speeches, books, classes, and references made by individual Church members in sacrament meeting talks, classes, and quorum meetings. Though such statements are not part of the curriculum, these members are often unrestrained in quoting from these writings when teaching Church lessons or giving Church talks. For example, a stake president recently used a stake conference talk to lambaste the Obama administration and suggest that Americans chose socialism when they voted for President Barack Obama in 2012. He explained that he was inspired to give this blatantly political talk.[7]

Meanwhile, other perspectives have been virtually absent in these forums. While some members may feel uneasy about the extreme political views of some LDS commentators, they have largely lacked alternatives. There is seldom another "LDS perspective" provided to counter those views and demonstrate breadth in approaches to government among members of the Church. In fact, some would suggest that there really is no other legitimate gospel perspective of the role of government. Indeed, the general absence of an alternative reinforces that conclusion.

Why has the discussion of the gospel and politics in the LDS community been so conspicuously one-sided? One reason may be that, once one set of political views was disseminated by some Church leaders, other Church leaders could have been reluctant to challenge that view in order to maintain the appearance of public unity. They likely worried that rank and file members could not handle political differences among "the Brethren."

Indeed, some Church members reacted with surprise when Elder Marlin K. Jensen of the Seventy gave a newspaper interview explaining that he was a Democrat and stressed that Church leaders do not want to leave the impression that the Church is a Republican institution. "There is a sort of a division along Mormon/non-Mormon lines. We regret that more than anything—that there would become a church party and a non-church party. That would be the last thing that we would want to happen." Of course, Elder Jensen was directed by the First Presidency to send the message that General Authorities

---

7. Peggy Fletcher Stack, "Mormon Stake President Gets Political at Church, Laments Election Results," *Salt Lake Tribune*, February 21, 2013, http://www.sltrib.com/sltrib/news/55876876-78/church-lds-political-devisser.html.csp (accessed April 3, 2014).

did not all think alike on political matters and that Church members could be diverse in their choice of political parties as well.[8]

Despite the cultural expectation that Church leaders think alike politically, the historical reality shows the opposite picture. For example, in 1898, Elder B. H. Roberts of the First Council of the Seventy was elected to the U.S. House of Representatives as a Democrat, although he was denied a seat because he was a polygamist. In 1902, Apostle Reed Smoot was elected a U.S. Senator as a Republican. Both men differed significantly on political issues of the day and made those differences public.

Other examples abound. In the early twentieth century, Church leaders took opposite positions on important issues of the day such as women's suffrage and the League of Nations. In the 1960s, President Hugh B. Brown typically took a more liberal position on issues such as civil rights and urged Church leaders not to oppose the civil rights movement—while Elder Ezra Taft Benson considered it to be part of a Communist conspiracy.

Despite this history of internal political difference and opposition, Church leaders may be reluctant to publicly counter Benson's political teachings, fearing that doing so might spur contention. They would rather communicate a message to members of unanimity among Church leadership than division. It is true that General Authorities are less likely today to publicly express political views than they were fifty years ago. For some members, silence can imply consent. It can leave the impression that what President Benson said in the political realm was Church doctrine and not just his own personal opinion—particularly when no other perspective is publicly presented.

In the rare cases where other Church leaders have responded, such alternative views have largely been oblique or even out of the public eye. For example, when Elder Ezra Taft Benson used the forum of a BYU devotional to express his right-wing political views, President Hugh B. Brown followed in a BYU commencement speech with a warning about not being dogmatic about one's political views.[9] Or a few years earlier, at the height of his political involvement, Elder Benson was assigned out of the United States to serve in Europe, a rare duty for a member of the Quorum of the Twelve. At the time, Elder Joseph Fielding Smith, President of the Quorum of the Twelve, said: "I

---

8. Dan Harrie, "GOP Dominance Troubles Church," *Salt Lake Tribune*, May 3, 1998, http://www.utahcountydems.com/content/view/178 (accessed January 16, 2013).

9. Ezra Taft Benson, "The Book of Mormon Warns America," BYU Devotional Address, May 21, 1968, audio available at BYU Speeches, http://speeches.byu.edu/index.php?act=viewitem&id=1619 (accessed January 16, 2013); and Hugh B. Brown, "God Is the Gardener," BYU Commencement Address, May 31, 1968, audio available at BYU Speeches, http://speeches.byu.edu/index.php?act=viewitem&id=111 (accessed January 16, 2013).

think it is time that Brother Benson forgot all about politics and settled down to his duties as a member of the Council of the Twelve. . . . He is going to take a mission to Europe in the near future and by the time he returns I hope he will get all of the political notions out of his system."[10]

Rather than directly addressing or differing with Benson's views, the Church instead emphasized the legitimacy of political differences. For example, in the fall of each election year, First Presidency statements have acknowledged that both political parties have principles of the gospel in their platforms, and the Church Public Affairs Department has consistently explained that members have the prerogative to individually choose from different political parties. However, these statements have not stated specifically what positions may reflect gospel values, nor do they directly provide a response to the exclusivity of libertarian or economically conservative models that members see in the writings and comments of Latter-day Saint politicians, writers, speakers, and even some Church leaders.[11]

In the past, some actions have given the impression that the Church endorses certain conservative political views. Deseret Book stores, owned by the Church, have prominently displayed writings of conservative authors such as Glenn Beck and Sean Hannity. Deseret Book Publishing Company, also owned by the Church, even published a book by Glenn Beck—although the book was not explicitly political. For nine years, Church-owned KSL radio aired the Sean Hannity show, a staunchly conservative program that strongly criticized political liberals. These, however, could have been business decisions more than indications of Church approval, as Church members in large numbers bought such books and listened to conservative talk show hosts. Because of criticism that Hannity's views were implicitly endorsed by the Church, KSL aired disclaimers during the program saying that the content of the show did not necessarily reflect the views of the station's owner. Ultimately, KSL dropped the Hannity program in 2010 and substituted more neutral programming.

The perception of an official conservative or libertarian political perspective was reinforced by the high status in the Church of some of the proponents of these views. These included President Benson, President J. Reuben Clark, Elder Marion G. Romney, Elder Verlan Andersen of the Seventy,

10. Joseph Fielding Smith, Letter to Ralph R. Harding, October 30, 1963, cited in Gregory A. Prince and Wm. Robert Wright, *David O. McKay and the Rise of Modern Mormonism* (Salt Lake City: University of Utah Press, 2005), 298.

11. Buddy Blankenfeld, "Political Neutrality: Whiteboard Animation Draws Out Church Position (video)," Newsroom Blog, May 3, 2012, http://www. mormonnewsroom.org/article/political-neutrality-whiteboard-animation-draws-out-church-position (accessed January 16, 2013).

and W. Cleon Skousen, who taught religion at BYU, founded the National Center for Constitutional Studies, and enjoyed an exalted status among many Church members as a political spokesman. In addition, BYU President Ernest Wilkinson used his position as university president from 1951 to 1971 to foster right-wing political views. For example, when asked at a student forum why he did not support deficit financing by government, Wilkinson replied that he would rather follow the "word of the Prophet on these things and that the Prophets had continuously warned us against the welfare state."[12]

This vocal group of conservative leaders may have led many members to believe that providing an alternative opinion would be in opposition to the Church. Indeed, those among the BYU faculty who took a different view on politics were considered suspect. Wilkinson feared that they were Communist sympathizers and recruited students to "spy" on political science and economics faculty members who held and sometimes expressed political views that were more moderate than Wilkinson's.[13]

Other Church leaders and members were not above suspicion. Some of the self-appointed spokespersons for the Church and politics implied that other Church members, perhaps even leaders, were not in agreement with their efforts to "save the Constitution." As a member of the Quorum of the Twelve, Elder Benson implied in a general conference talk that those who did not share his political views were opposing God: "Maybe the Lord will never set up a specific Church program for the purpose of saving the Constitution. Perhaps if he set up one at this time it might split the Church asunder, and perhaps he does not want that to happen yet, for not all the wheat and tares are fully ripe."[14]

Elder Benson was insistent on marrying a libertarian philosophy to Church doctrine and sometimes proclaimed it over the pulpit. In his view, the "function of government is to protect life, liberty, and property, and anything more or less than this is usurpation and oppression." Furthermore, he taught that government cannot "redistribute the wealth or force reluctant citizens to perform acts of charity against their will." According to him, such redistribution of wealth was "legalized plunder." He became even more specific at times, proclaiming that nobody "has the authority to grant such powers as welfare programs, schemes for redistributing the wealth, and activi-

---

12. Gary James Bergera, "The 1966 BYU Spy Ring," *Utah Historical Quarterly* 79, no. 2 (Spring 2011): 164–84, quotation on p. 169.

13. Ibid., 164–88.

14. Ezra Taft Benson, "Not Commanded in All Things," *Report of the Semi-Annual Conference of the Church of Jesus Christ of Latter-day Saints*, April 5, 1965 (Salt Lake City: Church of Jesus Christ of Latter-day Saints, semi-annual 1965), 121–25; quotation on p. 125.

ties that coerce people into acting in accordance with a prescribed code of social planning."[15] Benson was also quick to label others who felt differently. He railed against "would-be statesmen, socialists, and fellow travelers of the godless conspiracy" and condemned government officials who thought differently than he did: "It was the Lord God who established the foundation of this nation; and woe be unto those—members of the Supreme Court and others—who would weaken this foundation."[16]

The fact that he gave these talks in general conference suggested to members that there was no distinction between his personal political views and Church doctrine. His political and religious views were interchangeable: Libertarian politics were part of the gospel he believed in. That marriage in his mind made perfect sense to him. So even though Benson spoke for himself and not the Church when he discussed politics—even in general conference—those views were often interpreted by members as Church doctrine rather than an individual Church leader's personal views.

It is understandable that many Church members may have reached the conclusion that the Church tacitly endorsed these political views since an apostle was allowed to make political statements from the pulpit in general conference, and no other General Authority offered opposing views. Some members believe that the prophet's utterances are prophetic, even when they express his personal opinion. For example, a survey of priesthood holders' reaction to President David O. McKay's personal endorsement of Vice-President Richard Nixon in the 1960 presidential campaign found that while a plurality believed President McKay was not inspired when he endorsed Nixon, 27 percent were not sure whether or not he was and 30 percent believed he was. Perhaps not surprisingly, local church officers—such as stake presidencies and bishoprics—were more likely than average members to consider President

15. Ezra Taft Benson, "Americans Are Destroying America," *Report of the Semi-Annual Conference of the Church of Jesus Christ of Latter-day Saints*, April 6, 1968 (Salt Lake City: Church of Jesus Christ of Latter-day Saints, semi-annual, 1968), 49–54; quotation on p. 125; and Ezra Taft Benson, "The Proper Role of Government," *Report of the Semi-Annual Conference of the Church of Jesus Christ of Latter-day Saints*, October 1968 (Salt Lake City: Church of Jesus Christ of Latter-day Saints, semi-annual, 1968), 17–22; quotation on p. 19.

16. Ezra Taft Benson, "America—A Man and an Event," *Report of the Semi-Annual Conference of the Church of Jesus Christ of Latter-day Saints*, October 3, 1965 (Salt Lake City: Church of Jesus Christ of Latter-day Saints, semi-annual, 1965), 121–25; quotation on p. 122.

McKay's statement inspired.[17] That was true even though President McKay explained his statement as only personal and not a church endorsement.

Occasional Church statements have expressed the Church's distance from right-wing organizations, such as the John Birch Society, or regularly, during election years, reiterated the Church's position of neutrality in the use of Church facilities for political purposes, but official Church spokespersons, including other General Authorities, did not publically oppose the overall political philosophy that President Benson expressed—and only recently has the Church attempted to clarify that one set of views, such as President Benson's, are part of a panoply of views members could hold about politics.[18]

President Benson's teachings, however, should not be blindly accepted as official Church doctrine. As Elder D. Todd Christofferson explained in an April 2012 general conference talk, even prophets say things in conference that are not necessarily from the Lord.[19] "Not every statement made by a Church leader, past or present, necessarily constitutes doctrine."[20] Church leaders can express their personal preferences in the course of a conference talk, as well as in other settings, that do not necessarily reflect Church doctrine or policy. The Church has similarly reinforced this point on its website in defining what doctrine is (and is not).

To be clear, those who are Church members and espouse libertarian views have a perfect right to do so and can believe that those views are rooted in the gospel of Jesus Christ. What they should not do, however, is authoritatively assert that their interpretation of the intersection of the gospel of Jesus Christ and politics is the only one that Church members could correctly hold. Church leaders have made no such assertion. And the Church has made no such claim that there is a political gospel.

Does the Church Prefer a Certain Type of Government?

While Latter-day Saints look to a time when the Savior reigns personally on the earth and a theocracy is present, that day is not here. Instead, we have earthly governments that rule. If the Church does have any preference for

---

17. Dean E. Mann, "Mormon Attitudes Toward the Political Roles of Church Leaders," *Dialogue: A Journal of Mormon Thought*, 2, no. 2 (1967): 32–48.

18. Adding to this, President McKay publicly recommended one of Cleon Skousen's books, in general conference. David O. McKay, "Preach the Word," *Improvement Era*, December 1959, 912.

19. D. Todd Christofferson, "The Doctrine of Christ," *Ensign*, May 2012, 86–90; quotation on p. 88.

20. "Approaching Mormon Doctrine," Mormon Newsroom, May 4, 2007, http://www.mormonnewsroom.org/article/approaching-mormon-doctrine (accessed January 17, 2013).

types of governmental systems, it is those in which religious freedom allows for the gospel of Jesus Christ to be freely taught and practiced. The Church assigns missionaries to hundreds of missions across the globe. The nations where missionaries serve vary widely in their approaches to a host of policy matters involving macroeconomic policy, national defense, social issues, and so on. They range from wealthy social welfare states like Sweden, Denmark, and Norway to economically poor states such as Paraguay, Haiti, and Ghana. They include democratic nations such as the United States, Canada, and Japan, as well as dictatorships such as Ukraine, the Congo, and Mozambique. In addition to missions, wards, stakes, and temples are located across a wide array of political systems. As long as they allow religious freedom, the Church works with such systems to further the preaching of the gospel.

For many of these countries, the Church's presence is made possible through its cooperation with many types of governments. The Church seeks to follow the laws of these nations and has not encouraged the overthrowing of governments. Instead, Church members are encouraged to support their current government and work to improve it. This counsel is usually left intentionally vague, with specific policies only occasionally promoted—such as with the recent issue of same-sex marriage. On other issues—such as the role of the government in social welfare, economic regulation, or how political power is distributed within the political system—the Church has not dictated to members what their governmental system should look like.

Generally, the Church is ecumenical in its approach to governmental systems. This is particularly true in the area of concern for the poor. In addition to preaching the gospel across the world, Church leaders today recommend that everyone adopt a certain mindset toward our fellow human beings of helping those in need and has, in fact, made such a concern for the poor a key mission.

This mission of caring for the poor and needy neither requires nor precludes governmental role. In fact, a political system that includes governmental assistance to the poor assists the Church by providing care that the Church cannot. For example, where a nation institutes a national health care system, as in most industrialized nations, the Church can focus its energies on other needs besides basic health care. However, the Church has remained neutral on whether a society chooses to provide government assistance to the poor.

If the Church takes no official stance on a particular governmental model, how, then, should government be organized by a particular society? Clearly, that is a choice for each individual country to make. It is a choice that individual Latter-day Saints in various governmental systems must make in their roles as citizens. Those choices should be made by Latter-day Saints in conjunction with other citizens of other faiths or even of no faith at all, and they should reflect cultural realities, economic abilities, and public will. As a result, those decisions will be different across various societies.

Do All Governments Do Good?

Even though the Church takes no official position on a system of government, clearly some types of governments are not beneficial to their citizens. A government that does not respect freedom for individuals to worship as they please impinges on freedom of conscience. In such systems, people cannot do what they believe they should or avoid doing what they believe they should not. Religious belief and practice are basic human rights that government does not have divine sanction to deny. According to the Doctrine and Covenants, governments do not have "a right to interfere in prescribing rules of worship to bind the consciences of men, nor dictate forms for public or private devotion" (D&C 134:4).

Beyond religious freedom, a government that prevents individual citizens from participating in their own governance is not "for the benefit of man." Having the right to speak out in opposition to public policy or administrations they oppose is fundamental to the sovereignty of the people or their right to govern themselves. It is not surprising that a government that prohibits free expression is quick to allow its officials to commit other acts of compulsion or even violence against its own population. These include dragging a nation into an unnecessary war, rigging elections, imprisoning or even executing opponents, and enriching itself at the expense of its population. History records many examples of such governments and such leaders. In fact, for most of the world's history, the vast majority of humans have lived under such regimes. Some have gone to extremes in tyranny and cruelty, including Stalin's Russia in the 1930s, Nazi Germany in the 1930s and 1940s, Mao Tse-Tung's China in the 1950s and 1960s, and the rule of North Korea's dictatorial Kim family today.

Even when governments have not been overtly cruel, they have often neglected those they are supposed to serve. Many governments have failed to help their citizens in time of natural disaster or crisis. Some have gone to war over national pride or even because of miscommunication, resulting in the needless deaths of millions of people. Still others have reallocated national wealth to a relative few while forcing the vast majority of its citizens to live in abject poverty.

Many governments today inhibit individual rights and harm, rather than benefit, individuals. For example, North Korea spends money on national defense while millions of its citizens are malnourished. China offers its citizens broad economic freedom but prohibits them from choosing their own government and directing its policies through the people's will. Syria has bombed its own citizens, including unarmed women and children.

What Type of Government Benefits Human Beings?

Because bad government is a sorry chapter in the history of the world, it is easy to forget that government was instituted by God and that it is for our benefit. Indeed, government can, and does, benefit us. These benefits range from the establishment of basic order to the mechanism by which society takes care of its most vulnerable citizens.

At its most basic level, government provides public safety for a society. Without it, citizens would have to protect themselves, bringing society back to what it was before democratic governments. Rather than police forces, there would be individual weapon depots and fortress homes guarded by high walls. Requiring individuals to protect themselves is exactly the state of nature that government is intended to rise above. The greatest beneficiaries of government are the most vulnerable in society. Without government, most individuals would be subject to rule by the strongest. For example, those who have the wealth to protect themselves can hire private armies to do so, build homes that are fortresses guarded by private armies, and send their children to private schools. But those who lack such means are most susceptible to crime or become criminals themselves to survive. They also suffer from poor public education systems with the result that their children are destined to suffer the same lives of poverty and neglect.

Government that benefits its citizens does more than just provide a climate of public order. It goes beyond protection of public property and is dedicated to bettering the lives of all of its citizens. Indeed, there is no question that there is a strong linkage between promoting the welfare of its citizens and the existence of public order. A low-crime society is one where people do not view crime as their means for obtaining basic necessities of life or for achieving social and economic status. They have hope that they can secure a better life for themselves and their families in legitimate ways. They are optimistic about the future when they see society through its government being concerned about their welfare and not adopting a policy of neglecting those in need.

A society where citizens are well fed, well housed, well educated, well employed, and filled with hope for the future is one that also tends to be orderly. That is the kind of society that should be the objective of government. That is the society that improves people's lives and implements the objective of government as indicated by the Lord.

Unfortunately, many societies do not share this concern for the general welfare of all of their citizens. In those cases, such written constitutional promises about the "common good" remain unfulfilled and become mere rhetoric. In these societies, the lack of economic opportunity, which is usually caused by inaccessibility of education and the chance to work, breeds crime and hopelessness.

Government as the Tool of the Good Society

An important way to understand government, particularly in a democratic system, is to view it as the policy implementer for the decisions of a society. Society makes decisions about what it wishes itself to look like, how it acts, and what it does. A society that values self-centeredness will institute a government that downplays the importance of the community and creates a society based on survival of the fittest. On the other hand, a society in which people care about each other will choose government policies that enable all to be productive members of society and share in the society's goods.

Obviously, no society fits neatly into either of those categories. Instead, societies, like the human beings who make them up, are complicated entities that combine both virtues and vices. A government that assumes as an eternal truth what actually is not the case, i.e., that people are always virtuous, is one that is destined to fail. In fact, the real test of government is to function when virtue is in short supply. That test is particularly true when the missing virtue is a sense of selflessness.

The opposite of selflessness is self-centeredness—a concern only for ourselves and a disregard for the welfare of others, particularly others outside the limited circle of our immediate family and friends. Self-centeredness is corrosive to a society because self-centered individuals are atomistic and do not consider themselves part of a society. In such cases, society does not really exist.

Government cannot prevent or eliminate self-centeredness. However, it can be designed to restrain the effects of self-centeredness. For example, James Madison viewed the checks and balances in the American constitutional system as a process that would check "ambition with ambition." In other words, Congress's institutional ambition to rule the nation would check the president's similar ambition and vice versa. Pitting these two institutions against one another would provide a built-in check on governmental power.[21]

Madison understood human nature enough to know that self-centeredness was present in human beings. Therefore, he did not assume complete virtue on the part of people in governance. At the same time, he did not possess

---

21. Alexander Hamilton, James Madison, and John Jay, *The Federalist Papers* (New York: The New American Library, 1961), no. 51.

such a jaded view of humans that he concluded government by the people could not function. He took the path of seeking to harness self-centeredness to serve government's purposes.

Government can be the tool of a bad society that chooses evil governments or at least allows evil people to rule them. Societies can "sin" by veering off into policies that harm the society as a whole and individuals within it. Governmental systems reflect those "sins" because they reflect the society that formed the government. For example, 1930s Nazi Germany was the product of the German people's desire for order in the wake of instability in the 1920s. They also wished to restore their national pride, which had been wounded by their defeat in World War I. At first, Germans chose Nazism democratically, but democratic control waned as Germany degenerated into a bloody dictatorship.

In a democracy, as a society makes choices about its national direction, government becomes the tool to implement that policy. A society that values personal liberty will enact government policies to accomplish that end. Another society that cherishes civic interaction will use government for that purpose. Where people collectively are free to make decisions for their society, government becomes the means to put those decisions into action.

A society that is generally dedicated to the good of all its citizens will use government to improve the welfare of those citizens. That includes providing services that enable citizens to achieve their dreams in life. For example, by creating an effective free public education system, a society is equipping all members of the society to make meaningful contributions. Mechanics, doctors, teachers, and others do not magically appear. They are trained by a society that invests in its future (its children) to maintain and even improve the society. Also, a government that assists with decent housing offers children a chance to grow up in environments where they can feel safe. On the whole, a democratic government mirrors the society's decisions about how it will treat its citizens.

An old proverb is that a government is as good as the people who chose it. Indeed, where people are allowed to choose their own representatives and hold them accountable through elections, government is typically not an independent entity. Rather, it is a reflection of the people in the society.

Aren't Individuals Better at Providing Services Than Government?

The political rhetoric often heard today is that, while the government is inefficient and bloated, individuals and non-governmental organizational efforts are much more efficient and streamlined. Critics of government often argue that individuals or non-profit organizations (such as churches) can handle social welfare better than government, that because individual giving avoids bureaucracies, it will be less costly, and that taxpayers will not have to pay when individuals provide these important services to others.

In reality, the choice between private welfare and government welfare is false. Both have their place. The existence of both does not lead to the eventual displacement of the other. For example, some claim that the existence of government pushes out the private sector and that taxation precludes individual acts of charity. They argue that when tax rates are too high people do not have money to give to charity. However, to the contrary, charitable donations actually remain large in the United States—even where government also plays a role. This is true even in economic hard times. For example, in 2010, charitable giving in the United States was over $290 billion. Despite a recession, this was 2 percent higher than the previous year.[22]

The fact that government provides some social services does not mean individuals do not also give. Government can, and should, do only so much. The vast majority of acts of charity are those carried out by individuals, not by government. These include one-time financial donations from family member to family member or friend to friend, as well as simple acts of taking bread to a neighbor, watching someone else's children, or visiting a sick person in the hospital. These are things government cannot do, but which individuals can and should do.

At the same time, there are other things government can do that individuals alone find difficult to do. One example is health-care access. The private sector (i.e., health insurance companies, doctors, and hospitals) can provide health-care delivery services, but it does not automatically offer health care for all. Because many people cannot pay for those services and doctors cannot afford to treat them without getting paid, a segment of society is effectively denied health-care access.

The challenge of health care is particularly true when a family faces a severe illness. When a family without health insurance is hit with such a catastrophe, they can turn to extended family members, friends, neighbors, or even the whole community. However, neighborhood or community fundraisers typically provide only a fraction of the costs of expensive medical operations and treatment. Because of this, families often go bankrupt seeking to care for themselves in such situations.

Individuals may try hard to handle their own needs. I remember driving to work one day and seeing a man on the side of the road selling bottled

22. Katie L. Roeger, Amy Blackwood, and Sarah L. Pettijohn, "Non-Profit Sector in Brief: Charities, Giving, and Volunteering, 2011," *Urban Institute*, November 1, 2011, http://www.urban.org/publications/412434.html (accessed April 3, 2014).

water for a dollar. A sign he carried said that his wife had cancer. A woman in our ward struggled to care for her invalid husband by herself due to lack of money. It was only when she required her own surgeries caused by constantly lifting him did she seek hospice care for him. These people struggle to take care of their own family's needs, as they feel they should, but some problems are overwhelming for individuals, families, or even communities.

When a family in our neighborhood was faced with high medical costs for treatment of a child, they were able to turn to the bishop for temporary help. However, not every person has this opportunity. The vast majority of churches lack the centralized resources for such situations. Furthermore, it should not be the case that access to health care depends on whether a person belongs to a particular religion or any religion at all.

The cost of providing health care when spread across a whole nation or even an individual state or province is far more evenly distributed than when borne by a single family or neighborhood or even community. There are large-scale costs that individuals, families, and even small communities find difficult to bear. By spreading the costs across a nation, each individual pays a small amount for the betterment of others.

The principle is similar to the one the Church uses in supporting missionaries. When I served a full-time mission in the 1970s, the missionaries and their families had to bear the costs of a mission. As a result, the families of missionaries sent to expensive areas, such as New York City or London, faced much higher costs than those going to Fiji or Bolivia.

The Church does it differently today. By equalizing the costs and with each missionary paying the same amount regardless of their field of labor, families do not suffer financially because their sons or daughters are called to more expensive missions. The costs of missionary work are shared across many people within the Church, which reduces the expense for many missionaries and their families.

The best way to serve individuals and families in a society is through a combination of societal (typically via government) and individual or family action. Again, the vast majority of acts of service are performed at the individual or family level. Some are undertaken by organizations, particularly churches. In this way, government's role is part of a package of help, and it therefore supplements the roles of individuals, churches, and other charitable organizations.

Government is not the cure-all for economic, social, and political problems faced by individuals, including Latter-day Saints—but neither is the role of the government "off the table" as part of the total offering of service to individuals. Rather, it is the combination of government and individual or family service that characterizes a holistic approach to meeting the needs of our fellow human beings.

How Can We Get Beneficial
Rather Than Harmful Government?

If we assume that government can be either good or bad, how do we know whether we are going to get a government that is beneficial or harmful? That question assumes what I fear a lot of Latter-day Saints believe: that they are helpless in affecting government. Many of my students express cynicism about their ability to shape government. They simply despair, believing that they have no influence in molding their government.

Indeed, the result of such thinking can be a form of tribalism that goes something like this: I will just be concerned about my own family or people I know, typically those in my own ward; the larger community or even the nation is remote and beyond my influence and my efforts. Such thinking is reflected in a Church video I saw a few years ago. It showed a family inside a house with rain pouring down on the windows and loud thunder and bright lightning outside. The message was that there is a storm outside (the wickedness of the world) and we need to gather our families together in the shelter of our homes and protect them from the wickedness that exists in the world.

I thought the video had it wrong. A storm is not the right analogy. Perhaps a better one is a relief team for a natural disaster. When we see a need, our response should be to gather others together and clean up the disaster, not just hunker down in our individual houses and hope for the best for everyone else. This approach better portrays what Latter-day Saints can and should do. We have the potential to change government for the better. Our actions determine what government looks like. We should not sit back and allow others to play the role we should perform in making our societies better places for all to live.

We must work together to build a better society. Our combined efforts make change. We should not practice a tribalism that allows us to limit our concern for others. It also rules out NIMBY-ism (Not In My Back Yard) that prevents us from appreciating the need to sacrifice our resources for others, even others whom we do not personally know or who have not yet been born.

In reality, whether government works for the "benefit of man" or is harmful is really up to the citizens of a society—both individually and collectively. By our own individual attitudes and behavior about our own role and the role of others, we decide what our society will be like. And through our attitudes about government we determine whether the influences on that government will be positive or negative. In a democracy where people govern through majority rule, the nature of government reflects the nature of society. And the nature of our society mirrors us as individuals. The nature of government is our nature as a people in society.

The Proper Role of Government

Government is ordained of God. It is not inherently bad. As a vehicle for society to improve the lives of all—to benefit humankind—it has a positive role to play in our earthly existence. That role need not be purely minimal, as conservatives claim, or almost non-existent, as libertarians would argue. It can be substantive and it can be beneficial.

God, however, does not run earthly governments. People do. God has granted us—human beings—the authority to run earthly governments. I believe He will help those who run them, but He does not run them. Even governmental leaders who ask for God's help and desire to be instruments in God's hands can, through their incompetence and neglect, still run them badly, while others intentionally destroy societies by operating governments for their own selfish purposes. The actual operation of government is something for which individuals are responsible.

Indeed, the human nature of government makes it vulnerable as a target for those who oppose government role. It is easy to point to occasional human error, corruption, unintended negative consequences of policy decisions, or even incompetence as a justification for eliminating government role. Of course, all those justifications apply to any human endeavor at all. Humans are fallible and collective human activity is no different. Although far from perfect, government has the potential, particularly in partnership with groups and individuals, to help eradicate disease, alleviate poverty, extend life through decent health care, and educate people to play significant roles in society.

LDS writers from the ideological right wing have often written about the "proper role of government" to describe what they believe are the appropriate uses of government. To them, the proper role of government is to do little or nothing beyond maintaining law and order and national defense. In short, they see defending private property as the primary task of government.[23]

To the liberal soul, the proper role of government is to seek to improve the lives of its citizens—in other words, to benefit people. The appropriate role is to help meet the needs of people who live within the society. Those needs go beyond protecting private property. They also extend to caring for each other's well-being. While care is largely done by individuals, groups, and organizations,

---

23. See, for example, W. Cleon Skousen, *The Making of America: The Substance and Meaning of the Constitution*, 2nd ed. (Provo, Utah: National Center for Constitutional Studies, 1985); Ezra Taft Benson, *The Constitution: A Heavenly Banner* (Salt Lake City: Deseret Book, 1989); Ezra Taft Benson and H. Verlan Andersen, *The Proper and Improper Role of Government* (Orem, Utah: Sunrise Publishing, 2009); and Connor Boyack, *Latter-day Liberty: A Gospel Approach to Government and Politics* (Springville, Utah: Cedar Fort, 2011).

societies may collectively decide that those benefits should be extended to all. These could and should include adequate health care, a decent education, and a living wage, among others. The proper role of government, particularly in a society of liberal souls, is to assure that Doctrine and Covenants section 134 is fulfilled—that all benefit from divinely ordained government.

CHAPTER 2

YOU ARE TO BE EQUAL

Every Sunday, somewhere in the world, Primary children are singing the song "I Am a Child of God." This classic song for LDS children was written to reassure each Primary child that he or she has divine parentage and can return to Heavenly Father. The message of this song is universal. No child is exempted from that status.

It also has another message—as sons and daughters of God, we are also brothers and sisters. As siblings, we are all equal before God. Despite our skin color, socio-economic status, national origin, and even religion, we are alike in the eyes of our Heavenly Father. This raises a question for us to consider: If our Heavenly Father considers all of us as equal, why shouldn't we consider ourselves equal as well? Shouldn't we see each other the same way Heavenly Father sees us?

In practice, such a perspective has been extraordinarily rare in the annals of time. The history of the human race is filled with artificial inequalities set up by people to grade and rank each other. Unlike our Heavenly Father, today we still assess people based on characteristics such as ethnicity, race, gender, social status, income, or educational level. Wars have been fought over which nation is superior to another or which people should be the master race. Over the centuries, racial prejudice, with its ugly assumptions about inequality, has flourished across many societies. Historically, most cultures, often in the name of protecting women, have considered women as inherently inferior to men. And the scriptures are replete with instances of the poor being mistreated by the wealthy.

Over time and across the globe, there have been widespread attempts to promote greater social equality to end such discrimination. In India, political and social leaders have sought to eradicate the caste system that defined life-long class distinctions. In the United States, people in the civil rights movement demonstrated, lobbied, and sued to gain equal rights for African Americans. Similarly, South Africans protested against apartheid (racial segregation) and finally ended the practice in the early 1990s.

Yet discrimination based on these artificial categories is not a thing of the past. It is alive and real today—even in supposedly civilized nations. For example, Europeans often disparage the Roma, better known as gypsies, who travel across the continent. Women are discriminated against in many parts of the world, particularly in African and Middle Eastern nations. Governments use laws to limit a woman's right to own property or even act independently of her father or husband. Indeed, women are the most vulnerable of all in wartime, when they are often raped and murdered by marauding guerillas or soldiers. Also, despite major gains in Western industrialized nations, gays and lesbians are still commonly discriminated against across the world. Some nations, such as Pakistan, Nigeria, and Zimbabwe, still ban homosexuality.

Such discriminatory behavior is contrary to the gospel of Jesus Christ. Christ's teachings value the worth of each individual—regardless of race, gender, nationality, or other such categories. We are admonished to see the beauty of all: "Remember the worth of souls is great in the sight of God" (D&C 18:10). The scope of this verse is not limited to certain races or religions; rather, it is universal. Indeed, we are all made just "a little lower than the angels" (Ps. 8:5). In fact, our Heavenly Father's love for all is not even diminished by the sinful acts his children might commit, as captured in the parable of the prodigal son.

Most importantly, the Atonement has universal application. No one is excluded from the Father's love and the Son's atoning sacrifice. There are no bounds to the Atonement's reach, because the Savior's love and compassion are comprehensive. All of this demonstrates to us that, if our Heavenly Father loves all of His children, who are we to play favorites?

There are, however, many temptations to adopt worldly attitudes about others rather than to take the Lord's perspective. As Latter-day Saints, we live in cultures where attitudes of discrimination are widely shared and left unchallenged. Our societies socialize us as young people to adopt these views without question. They are so engrained in us that we may not even realize that they lead us away from the gospel.

One example is racism, which Elder Alexander Morrison called "one of the abiding sins of societies the world over."[1] Racial prejudice may range from discriminatory language to violent acts. According to President Gordon B. Hinckley, "No man who makes disparaging remarks concerning those of another race can consider himself a true disciple of Christ."[2] But language usually is preceded by attitudes—mistrust, suspicion, and outright fear—that manifest themselves in actions such as avoidance, exclusion, and even violence.

---

1. Alexander B. Morrison, "No More Strangers," *Ensign*, September 2000, 16–20, quotation on p. 16.

2. Gordon B. Hinckley, "The Need for Greater Kindness," *Ensign*, May 2006, 58–61, quotation on p. 58.

Another is homophobia—a fear of, and even hatred toward, homosexuals. This prejudice has been transferred from generation to generation in society generally and within the Church. At times, teenage boys in my ward have called other boys "gay" as a derogatory remark. This wasn't something these young boys picked up on their own; it was taught them at home, school, or church.

In the past, I have frequently heard anti-gay comments in Church meetings. Then, something happened. As more people with same-sex attraction began to admit this feeling to others and to openly express that attraction, people began to realize that those they hated were among their own family members and close friends. A friend of mine, who is a former bishop, admitted to me that he began to change his mind about gays when a former missionary companion of his announced that he was gay and was married to a gay man in California. My friend admitted that he was confused. This was his friend; he was not a monster. To my surprise, he also admitted that he now did not understand the Church's stance on same-sex marriage, even though he has a strong personal testimony of the Church, nor could he see how his traditional marriage was threatened because his former missionary companion had entered into a same-sex marriage.

Many Church members may not have come to the point of questioning the Church's position on same-sex marriage, but they have experienced a transformation in their attitudes toward homosexuals. For many families, gays have become less the "them" and more the "us." Many have come to see those with same-sex attraction as children of God just as are those who are heterosexuals.

What has occurred gives me hope that long-entrenched worldly attitudes can be transformed. Even those cultural attitudes that are deeply entrenched can be discarded in favor of other attitudes that are more Christ-like. With the help of the Savior, we can see each other as equal sons and daughters of God and brothers and sisters.

Why are these cultural prejudices so dangerous for us? They lead us to foster false attitudes of superiority or inferiority. One group considers itself better than another and seeks to inculcate in the other group a sense of mediocrity and subordination. Neither attitude conforms to the Apostle Paul's instruction that we should have "lowliness of mind" and "let each esteem the other better than themselves" (Phil. 2:3).

Our prejudices both stem from fear and fill us with fear rather than faith and hope. They produce unrighteous judgment of others based on less important attributes such as skin color, ethnicity, gender, and sexual orientation, rather than appreciation for the nature of their souls. In simple terms, they distract us from Christ. Through cultural prejudice, we forget the worth of each individual in the eyes of the Lord. That prejudice drives out our ability to "love one another." We cannot love others while we are also fearing and mistrusting them at the same time.

On the other hand, equality is a gospel concept that enriches us. It opens our eyes to the world as it is rather than how our culture wants us to see it. It helps us understand who we are and who others around us really are as well. The reality that everyone is a child of God becomes apparent to us, perhaps for the first time.

But what does equality mean? How does the liberal soul view equality? Is equality limited to issues of race or gender or sexual orientation? Or it is something more, perhaps much more?

Equality is a much broader term with application beyond demographics. It crosses economic, social, legal, political, and even spiritual lines. Let's take each of these types of equality in turn and relate it to the attitudes of the liberal soul.

Economic Equality: "And You Are to be Equal"

The admonition to be equal was given to the Saints as they attempted to live the United Order in the 1830s (D&C 82:17). This wasn't the only time the early Saints were urged to be equal, nor were they ignorant of what would happen if they were not equal. They were told that if they were not equal in their respective stewardships on earth, they would not be able to enjoy heavenly things (D&C 70:14, 78:6).

This admonition may seem harsh, but the logic is easy to comprehend. It would be difficult to view our brothers and sisters as equal in a heavenly sense if we cannot do it first while we are on earth. How can we enjoy heavenly association there if we do not strive for it here first?

The example of the early Saints is not the only one in scripture. The most idyllic time in the history of the Book of Mormon peoples was the period following the visitation of Jesus Christ after His resurrection and the establishment of Zion among them. Fourth Nephi tells of a society where the people had "all things in common among them; therefore there were not rich and poor, bond and free, but they were all made free, and partakers of the heavenly gift" (4 Ne. 1:3).

Immediately following the resurrection of Christ and the day of Pentecost, the Christians in the New Testament Church were practicing economic equality. The Book of Acts tells us that "all that believed were together, and had all things common; and sold their possessions and goods, and parted them to all men, as every man had need" (Acts 2:44–45). They were "of one heart and of one soul: neither said any of them that ought of the things which he possessed was his own; but they had all things common" (Acts 2:32). These early Saints took their possessions and "laid them down at the apostles' feet." These goods were then distributed according to the needs of the people. This was so important that when Ananias and Sapphira lied to Peter and kept back some of their property for themselves, Peter accused them of having Satan in their heart and they both fell down dead (Acts 4:35, 5:1–10).

Early Latter-day Saint Efforts toward Economic Equality

Following the admonition in the Doctrine and Covenants to be equal, Church leaders in the nineteenth century tested various social and economic arrangements in order to live the law of consecration and form a Zion society. Joseph Smith attempted to institute the law of consecration in Kirtland, Ohio, and Jackson County, Missouri, in the early 1830s through an organization called the United Firm.[3] He sought to do so again in Missouri in the late 1830s. Neither effort succeeded.

A cardinal principle of these efforts was the sharing of wealth, as in the New Testament days. The objective was to attain economic equality among the Saints and thus avoid the sins that arise from economic disparities. The question, then, was how to achieve it.

The revelations in the Doctrine and Covenants were a guide for them. Every individual was made "a steward over his own property, or that which he has received by consecration" (D&C 42:32). It is easy to interpret that revelation as stating that all individuals had a responsibility and, as is common in the world today, had economic incentives to succeed so they could enjoy the fruits of their own labors as much as they wished. But the rest of that verse qualifies that stewardship's role. It is not for individual economic gain. Instead, the wealth generated by that endeavor was kept back by the individual only "as much as is sufficient for himself and family" (D&C 42:32).

The objective was communal wealth. Church leaders and members were commanded: "If there shall be properties in the hands of the church, or any individuals of it, more than is necessary for their support after this first consecration, which is a residue to be consecrated unto the bishop, it shall be kept to administer to those who have not, from time to time, that every man who has need may be amply supplied and receive according to his wants" (D&C 42:33).

Church leaders in the 1830s expected members to attain economic equality by following these divine prescriptions. In May 1831, Presiding Bishop Edward Partridge was told to "appoint unto this people their portions, every man equal according to his family, according to his circumstances and his wants and needs" (D&C 51:3). That counsel was repeated the next year with

---

3. See Max H. Parkin, "Joseph Smith and the United Firm: The Growth and Decline of the Church's First Master Plan of Business and Finance, Ohio and Missouri, 1832–1834," *BYU Studies* 46 (2007): 5–66.

the revelation that all would have stewardships and they would be responsible for managing those stewardships through the Church. "You are to have equal claims on the properties, for the benefit of managing the concerns of your stewardships, every man according to his wants and his needs, inasmuch as his wants are just" (D&C 82:17).

As each individual wisely administered his or her own stewardship, that Latter-day Saint would prosper and the excess of that prosperity would "be cast into the Lord's storehouse to become the common property of the whole church" (D&C 82:18). Rather than being selfish, each Latter-day Saint would take what he needed and give the rest to the Church for the good of others. Those needs might vary from household to household, but all would enjoy a similar economic status.

Of course, there were intangible, spiritual benefits to this plan. This law would not only provide economic benefits for all but also would transform Church members from a worldly people with only a self-centered interest in their own economic well-being to a Zion society in which members manifested care for others: "[E]very man seeking the interest of his neighbor, and doing all things with an eye single to the glory of God" (D&C 82:19).

For various reasons, the United Firm failed in Kirtland. However, once again, in Missouri in 1838, an attempt was made to live the law of consecration, although in somewhat modified form compared to the first attempt. In this case, the Saints were directed to bring "their surplus property to be put into the hands of the bishop of my church in Zion" (D&C 119:1). This arrangement was called "tithing," but it was not a tithing of 10 percent. Rather, it was a tithing of all beyond what was necessary for the stewardship of each Latter-day Saint family. After making this initial "tithe," they then tithed "one-tenth of all their interest annually" (D&C 119:4).

A "good of all" approach was a novel concept for early Americans who had become accustomed to thinking as individuals rather than as a group. It required a shift in mindset, one that even Church members acting under revelation had a difficult time living. One of the challenges was the fact that equality required the redistribution of wealth within the Church from the rich to the poor. Bishop Newel K. Whitney was told to travel around the churches "searching after the poor to administer to their wants by humbling the rich and the proud" (D&C 84:112).

A key concept was economic stewardship. However, the management of that stewardship varied. Under the United Firm established by Joseph Smith in the 1830s, legal ownership of the stewardship properties was held by individuals who were responsible for them. In the 1850s, Brigham Young again attempted to institute a form of the law of consecration using basically the same plan. Under Brigham Young's plan, however, Church members technically deeded over properties to the Church, even though actual management of the property would be retained by the individual. The owner of the property—whether a business, ranch, home, or vacant land—would be the Church, and not the individual. The individual member would be the steward of the property and responsible to the Lord for using that property to serve the kingdom of God generally. That kingdom included the society of Saints. Brigham Young's experiment, however, was short-lived, and legal ownership never really transferred to the Church.

These experiments may have been instituted as a test of the loyalty of some members. In both versions—1830s and 1850s—each individual had an obligation to tend to that stewardship. The term "steward" is a vital one, and it is purposely used in revelations instead of "owner." A "steward" implies responsibility for financial affairs in the name of someone else. The Lord was making clear that their stewardship was to Him. Also, the Lord wanted the Saints to understand that material wealth was not theirs, but His. And His command was for them to make sure each Latter-day Saint had what he or she needed economically and would not be abandoned in poverty.

Through these stewardships, all would be economically equal. No one would have more than anyone else. All would understand that their possessions were not theirs at all, but the Lord's. In that sense, all would be the same in their role as stewards, even though the respective stewardships were different.

For a brief time, Brigham Young tried an even more radical experiment—communitarianism. This was not the communism of Karl Marx or Vladimir Lenin but was instead a form of communal living similar to the various Utopian social experiments of the nineteenth century adopted by Robert Owen in upstate New York, John Humphrey Noyes's Oneida Community, and the Shakers settlements throughout the eastern United States. This approach included actual communal property ownership rather than individual ownership. Living arrangements were "common" in the sense that all participants were allocated their residences, not based on household income, as today, but on family size. The members of these communal societies created in Utah dressed commonly in homespun clothes made by and for the community.

The best known of these communal societies was the southern Utah town of Orderville, which operated like a small commune. Each family lived in its own community-owned house, but ate in a communal dining room, and worked for equal pay at jobs assigned by the order's leaders. Orderville operated for about ten years from its founding in 1875 until Church leaders ended the experiment and told the Church members to dissolve the commune.[4]

---

4. For a discussion of the United Order efforts in the 1870s and 1880s, see Leonard J. Arrington, Feramorz Y. Fox, and Dean L. May, *Building the City of God* (Salt Lake

Experiments like Orderville may seem surprising to many Latter-day Saints today because of the emphasis on individualism that has pervaded LDS culture in the last century. Terms like "self-reliance" and "individual (and family) temporal responsibility" have become far more common than "economic stewardship" and "communitarianism." But early Church leaders and members attempted to live the law of consecration as it had been practiced in earlier times by pooling common wealth or even by creating economic equality.

These early communal efforts by Church leaders were close to the ideal of economic equality—the concept that all would be alike economically and that each would serve the other from a position of equality, not from positions of economic superiority or subordination. These experiments were intended to prevent the Saints from mimicking the materialism of the world. President Brigham Young worried about the effect individual wealth would have on the Saints: "The worst fear I have about this people is that they will get rich in this country, forget God and His people, wax fat, and kick themselves out of the Church," he lamented. In 1878, the year after Brigham Young's death, George Q. Cannon praised the Church's policy of giving immigrants no more land than they could work, remarking that Utah was a "land in which men cannot, from the very nature of things, monopolize large bodies of land to the exclusion of their poorer neighbors."[5]

Besides caring for the poor, economic equality had two other vital goals. One goal was to avoid the creation of a class-based society—something that the Book of Mormon repeatedly condemns. Throughout the record, the rich are described as "puffed up," filled with "pride," and disdaining the poor. As the Nephites moved closer to achieving a class-based society, the cycle repeatedly ended in personal and societal wickedness and eventual destruction.

The other goal was the spiritual preparation of Church members through a refining process that would make them eligible for gifts from Heavenly Father. The Lord reminded the people that "if ye are not equal in earthly things, ye cannot be equal in obtaining heavenly things" (D&C 78:6). Our own exaltation seems to hinge on how much we are willing to share of our earthly goods.

Economic Equality and the Church Today

Economic equality was never achieved in the early Church. Indeed, since the late nineteenth century, it has not even been attempted. Church lead-

---

City: Deseret Book, 1976).

5. Preston Nibley, *Brigham Young: The Man and His Work* (Salt Lake City: Deseret News Press, 1936), 128; and Elder George Q. Cannon, July 7, 1878, *Journal of Discourses*, 26 vols. (London and Liverpool: LDS Booksellers Depot, 1854–86), 20:34.

ers more recently have emphasized individualism and economic self-reliance rather than a communal effort to implement the law of consecration. The communal nature of early Church experiments has been downplayed somewhat, while attention has been focused on individuals and families. For several decades beginning in the 1930s, Church leaders counseled families to acquire a year's supply of food storage, although that has been modified in recent years to some level of preparation for emergencies. President Spencer W. Kimball repeatedly urged members to grow gardens, be self-sufficient, and prepare for catastrophes. The rhetorical focus has revolved around the individual and the family.[6]

This shift from communal to individual and familial needs may be the result of the separation of Church and state in Utah. While the two were tightly joined in the Church's early years—both in Nauvoo and in Utah—that connection was loosened by the end of the nineteenth century. No longer was the Church able to control politics or the local economy. Economic individualism was spurred by "gentile" businessmen who did not participate in the United Order. With the growth of mining, the coming of the railroad in 1869, and the influx of non-members, Church influence became more limited in economic matters.

Another problem, however, was the failure of these economic experiments. Many members had difficulty living the United Order. It was not easy to deed over personal property to the Church, even if it was primarily symbolic in terms of property management. Nor did some people take well to the strictness of communal living.

Nevertheless, the seeds of the eventual practice of consecration are still stressed today. Church leaders still attempt to cultivate a willingness to sacrifice material things to further the gospel. In that vein, a message of anti-materialism has emerged in recent years. For example, Elder Russell M. Ballard explained in 2009 that technology and science have "contributed to the rise of materialism and self-indulgence and to the decline of morality." In 2008, Elder D. Todd Christofferson warned that "materialism is just one more manifestation of the idolatry and pride that characterize Babylon." Similarly, Elder Joe J. Christensen in 1999 preached against a rampant materialism that saps our souls and urged Church members to "have the courage to examine honestly where our treasures lie and avoid the pitfalls that result from greed, selfishness, and overindulgence."[7]

---

6. Spencer W. Kimball, "A Report and a Challenge," *Ensign*, November 1976, http://www.lds.org/ensign/1976/11/a-report-and-a-challenge?lang=eng (accessed April 3, 2014).

7. Russell M. Ballard, "Learning the Lessons of the Past," *Ensign*, May 2009, 31–34, quotation on p. 33; D. Todd Christofferson, "Come to Zion," *Ensign*, November

The Church welfare program is based on principles of communal economic welfare similar to those emphasized in the nineteenth century. Today's program does not match the communistic arrangement of Orderville or even the handing over of a property deed and assuming legal stewardship of one's property and business from the nineteenth century. However, it continues to stress the need for all to be concerned for each other's economic welfare. Those who are most in need are provided with temporary Church assistance through the Church's extensive economic welfare system; and that system is sustained with not only the financial contributions of members but also by the volunteer time and labor of many who work in canneries, storehouses, and farms owned by the Church.

The goal of being economically equal may not be possible today given broad acceptability of seeking personal gain over community good. Of course, that social norm may also be an excuse for selfishness that leads to an abandonment of the goal. (It doesn't help that the repeated rationale of economic self-reliance can too often be transformed into rhetorical reinforcement for material self-centeredness.)

The objective of the self-reliance rhetoric is to keep Church members out of debt, and off government and Church welfare rolls as much as possible. Moreover, it is intended to prepare members for catastrophes, ranging from natural disasters to job loss, chronic illnesses, or other challenges. This emphasis is easy to understand: People who are economically self-sufficient will not be a drain on the resources of others—be it government or the Church. Then, such aid can go to others who are needy in difficult economic times or at moments of natural disaster. "Be prepared" is wise counsel, not just for Boy Scouts, but for everyone.

Many members perceive eschewing debt and having food storage and a financial emergency fund as providing solely for their personal security. Undoubtedly, caring for one's family and avoiding being a burden on others are worthwhile reasons for building up an economic surplus. However, another purpose of economic preparedness also exists: It is the connection between having a personal economic surplus—be it in the form of money or goods—and being in a position to assist others in need.

Having a surplus also allows us the means to be of assistance. "Being prepared" means more than just being prepared for our own needs; the possession of some wealth puts us in the position of being able to help others who, for whatever reason, face financial difficulties. Early Latter-day Saints were urged to place their surplus in the bishop's storehouse for the use of others: "Let all

2008, 37–40, quotation on p. 39; and Joe J. Christensen, "Greed, Selfishness, and Overindulgence," *Ensign*, May 1999, 9–12, quotation on p. 12.

things both in money and in meat, which are more than is needful for the wants of this people, be kept in the hands of the bishop" (D&C 51:13). Similarly, when the pioneers trekked west, they were admonished to share their property with the "poor, the widows, the fatherless, and the families of those have gone into the army that the cries of the widow and the fatherless come not up into the ears of the Lord against this people" (D&C 136:8). President Spencer W. Kimball was referring to this principle when he urged members who could give more in fast offerings than the actual amount of two meals to dramatically multiply those offerings. He was saying, in other words, that we should be willing to divest ourselves of our surplus in order to help the Church (and the Lord) take care of those in need—precisely the same instruction that the Lord provided in the opening verse of Doctrine and Covenants 119.

Redistribution of wealth is not inherently evil. In fact, the initial distribution of wealth is often simply arbitrary. For example, many become rich because they have inherited their wealth. Others were lucky enough to be in an economically advantageous time and place—a situation in which the vast majority of people on this planet will never find themselves. Given such randomness, the requirement for redistribution should not be surprising.

Furthermore, the need to redistribute is not just societal; it also is individual. Giving to others is something each of us must learn to do. It is a sign of our movement toward Christ-like attitudes and behavior. Perhaps one of our greatest tests as Latter-day Saints is our individual answer to the question: Will I share with others?[8]

Unfortunately, what motivates the vast majority of people to acquire wealth is not concern for others. Usually it is a driving need for economic security, the lust for material things, or sometimes a means of attaining power. Rarely do those seeking riches really do so for the good of all humanity, despite occasional rhetoric to the contrary.

The scriptures are crystal clear on this point. Followers of Christ have only one legitimate reason for seeking wealth: It is to be able to aid others in need:

> Before ye seek riches, seek ye for the kingdom of God. And after ye have obtained a hope in Christ ye shall obtain riches, if ye seek them; and ye will seek them for the intent to do good—to clothe the naked, and to feed the hungry, and to liberate the captive, and to administer relief to the sick and afflicted. (Jacob 2:18–19)

---

8. As three LDS writers on this topic have noted, "When significant inequalities exist, it is a sign that we have erred." This type of inequality is due to "inattentiveness of the rich to their responsibility to create equality of opportunity." Warner Woodworth, Joseph Grenny, and Todd Manwaring, *United for Zion: Principles for Uniting the Saints to Eliminate Poverty* (Orem, Utah: Unitus Publications, 2000), 37.

Those admonitions, if put in practice, might result in more charitable giving by members, which means that the Church and other charitable organizations will have the capability to accomplish more good. Perhaps more importantly, it might cultivate in all of us a "new heart" that sees the process of redistribution of resources as benefiting both the recipient and the giver.

The Government's Role

Does government have a role in bringing about economic equality? How should the liberal soul treat the government's role? Must the liberal soul choose between laissez-faire capitalism—where economic equality is never achieved and is not even sought—and state-sponsored communism—in which economic equality can be the equivalent of poverty for all except for leaders of the ruling party?

In our time, economic equality is an idealistic goal that is, in practical terms, out of reach for today's society, including the communities of Latter-day Saints around the world. Whether such equality will ever be possible in this current world is unknown. However, Latter-day Saints can help bring about the nearest thing to economic equality—that is, economic opportunity for all. That means providing the means for all to succeed economically—particularly in terms of achieving decent living conditions for all families. That is a practical goal for Latter-day Saints and is the objective of the Church today.

An essential aspect of economic opportunity is maintaining a floor or baseline for economic sustenance beyond which people will not sink. This goal is basically what the Church Welfare System is intended to achieve. Church members are provided with basics to help them in time of crisis in their lives. For those with long-term and even lifetime temporal needs, that assistance may be continual.

The liberal soul, however, does not believe that this threshold should be reserved only for Church members. All should be given the opportunity, regardless of their religious affiliation. Basic human needs are universal, not limited by religion.

At the same time, the Church institutionally cannot be the vehicle for providing that economic opportunity for hundreds of millions of people who are not LDS Church members. It would be an impossible burden. Nor should the liberal soul conclude that all should join the Church in order to receive the benefits of the Church's system. Not only is it an unrealistic idea, but it would promote joining the Church for the wrong reason.

Therefore, the liberal soul must advocate other means, beyond Church welfare, to provide economic opportunity for all. But what is "economic opportunity"? What are its components?

Apostle Paul gave us a clue when he advised his fellow Christians to be fair toward each other: "Masters, give unto your servants that which is just and equal; knowing that ye also have a Master in heaven" (Col. 4:1). According to Paul, both sides in an economic relationship have a responsibility to assure fairness in their relationship. But the greater obligation is upon the "master," because that person has the upper hand in the relationship. That power differential, unless it is governed by an ethical commitment to fairness, can lead to inequality rather than a relationship that is "just and equal."

What is "just"? What is "equal"? The definitions of such terms would vary from person to person and even from situation to situation. However, a baseline of justice and equality would include at least a decent living wage—the ability to purchase an adequate and safe dwelling for a family, to buy enough food, and to meet other necessities of life. In addition, it would mean access to adequate health care for the worker and his or her family, educational opportunities, and retirement benefits. Equality and justice also imply that workers have limits on their work hours so that they can enjoy time with their families, engage in wholesome recreational pursuits, and also pursue goals of self-improvement.

A decent living wage may vary from place to place, but it is not a mysterious figure. When employees working full time are forced to turn to government welfare for economic sustenance, cannot get access to health care, lack the means to afford safe and comfortable housing, or are unable to educate their children, they are not being paid a decent wage.

Complicating the ability for persons and families to receive living wages is the passing of responsibility to someone else to help secure that decent wage. The employer usually holds the power to offer a wage that allows an employee to live decently. Unfortunately, too many employers adopt the approach that, if employees lack the basic necessities of life, it is their problem, not that of the business. After all, the employer is merely paying the market wage.

The growth of big business has exacerbated this problem. While small business owners are able to see their employees as human beings and not just as names or statistics on a page, owners, shareholders, and executives in large corporations lack that personal approach. They are far more likely than small businesses to adopt bureaucratic rules that emphasize the bottom line of profits that will satisfy shareholders. As a result, the practices of large corporations can foster an attitude of inhumanity toward workers in need.

Of course, this is not always the case for large corporations. In 1914, Henry Ford, then head of Ford Motor Company, shocked the business world by lowering his average working period to eight hours a day rather than nine and doubling the minimum wage his company paid many of his employees.

He considered this behavior an act of social justice and was pleased that he had made so many of his workers happy through this move.[9]

Granted, Ford knew that his company would also sell more cars because his own workers now had enough money to buy those cars. Yet, it also meant that those workers could buy other things as well—better houses, college education for their children, and so on—and would have more time to spend with their families and for leisure as well.

Unfortunately, Ford's views are not shared widely enough by corporate employers today. The accepted business practice for many companies is to hire employees at the lowest wage possible. Where demand for jobs is high, companies get low-paid workers. When demand for workers is high, employers must pay more. The tragedy for families is that it is precisely in economic hard times (when jobs are at a premium) that employees have the most difficulty in providing basic necessities for their families. Employers typically offer the lowest possible wage that the market will bear, regardless of its consequences for the worker and his or her family. When money is tight and jobs scarce, employers can use that leverage to lower salaries and reduce or eliminate benefits. They know they can do so because most people are willing to work under those conditions rather than not work at all. Even the best of employers may find themselves taking this approach because they must compete against other companies that cut their costs (and their prices) by lowering employees' wages.

The scriptures are clear in condemning inadequate wages paid by employers who have the ability to offer fairer salaries. According to the New Testament Epistle of James, the wealthy who deny decent wages to their employees will lose the riches they have sought after, and their unrighteous deeds will testify against them (James 5:1–6). Unfortunately, because this judgment does not necessarily happen in this life, it does not ensure relief for those who are oppressed by these practices today.

So how is relief provided in this life? How can future generations prevent the suffering inflicted by an unrighteous employer? And how can employers who are tempted to place the bottom line ahead of their obligation to their employees be prevented from succumbing to that temptation?

One answer is to call out such employers and publicize their deeds. They could be identified and chastised by groups seeking better living conditions for employees. Perhaps their goods and services could be boycotted. However, social pressure alone is not enough. Rather, it is government that plays the role of compelling employers to do what they should do without compulsion. For example, government regulations create salary thresholds of a minimum

---

9. Henry Ford, *My Life and Work* (New York: Classic House Books, 2007), chap. 8.

wage or require employers to provide health care benefits for employees. Government regulation helps curb bad employers from acting badly and good employers from being tempted to act badly.

Because employers are subject to the same minimum wage rate, this regulation levels the playing field for employers by minimizing competitive advantage in terms of lowering wages. Granted, that wage rate must be high enough to provide a decent living. Too often, the regulations of minimum wage lag far behind the real costs of living. As a result, the floor is too low for a family to live on and poverty exists even among those who work full-time.

The presence of laws further reminds us of the consequences of bad behavior when we are tempted to violate them. Their existence also is necessary to assure fair treatment by employers. Due to government regulation on matters such as maximum working hours, workplace safety, minimum wage, and other issues, workers are more likely to have and potentially exercise an equal opportunity for economic success than if those regulations were not present.

Additionally, government plays a role in economic opportunity by legally prohibiting biases from inhibiting individuals' opportunities to better themselves economically. For example, an employer cannot use race, religion, or gender as reasons for not hiring or promoting an employee. As a result, even though the employer may hold certain prejudices, he or she cannot legally implement them to hold back people from economic opportunities.

This is why the liberal soul realizes that, due to the presence of "bad apples" in every group and the continual temptation to act badly for our own purposes, government must play a role in helping bring about opportunity for all and protect workers from unrighteous employers. Without society's intervention through government, economic opportunity would be a dream, and not a reality—or even possibility—for many. Such exclusion offends the liberal soul.

Social Equality

When the Saints gathered together to learn the gospel in Kirtland, Ohio, they were told to "let one speak at a time and let all listen unto his sayings, that when all have spoken that all may be edified of all, and that every man may have an equal privilege" (D&C 88:122). Similarly, Church members in the Book of Mormon were described as having a similar equality: "the priest, not esteeming himself above his hearers, for the preacher was not better than the hearer, neither was the teacher any better than the learner; and thus they were all equal" (Alma 1:26).

The Church of Jesus Christ of Latter-day Saints is a place in which Latter-day Saints can practice that concept of equality. In fact, it is one of the most important venues for Church members to learn what social equality means. Once learned in that setting, it can be extended beyond Church members to all of God's children.

The Church's teaching of social equality is communicated in small and subtle, but nevertheless important, ways. For example, the policy of rotating callings—a Primary teacher may become a bishop or a stake president and then a ward chorister—mitigates the hierarchal distinctions that can easily arise in any organization. Another example can be found in the temple, where all wear very similar clothing that breaks down the class distinction that is often marked by the clothing one can afford to wear.

However, we live in a society much broader than our Church environment. We live in a world where few, relatively speaking, are Latter-day Saints. We cannot consider ourselves followers of Christ and believe that brotherhood and sisterhood is defined by Church membership. Equality does not stop at the chapel door or the ward directory. Our sense of equality must be applied to all we come in contact with, all who share our humanity. All deserve the title of "child of God" and of "brother" or "sister." Equality applies to all, regardless of who they are or what religion they have. Since all people are brothers and sisters, all should be accepted as socially equal as well. There can be no exceptions.

Challenging Our Own Biases

Where the challenge lies for each of us is dealing with our own prejudices. Through culture or our experience with particular individuals, we can become biased in certain ways. Some of those biases against certain things can be good because they keep us from what is bad. A bias against food that upsets our stomach helps us stay healthy. If we suffer from alcoholism, a bias against bars and pubs where we may be tempted to imbibe is a good thing.

However, other biases related to people, particularly groups of people, lead us away from desirable traits such as acceptance, compassion, and love. For the liberal soul, discriminatory practices that target people based on their membership in a particular demographic group (nationality, race, ethnicity, etc.) are not in keeping with the gospel of Jesus Christ. Discrimination on such grounds means prejudging an individual according to his or her category, before even knowing the individual. Judging others is dangerous. Judging them unrighteously is sinful.

Discrimination can exist not only on an individual level, but also on a societal level. A whole society, through its attitudes, its practices, and then its laws, can exhibit prejudice against certain groups within the society. This happens in nations around the world. The caste system in India, slavery in many nations, apartheid and Jim Crow laws in South Africa and the United States, and legal discrimination against women practiced worldwide are all examples of societal prejudice that have been bolstered by law.

Various movements have emerged to eradicate these discriminatory practices. They have sought to end society's acceptance of prejudice, particularly through law. For example, the civil rights movement in the United States sought to change laws that prevented African Americans from voting, enrolling in certain schools, or even eating in certain restaurants. These were efforts to replace societal discrimination with justice that, in turn, helps bring about social equality.

Unfortunately, some detractors see these movements, not as progress, but as threats. For example, one LDS political commentator once urged his listeners to leave a church that preaches social justice.[10] But far from being sinful, social justice is the essence of the behavior of a Zion society practicing the gospel of Jesus Christ. Just as one-on-one discrimination is bad for the soul, discrimination writ large in a society is bad for the society. For example, apartheid in South Africa corrupted the whole nation. Every person was required to participate in discriminatory laws passed by the government. Everyone had to think about race on a constant basis and perpetuate the inequitable practices that denied equality. Each new generation grew up learning racist prejudices legitimated by the society through its government.

Of all religious groups, Latter-day Saints should be among the most sympathetic to the cause of social justice. By remembering Church history, we are reminded of what it is like to be persecuted and rejected by society. For some Church members, history is still alive with the religious discrimination they feel today in the societies where they live. In the 1990s, for example, Church members in Ghana were persecuted by a government determined to disband the Church and scatter its members.

Unlike the vast majority of Americans, Church members can understand the devastating power of social discrimination enforced by government. The history of the Church has been one of discrimination based on religion. Examples include hostility and scorn toward Joseph Smith in Palmyra, persecution in Kirtland, pillaging and murder in Missouri, expulsion from Nauvoo, and the harassment of LDS missionaries in various parts of the world even today.

And of all people, Latter-day Saints should realize that such persecution is not just individual-based; it can be directed at a group. As a group, and not just as individuals, Latter-day Saints were driven from their homes, beaten,

---

10. "Glenn Beck: 'Leave Your Church,'" *Christianity Today*, March 12, 2010, http://www. christianitytoday.com/ct/2010/marchweb-only/20-51.0.html (accessed April 15, 2013).

and even murdered by Missourians in the 1830s. The state's governor used the power of government to articulate and encourage such behavior by issuing an extermination order.

The national government did nothing to intervene. When Joseph Smith appealed to the president of the United States, Martin Van Buren told the Prophet that the federal government lacked the power to intervene in the internal affairs of Missouri. The Prophet Joseph was irate over the federal government's failure to protect the Latter-day Saints from oppressive state and local government action.[11] Nor did Van Buren reflect on the larger issue on civil rights for a religious minority. Instead, according to Joseph Smith, Van Buren "treated me very insolently, and it was with great reluctance he listened to our message, which, when he had heard, he said: 'Gentlemen, your cause is just, but I can do nothing for you.'"[12] When Joseph ran for president in 1844, it is not surprising that one plank in his platform was greater power for the federal government to protect the rights of individual citizens when violated by the states.[13] Eventually, the U.S. Supreme Court would also rule that individual religious rights took precedence over state legislation, but not for nearly another century.

The persecution of the Saints did not stop after the Missouri experience. The Mormons were driven out of Illinois in the 1840s. In 1857, U.S. troops invaded Utah to bring the supposedly rebellious Mormons to heel. During the 1880s, U.S. federal officers raided homes to find polygamists, with and without search warrants. Congressional legislation disestablished the Church and disfranchised its members. In the twentieth century, communities across the nation passed ordinances to prohibit door-to-door religious proselytizing, a key contacting tool for LDS missionaries. It was not until 2002 that the U.S. Supreme Court ruled definitively that cities and towns could not block such contacting.

Fortunately, that discrimination has eased over time. The two presidential campaigns of Mitt Romney (2008, 2012) and the U.S. Senate leadership of Harry Reid are symbols of the change. But even today, Latter-day Saints may feel societal discrimination. Indeed, in a 2011 survey of Latter-day Saints, two-thirds said they do not feel accepted in the mainstream of American society and 46 percent agreed that there is "a lot of discrimination

---

11. Joseph Smith, et al., *History of the Church of Jesus Christ of Latter-day Saints*, edited by B. H. Roberts, 7 vols., 2nd ed. rev. (Salt Lake City: Deseret Book, 1948 printing), 3:40–43.

12. Ibid., 4:80.

13. See *The Prophet Joseph Smith's Views on the Powers and Policy of the Government of the United States* (Salt Lake City: Jos. Hyrum Parry & Co., 1886), 18.

against Mormons" in the United States today.[14] The liberal soul remembers the persecution Latter-day Saints have experienced and still experience today; our theological understanding interprets such activities as efforts of Satan to thwart members from living the gospel by prompting acts of individual and society persecution. Building on that understanding, the liberal soul should empathize with others who also are discriminated against. The liberal soul is sensitive to all who, like Latter-day Saints, suffer from various types of discrimination. And the liberal soul views that discrimination as something society is morally and ethically called to attempt to stop.

However, the liberal soul does not stop there. Liberal souls also are aware that Latter-day Saints have not been the only religious group discriminated against. Catholics were a persecuted minority for years, as evidenced by anti-Catholic legislation in various nations in the eighteenth and nineteenth centuries, political slogans against "rum and Romanism," and religious opposition to the presidential candidacies of Al Smith in 1928 and John F. Kennedy in 1960. Members of other religious groups such as Jehovah's Witnesses, Sikhs, and Muslims still suffer much religious discrimination today.

Not only has minority religion status made people targets for discrimination, but so have a number of other factors—gender, race, ethnicity, nationality, and sexual orientation. For many years in the United States, women could not vote or hold office, some states banned them from owning property or having a separate income, and they were excluded from certain occupations. Racial and ethnic discrimination was common in the South and the West against African Americans, Hispanics, and Native Americans. Gays were fired from certain jobs if their sexual orientation was known; and until recently, homosexuals in the military could be dishonorably discharged if their sexual orientation became known.

What can the liberal soul do to help secure social equality? We can examine this problem from the three levels. At the individual level, the liberal soul can seek to banish such prejudices from his or her mind and lips. This means avoiding discriminatory remarks—even allegedly "joking" comments—against groups of people based on their race, religion, nationality, gender, sexual orientation, and other categories. Another is to gently admonish those who do make such remarks, particularly when they have chosen the path of discipleship of Christ. Yet another way is to get to know people of different races, nationalities, religions, etc. in a sincere effort to view people as individuals and not as members of groups.

---

14. "Mormons in America: Certain in Their Beliefs, Uncertain of Their Place in Society," The Pew Forum on Religion & Public Life, January 12, 2012, http://www.pewforum.org/Christian/Mormon/mormons-in-america.aspx (accessed April 15, 2013).

One should slow down the process of judging others. This includes avoiding discriminatory attitudes that perpetuate social inequality such as harboring stereotypes that assume certain types of views or behavior because of group membership. I remember a blogger reviewing a book I had written, which was an academic study of political blogging. Some of the findings from the research supported the positions of political conservatives about bias in news media use of blogs. This blogger did not attribute these conclusions to my findings but concluded that I must be politically conservative because I worked at BYU. When I pointed out this unfounded assumption to the blogger—since he had provided no evidence for his assertion except my place of employment—he apologized for jumping to such a conclusion. He was not alone. Making such judgments based on membership in a particular group is common.

Next is change in our practices. If we are reluctant to hire someone because he or she belongs to a certain racial group or are not willing to socialize with someone because he or she belongs to a certain religion, we are practicing discrimination based on group membership. A few types of discrimination make sense in some ways if the group's positions are clear. For example, it is best to avoid serving pork to an Orthodox Jew. But in most cases, our discriminatory practices tend to focus on assumptions, not on facts.

We need to consider whether we unconsciously perpetuate biases. Do we assume that people can or cannot do certain things because of their race, color, ethnicity, gender, or sexual orientation without even thinking of the consequences of our assumptions? Do we favor certain people because they fit certain images in our minds—assuming that only a person of a certain race, gender, or particular age can do a certain job adequately or only a candidate of a certain religion could be a public official or even president?

Social equality also needs to be furthered by organizations and not just individuals. Organizations can become collective, and therefore more powerful, forces for discrimination. These include such obvious ones as the Ku Klux Klan with its blatantly anti-black and anti-Catholic membership qualifications or various social clubs that ban women. Today, such groups are relatively easy to point to as discriminatory.

More difficult is a work climate in an office, or even a whole company, that fosters a discriminatory culture. This might consist of an unspoken understanding that women are not promoted to top management positions. Or it might be a social tradition of mocking someone who belongs to another minority religion, often presented as a joke. Sometimes, the discrimination can be against religious believers generally.

How does the liberal soul promote social equality at the organizational level? One way is to refuse to join it. That means resisting the temptation to impress others in the office or social club who discriminate by being intolerant as well. It also means seeking to guide the organization to adopt policies that promote social equality, such as suggesting changes in corporate policy to remove discriminatory policies or practices.

The third level is the society in which we live. Society is the amalgamation of views of individuals and groups. If social justice is the objective of individuals, it will be the aim of the society as a whole as well as of its government.

The liberal soul can urge the passage of laws that diminish social inequality and respect the contribution of every member of society. The liberal soul can seek out parties or candidates who promote policies that will be inclusive of people regardless of religion, ethnicity, race, etc., rather than exclusive. The liberal soul can examine how parties and candidates treat those who have been discriminated against. Do they engage in discriminatory language and behavior themselves? Do they pretend discrimination has not existed? Do they downplay it? Are they inclined to see prejudice as merely an individual and perhaps isolated problem, and not as one that society deals with as a whole? All of these are questions that the liberal soul should be addressing.

Legal Equality

When school children in the United States stand to recite the Pledge of Allegiance, they end it by saying "liberty and justice for all." This is legal equality—justice for all. It means that everyone has equal claim to the protections of the law. This legal equality allows Americans to live our lives freely and enjoy all the opportunities available within society. If the social equality discussed above was practiced across a society, legal equality would not be a question. Instead, legal inequality is a product of social inequality. Ultimately, the cure is to bring about social equality.

However, legal equality must occur even without universal acceptance of social equality. One person's continued prejudice cannot become the barrier for someone else's ability to live their life fully. For example, a white police officer who is prejudiced against Latinos cannot be allowed to stop Latinos on the street and question them arbitrarily because he or she dislikes Latino people. A school principal does not have the right to refuse to hire someone who is homosexual because he or she is uneasy about homosexuals and equates homosexuality with pedophilia.

One reason that legal inequality exists is because, over time, many government policies have reflected social attitudes that favor inequality. When society believes certain minority groups should not have equal rights, then laws are enacted to codify that inequality and enforce it through government. Government has been a powerful tool of society's discriminatory attitudes in the past. Slavery, restrictions on the rights and activity spheres of women, and intolerance toward minority religions are examples of society using government to enforce its prejudices.

Legal practices designed to discriminate are not harmless. They have enormous consequences for a society as a whole and for all the individuals in the society. It is society's great loss. The potential for individuals of certain groups to contribute to society is wasted because they are relegated to inferior positions. A society loses doctors, teachers, and business leaders from among those minority groups—people who could have cured diseases, enlightened and encouraged young minds, and created jobs for others. They could have made important contributions to society but were not allowed to do so.

Not only does the society harm itself by restricting certain members from making a full contribution, but it inflicts psychological damage on itself. Laws upholding racism, for example, encourage even more racism by the members of the society. Young people absorb these conventions and traditions of racism, then perpetuate those attitudes as they raise their own children. Such laws legitimate and reinforce racial attitudes for the whole society. A racial majority adopts inaccurate views about a racial minority, which are perpetuated over time. The majority becomes wedded to the idea of racial superiority, a wrong-headed concept that warps people's minds about themselves and others of different races.

Unfortunately, the minority often emotionally accepts that racism as well. Indeed, a minority group who accepts discrimination would have great difficulty in not absorbing a false attitude of self-inferiority. For example, an African American civil rights leader related that, when he boarded a plane in 1970, he saw a black man in the pilot's seat. His first thought was to wonder whether he would be safe on the plane with that pilot. He then realized what had happened. He had subconsciously accepted the inferiority he had long been taught by a white majority. A famous study of pre-school children's preferences for dolls conducted in the 1940s found that both white and black children preferred white dolls. When the study was replicated in the 1980s, even after the civil rights movement, the findings were still the same.[15]

The effects of such prejudice may linger long after certain racist acts and policies have been banned. The effects of racism—apathy, despair, crime, poverty, and the breakdown of the family—do not suddenly disappear when racially discriminatory laws are overturned. The conditions those laws created remain—potentially for generations. South Africa still wrestles with the effects of racial discrimination that produced poor townships where black South

---

15. Daniel Goleman, "Black Child's Self-View Is Still Low, Study Finds," *New York Times*, August 31, 1987, at http://www.nytimes.com/1987/08/31/us/black-child-s-self-view-is-still-low-study-finds.html (accessed March 23, 2014).

Africans were legally confined by white leaders. Similarly, the United States is still a racially divided nation where many blacks and whites live in separate neighborhoods, communities, and even towns. Even in a nation which has elected its first black president, there are still stark differences along racial lines in areas such as educational level, occupation, and household income.

Society must address the issue of what to do about the lingering effects of discrimination, even when it is no longer practiced. In the United States, one policy proposal has been affirmative action, or an attempt to rectify effects of past discrimination. Launched in the late 1960s, affirmative action became the basis of law, bureaucratic regulation, and business and education policies.

Some of my students at BYU complain about affirmative action. They consider it unfair for African Americans to expect compensation for wrongs committed in the past, and they refuse to support actions to help a particular group of people discriminated against in the past. They think any remedial action should only apply on a case-by-case basis to individuals.

Yet affirmative action has a parallel with LDS Church history. When the Prophet Joseph traveled to Washington, D.C., to petition the federal government for redress, he did so because Missourians had expelled Mormons, appropriating their land and property, under the thin legal fiction that the Mormons had (though at bayonet point) signed over their property to pay the expenses of the Mormon War. In behalf of Church members, Joseph asked the president to force the Missourians to return the real and personal property that had been appropriated by their enemies.

Relating the history of persecution against the Church is significant, not only as a reminder of religious persecution but also as a lesson in how such persecution can be dealt with regardless of who is the object of persecution. First, Joseph turned to government to solve the problem. That is significant because he felt that government had a legitimate role in resolving a dispute between two parties—Mormons and their persecutors. The Prophet concluded that government action was a reasonable expectation because government action (the mobilization of the state militia and the governor's extermination order) had legitimated persecution that had begun as vigilante action. He believed that the constitutional rights of Latter-day Saints had been violated and should be restored. Who but the government had the power to compel Missourians to return the property of the Latter-day Saints?

Second, the government level to which he appealed was the federal level, not the state. The fact that Joseph asked for federal government help suggests that he saw such federal intervention as a legitimate government activity, despite the state's obvious disagreement. Given his actions, it seems likely that Joseph would not have agreed with many today who argue that state sovereignty is supreme and that the federal government should not intervene in a state's business.

An important point to remember relating to affirmative action is that Joseph was requesting positive action on the part of the federal government to rectify group discrimination. He wanted remedial action by the federal government to restore rights to a discriminated group, in this case the right to live peaceably and maintain their property. Importantly, his appeal was not just for discriminated individuals within the group, but for the group as a whole. The confiscated possessions had been taken because they belonged to a group—the Latter-day Saints—and had been taken precisely because they belonged to that group.

This sounds much like affirmative action. Again, affirmative action is a positive government policy intended to rectify the effects of past societal discrimination. The effects of past discrimination not only include the sense of inferiority discussed earlier but also the tangible damage inflicted through the loss of educational and job opportunities. For example, for many years African Americans were consigned to live in certain areas, nearly always undesirable sections of cities or rural areas. They were forced to attend black-only schools, which were underfunded by white school boards and white taxpayers. They were not able to go to the higher education institutions they paid taxes to support. Without the same education as whites, they were unable to get the jobs whites received.

Affirmative action cannot go back in time and undo what was done then. But the effects of that past linger. The consequences of the treatment of racial minorities or discrimination against women did not end with the prohibition of legal discrimination. They still remain, potentially for generations after.

It is critical to remember that the past history of official discrimination is not from a history long past. This is recent history. There are many alive today who lived through it. The desegregation of schools in the United States did not occur for many parts of the nation until the 1970s. For example, my sophomore year of high school in the 1970s was the first year the high school in my town was desegregated.

Those who lived through such racism can be relieved to know their children and grandchildren are not likely to suffer the same levels of prejudice they did, but most of those who were discriminated against, along with those children and grandchildren, still live in the residential areas previous generations were relegated to because of skin color. They still go to the schools created for that group because they live in those neighborhoods. And they live in poverty because of the limited and low-paying jobs their parents and grandparents were forced to take rather than having broad discretion to seek, train for, and exercise more preferred professions. They are further handicapped by living in an environment where authority figures they respect and who could be role models to a rising generation lack the educational skills to succeed. Perhaps even more dangerously, in some cases, they do not believe that people in their situation have the ability to succeed. That attitude can be transferred powerfully to succeeding generations, even when the legal constraints on advancement are removed.

I remember encountering this attitude when I taught a college course at a maximum security prison. I got into a discussion with my teaching assistant, who had been convicted of murder, about the reality of the American dream. My argument was that if someone worked hard, he or she would eventually succeed. He posed the question: "But what if they did not succeed? What if they worked and worked, but remained in a situation of poverty or oppression?"

It dawned on me that our cultures were quite different. I had grown up with the optimistic approach that potential accomplishment and success were available to me. If I put my hand to something, I would succeed. Only my personal limitations, preferences, willingness to exert effort, and ambitions restricted me from achieving such goals. But he had been raised in an environment of likely failure, regardless of effort. His views probably came from seeing others work hard yet remain unable to achieve significant economic or social advancement.

Children who grow up in such an environment almost certainly absorb such views even before they develop the critical thinking skills to appraise their source, their mechanisms of enforcement, or strategies for change. They may conclude that education is useless and that the job awaiting them involves wielding a broom or a shovel. Unless an extra effort is made to assist them, they are likely to remain cynical and unconvinced that educational and economic opportunities are available to them.

Affirmative action programs are used to minimize those discriminatory effects by providing positive action for those suffering from them. School integration, outreach to recruit minority employees, scholarship funds for minorities, and admissions standards that take race and ethnicity into consideration are all designed to help those that have been disadvantaged by our discriminatory and racist past. Affirmative action has been applied to the consequences of past discrimination against women and various racial and ethnic minorities to provide a form of restitution for that official discrimination.

Critics of affirmative action have argued that the focus of rights should be on individuals, not on groups. Yet Joseph Smith's appeal to Washington was for group rights—the rights of Latter-day Saints as a group to worship freely, live where they wished, and be protected from harassment by those who found their beliefs repugnant. Affirmative action by government (a positive response to restore lost property) was being requested because those basic rights were being violated by one group of people against another group of people—just because they were members of that group.

Moreover, like proponents of affirmative action today, he was requesting remedial action. He wanted restitution of what had been lost. During the conflicts between Missourians and Latter-day Saints, the Missourians had appropriated the lands and properties of the Latter-day Saints with the express approval of the state government; and Joseph wanted those back. Today, it is educational opportunities, economic advancement, and even decisions about neighborhoods in which to live that were denied certain groups of people for many years in the United States. They seek restitution of those things long prohibited them.

Critics of affirmative action often argue that there is no equality when it comes to affirmative action programs, claiming that it places certain groups above other groups and is simply a new form of discrimination. By definition, it does provide a temporary favoritism to certain groups. Much as when a scale is out of balance, additional pressure or weight needs to be applied to one side to reestablish balance. Racial discrimination put society out of balance, and affirmative action rights things once again. Granted, the issues are not easy to wrestle with, nor are the programs that institute affirmative action perfect. Like all institutions or processes devised by humans, they incorporate flaws. There is no gospel answer for how or whether to use specific affirmative action programs.

However, there are ways to think about affirmative action that correspond to the nature of the liberal soul. In considering these issues, it is important to remember gospel teachings regarding how we treat others in society. Specifically, does the Lord treat people equally? Are the ways of the Lord always equal? An Old Testament passage may be helpful in this regard. Ezekiel 18 portrays a hypothetical conversation between God and the people of ancient Israel. The people were complaining that the Lord's ways were not equal, because he did not punish repentant sinners but forgave them. The critics protested that those sinners were not getting their just desserts.

These Israelites complained because they did not understand the Lord's mercy. The Lord's way is not always equal. His plan of salvation is weighted toward helping those who are in the greatest need of it. For example, because He is merciful, His attitude toward His children is to give special consideration to those who have sinned and come back.

Jesus spelled out the claims of this "inequality" in our behalf in the parable of the workers in the field (Matt. 20). The master returned several times during the day, each time hiring a different group of workers. At the day's end, he paid each worker the same daily wage even though some had labored all day while others had worked for only the final hour. Was it just to give

YOU ARE TO BE EQUAL

the same pay to all, regardless of how long they worked? Is anything different really fair? Indeed, this circumstance is *not* equal, and that is exactly the point.

Equality is not the same as fairness. Rather, this parable is a wonderful illustration of how the Lord uses inequality to bless our lives. He dismisses the complaints by pointing out that he did not begin with a "contract" agreement of how much each worker would be paid an hour. Rather, the workers manifested trust in the master's general fairness and did not haggle about the terms. As a result—as the master tellingly pointed out—he was free to distribute his resources as he saw fit. If the daily wage is our opportunity to return to live with our Heavenly Father in the celestial kingdom, then it becomes clearer that the Savior not only wanted everyone to have that ability but took steps to extend that opportunity to all. Those who labored in the Lord's kingdom throughout their lives can receive all the blessings of heaven; and those who did not, for whatever reason, can still access the Lord's mercy and receive that same reward.

Let's personalize this concept. If we have a child, a spouse, or friend who strays or lives without regard to gospel principles, how grateful we should be that the Lord will extend the invitation to return to Him, even at the end of their lives. If we lose our way throughout our life, we can repent, be forgiven, and experience the same acceptance from our Heavenly Father and Christ as well.

Those who worry that this is not equality are exactly right. It is not. In essence, the Savior is giving a break to those who are wicked but who come back to him. Those who get "the break" do not constitute someone else. Rather, it includes us as well because it includes all who commit sins. Those resisting this generous mercy are not losing any blessings by living long lives of purity, righteousness, faith, and service. It is the development of these very godlike qualities that should underscore the appropriate response: rejoicing in the mercy and power of our God rather than complaining that we have been somehow mistreated. Do we *really* think that a long life of devotion and righteousness means that we have earned our salvation? Indeed, no. For all of us, it is grace, not our good works, that intervenes to treat us mercifully instead of the "justice" that our sins really merit.

Another example of this inequality, again with wonderful results, is the parable of the prodigal son in Luke 15. Jesus tells of a young man who requests his inheritance from his father, then rushes away from his home to waste his patrimony on sinful self-indulgence with a group quickly attracted by his affluence. It does not last long, and neither do his friends. When he comes back, suffering, destitute, and in sorrow, his father embraces him and welcomes him back with fine apparel, a banquet, and a celebration. The young man's brother is jealous. He protests to his father that he has worked long and hard for his father and never received such attention. It isn't fair, he is saying. Indeed, it was not fair in strict terms of justice. But the father gently reassured him of the father's unwavering love for him, his unchanged heirship, and the joy that was being poisoned by his envy. Rather, he should show mercy and be grateful for his brother's return.

In that same chapter, a man left ninety-nine sheep in safety to seek one lost sheep. He made a special effort to recover what had been lost. It seems from the story that he quickly intervened to leave the ninety-nine in safety while he sought—doubtless over many miles, during the darkness, and despite his own weariness at the end of a long day—to bring back the sheep who had strayed. At that point, he did not treat all the sheep equally. He reached out for just one.

There are differences between heavenly and earthly things in this regard. Exaltation is not a zero-sum game like slots in a certain medical school or the numbers of people that can be hired or promoted. Heavenly Father's eternal gifts are available to all. One person's obtaining the celestial kingdom does not limit someone else's ability to do the same. Earth life often does not follow this same pattern of divine and unfailing abundance. A particular opportunity attained by one individual often means that another candidate will not have that opportunity. Nevertheless, there usually is enough on earth to go around. Ensuring that all individuals in all groups become fully integrated into society and achieve full equality is part of God's plan. In order to obtain equality for all, the Lord's way is not equal. Sometimes, on a temporary basis to rectify past sins, that is necessary on earth as well.

Political Equality

In the Book of Mormon, King Mosiah proposed that the government consist of judges rather than a king. He also urged that those judges be chosen "by the voice of this people." He admonished the people to "observe and make it your law—to do your business by the voice of the people" (Mosiah 29:25–26). Democracy rests on the concept that the people will ultimately choose wisely. Mosiah believed that "it is not common that the voice of the people desireth anything contrary to that which is right; but it is common for the lesser part of the people to desire that which is not right" (Mosiah 29:26).

Nevertheless, democracy has its critics, even among people who enjoy the benefits of living in democratic governmental systems. Some of my students refuse to call the United States a democracy, insisting that it is, instead, a republic. (A republic is a democracy in which citizens choose others to represent them in government.) "Democracy," with its implications that all citizens are essentially equal in their rights and responsibilities as citizens makes them uneasy, and it is, in fact, a description of radical (and probably unattainable) equality. Indeed, many early American political leaders, including some framers of the U.S. Constitution, who were primarily familiar with monarchies, shared this uneasiness, considering democracy as similar to mob rule.

However, most people around the world today see democracy as a good thing. It certainly should be praiseworthy to Latter-day Saints. The preaching of the gospel of Jesus Christ generally flourishes in democratic nations. Democratic nations almost always allow broad religious freedom and accept LDS missionaries as part of that freedom.

The very foundation of democracy is the concept of sovereignty of the public, in other words, a government where the people rule. "We, the People," the first words in the preamble to the U.S. Constitution, are not there for decoration. They describe people making decisions about how they will be governed and not leaving that decision to someone else. Each citizen is part of that "people" and therefore possesses the power to shape his or her own destiny as a participant in a democracy.

However, democracy does not work if political equality is not present. Political equality means the right of every adult to have an equal voice in the decision-making process of the governance of the society in which he or she lives. Any system that favors one individual or group above others is not, at heart, a democracy.

Democracy rests on the assumption that the people govern. That makes the people the sovereigns, rather than an individual monarch. Each individual is part of that popular sovereignty in a democratic society. It means that each individual must be allowed to play his or her respective role as a sovereign. Each person must be able to participate in his or her own governance.

There are those who believe that not all should participate in democratic governance. They would exclude people who they believe should not be able to participate, including the uninformed, uneducated, or those who do not seem to have a stake in society because they do not own property or businesses.

Such reasoning can often lead to dictatorships (rule by one), oligarchies (rule by a few), or aristocracies (rule by a certain privileged class), because, if the people are generally seen as unfit to make their own decisions, then someone must make those decisions for them. Democracy, on the other hand, sees the collective masses as fit to govern rather than be governed by someone else.

The liberal soul seeks to create a society where political equality, democracy's foundation, is a reality, not just a dream. This means seeking a system where all possess equal potential to affect public policy regardless of their income level, intelligence, or level of education. It also requires encouraging broader participation rather than seeking to diminish it. It also includes promoting policies that lower barriers for voter participation rather than raise them.

A major obstacle to political equality is the role of money in politics. It does not take a mathematician to figure out that, when the very ability to campaign for office requires huge sums of money, the person with more money will be more influential than the person with less. Political equality is eliminated in such a system. The liberal soul supports government policy that promotes full political equality and seeks to create an electoral system that gives equal voice to the rich and the poor since both are sovereign in a democratic society. The system of democratic decisions thus cannot rest on the power of money. Instead, the structure and rules of elections must promote an equal role for all in the society.

Spiritual Equality

In no other area of life are Latter-day Saints more torn between the "natural man" and the "disciple of Christ" than in attitudes about equality. What we conclude about others and how we implement those conclusions says a lot about what kind of person we are. It also defines our relationship with our Heavenly Father.

We know that because, if others are equal in the eyes of God, they should be equal in our own eyes as well. But do we see all others equally? In addition to the prejudices based on skin color, religion, or sexual orientation, do we also harshly judge and categorize individuals we encounter—or even those we don't know personally but see as belonging to groups of diminished worth? Do we consider the beggar on the street to be equal to us? How about the passerby with legs and arms solidly tattooed and a mohawk haircut? Or maybe the woman who wears a short skirt and a halter top?

Elder Alexander Morrison once told a story about how he judged a group of people he saw on a street in France. Friends had warned his family of the dangers of thieves who preyed on tourists. As he watched people passing on the street one day, a wallet fell out of another tourist's pocket, and a group of young boys lunged to pick it up. He fully expected they would run away with it; but instead, one of them held the wallet up and yelled to the tourist, "Excuse me, monsieur. You lost your wallet." He admitted: "I hung my head in shame, chagrined at my too-eager willingness to prematurely judge others. The experience taught me an important lesson: we must look beyond the superficial stereotyping which influences too much of our thinking about the worth of those who seem on the surface to be different than we are."[16]

I had a similar experience several years ago when I happened to be in Boston on a business trip and decided to walk around the Boston Commons,

---

16. Morrison, "No More Strangers," 20.

a large park in the center of the city. I noticed a man stumbling around the park. He was wearing an expensive suit, but appeared to be drunk. I was concerned that the man might hurt himself. Another man sitting on a park bench, noticing my concern, told me the inebriated man had been a prominent lawyer in Boston who had become an alcoholic. My first reaction was to judge him as a weak man who had succumbed to this self-inflicted disease. Instead, I should have wondered what agony this man might have gone through in his career or with his family that drove him to find solace in a bottle. I should not have condemned him.

How does our Heavenly Father feel when we judge others and consider others to be inferior to us? Jesus told us to "judge not, that ye be not judged" (Matt. 7:1). When we judge others, we are taking on a responsibility that belongs to God, and not to us. Also, as these two examples show, our usual tendency is to judge unrighteously. As a consequence, our ventures into the zone of judgment usually result in too-quick, too-easy, and too-inaccurate judgments. That is why we are not the right person to judge others' spirituality or their relationship with God; only He can do that.

The basis for all of the forms of equality discussed in this chapter is an appreciation of our spiritual equality. That spiritual equality transcends the temporal. The liberal soul understands that we are all children of our Heavenly Father. Whatever worldly differences exist between us in this life—social, economic, national, etc.—they are merely temporary. They are not important in the next life and therefore should not be considered vital in this life.

While we are in this life, cultural differences among people do test our willingness to embrace fully the concept of spiritual equality. The tendency to think of others as inferior to us is a continual temptation that we suffer as part of our mortal existence. Just as our flesh is weak, so are we when it comes to cultural prejudices. The pull of these prejudices is one of the trials we all face in this life, and for some it is a vexation throughout life. Overcoming them is a continual struggle.

In wrestling with these cultural prejudices, one of the worst things we can do is perceive them as the preference of God and not as the invention of people. For example, slavery was often defended as a divinely established condition by many Christians, including some Latter-day Saints. Today, greater affluence or social status often is attributed to our Heavenly Father's approval. Therefore, we may conclude that not only are pride and condescension justifiable but that withholding our sense of equality toward others is even righteous behavior because it is in accordance with God's will.

The liberal soul, however, sees the temptations of inequality for what they are—artificial labels. He or she strives to rise above the "natural man or woman." By doing so, the liberal soul becomes a disciple who follows Christ's example of love for all. He or she also realizes that even though we do not carry "under construction" labels as part of our visible garb, we are all, indeed, works in spiritual progress. For some, the task of overcoming prejudice is still a work very much in progress. When surveying the world facing a constant temptation to judge others, the liberal soul must develop the spiritual discipline and grace to forgive others and also to forgive oneself in the quest for achieving the Lord's admonition to be equal.

CHAPTER 3

THE POOR ALWAYS HAVE YE WITH YOU

When a woman poured ointment on Jesus's head while he sat in the house of Simon, some of those present murmured against her, complaining that the expensive oil could have been used for the poor. Jesus responded by admonishing them to leave her alone: "For the poor always ye have with you; but me ye have not always" (John 12:8).

Poverty is an unfortunate fact of this world. There always have been and will be those who suffer ill-fortune, lack the skills to take higher paying jobs, are physically or mentally unable to take care of themselves, or refuse to work and simply hope to rely on others for a living. The presence of the poor has been the reality of human existence for all of human history, with the exception of golden moments of communalism like the early New Testament times, the city of Enoch, and the Nephites immediately after the visitation of Jesus. In our current world, it is unlikely that poverty will be eliminated anytime soon, despite repeated efforts by government and nonprofit organizations toward that end.

The continual presence of the poor is a challenge and an opportunity to the liberal soul. The poor challenge our commitment to the gospel and our willingness to keep the commandments. The poor also test whether we possess mercy and compassion. They make us question whether we are willing to help or if we will merely stand on the sidelines and criticize. The poor make us consider how judgmental we really are.

At the same time, without the opportunity of the poor, we would not know whether we would share of our worldly possessions for the benefit of others in need. We could only guess whether our love of others would trump our materialism. The trial of our faith, in this respect, could never occur. Our own status as disciples of Christ is questioned or reaffirmed based on how we deal with those who are poor.

The Individual and the Poor

While, at first, Jesus's statement concerning the poor may seem callous, it is really just a statement of fact of our mortal condition. In proclaiming that the poor are always with us, Jesus was not suggesting that we have no obligation toward them. Jesus's own life and teachings show that he had an inherent concern for the poor. It was no coincidence that Jesus was born in the humblest of circumstances. He spent his life around the poor and downtrodden of his society, mingling with them constantly in the crowded streets and on the dusty roads. He told the rich who sought to follow him to sell their goods and donate to the poor. He praised a poor widow who gave almost nothing at the temple over rich men who gave much more.

Jesus's teachings emphasized the transient nature of riches. He taught his disciples not to worry much about material things, and his parables favored the poor over the rich. It is impossible to review the earthly life and teachings of Christ without noticing his concern for the poor, as well as his repeated condemnation of those who seek after riches for themselves.

Other scriptures also affirm the need for Christ's disciples to not focus on riches or ignore the poor. In the Old Testament, the Israelites were commanded not to harvest their fields so extensively that there would be no grain left "unto the poor and to the stranger" (Lev. 23:22). They were also supposed to relieve the poor among them and were instructed that concern for the poor distinguished the righteous from the wicked: "The righteous considereth the cause of the poor; but the wicked regardeth not to know it" (Lev. 25:35). In the New Testament, James condemns rich men for relying on earthly treasure as their salvation and oppressing the poor. According to him, at the heart of the gospel is to care for those in need: "Pure religion and undefiled before God and the Father is this, To visit the fatherless and the widows in their affliction" (James 5:1–6, 1:27).

The Book of Mormon also shares this concern for the poor. In 2 Nephi, the prophet Jacob warned the Nephites: "Wo unto the rich, who are rich as to the things of the world. For because they are rich they despise the poor, and they persecute the meek, and their hearts are upon their treasures; wherefore, their treasure is their god. And behold, their treasure shall perish with them also" (Mosiah 4:16, 26; see also 2 Ne. 9:30). At the end of his administration, King Benjamin taught the Nephites that they should "impart of [their] substance to the poor, every man according to that which he hath." This was their Christian obligation, to "succor those that stand in need of your succor." He spelled out the behavior that obedience to this commandment involved: "Ye will administer of your substance unto him that standeth in need; and ye will not suffer that the beggar putteth up his petition to you in vain, and turn him out to perish" (Mosiah 4:16)

The commandment to give to the poor is both a collective one and an individual one. It is directed at each individual as well as to the Church and to society as a whole. We cannot "get off the hook" because we belong to a Church that has a welfare system for the poor. Our relationship to the poor affects each of us individually. We are shaped by their presence and in how we respond to their needs. Without them, and our individual interaction with them, the Lord's blessings would not be poured out on all.

One of the blessings we receive by caring for the poor is overcoming the temptation to consider them as aliens, different than us. Indeed, the truth is they are us. Nearly all of us are materially poor according to the standards of our society at some point—many of us throughout our entire lives. And regardless of our present situation, any one of us may become poor at any time due to unexpected circumstances. The stock market crashes, a natural disaster destroys our home, a major illness depletes our savings—all of these are real possibilities and should make us realize how tenuous our riches really are.

Another blessing is developing an attitude of service. Not only are we commanded to care for the poor and the needy, but we are also encouraged to relish the opportunity. It is easy to resent having to give to the poor. Sometimes we can view it as an unpleasant sacrifice that we wish to avoid. However, as President George Albert Smith urged, we can "find joy in ministering to the needs of the poor."[1] As we serve others, especially the poor, we learn to better love everyone around us and develop the type of love that God possesses.

We also are blessed with an increasingly close relationship with our Heavenly Father. How we treat the poor affects our own exaltation. For example, Jesus told the rich man that if he gave to the poor "thou shalt have treasure in heaven" (Mark 10: 21); and he told his disciples that they would "inherit the kingdom prepared for you" if they fed the hungry, clothed the naked, and visited the sick and imprisoned (Matt. 25:34–36). Conversely, those who do not care for the poor and needy are actually sinning against God. Their wickedness is in their neglect of the poor when they possess the ability to make a difference. In the Book of Mormon, Alma condemned the people of Zarahemla for "turning [their] backs upon the poor, and the needy, and in withholding [their] substance from them" (Alma 5:55).

The condemnation of ignoring the poor should ring true because it is difficult to imagine our having Christ-like qualities without possessing compassion for others who are in need. How can we expect to dwell with God

---

1. *Teachings of the Presidents of the Church: George Albert Smith* (Salt Lake City: Church of Jesus Christ of Latter-day Saints, 2010), 1.

if we still have hardness in our heart toward others? How can we be trusted with celestial glory when we are still obsessed with material things? How can we love as God loves if we are judgmental toward others? Fortunately, our Heavenly Father gives us time to develop those qualities. But the presence of the poor in our lives helps us become Christ-like.

Of course, those who benefit the most from caring for the poor are the poor. Giving is a way for us to actually assist our brothers and sisters in need. In doing so, we are the Lord's hands and become part of His plan to succor those in need and to be succored in turn when we are in need.

The Church's Fourth Mission

Since the early days of the Church, members have been instructed to help the poor. To make this even more explicit, in 2010 the Church added a fourth mission to its previously three-fold purpose: care for the poor and needy. Supplementing the previous missions of the Church to perfect the Saints (member welfare), preach the gospel (missionary work), and redeem the dead (temple work), the new fourth mission was directed at those in material need.[2] Unlike the first-mentioned mission, perfecting the members of the Church, this mission was not limited to Church members but included all peoples across the world.

When this fourth mission was made official, the Church as an institution already had an impressive history of fulfilling this task, particularly in relation to Church members. In 1936, the Church instituted the Church Security Program (the name later changed to the Church Welfare System) to help members in economic distress because of the Great Depression. By 2010, the program included a network of canneries, storehouses, and farms that produced and distributed food to hundreds of thousands of people. As of 2011, for example, there were 143 storehouses, 326 employment resource centers, and 43 Deseret Industries thrift stores, as well as over 8,000 missionaries serving in the Welfare Services program.[3]

Individual Latter-day Saints also have been generous with their time and resources in caring for others. Church members are instructed to fast once a month and donate at least the equivalent of missed meals (and more, if possible) to the Church for the care of the poor. In 1977, President Spencer W.

---

2. "The Purpose of the Church" in *Handbook 2: Administering the Church*, 2.2, https://www.lds.org/handbook/handbook-2-administering-the-church/priesthood-principles (accessed May 16, 2013).

3. Scott Taylor, "2010 Mormon Church Welfare Statistics," *Deseret News*, April 3, 2011, http://www.deseretnews.com/article/700124060/2010-Mormon-church-welfare-statistics.html?pg=all (accessed May 16, 2013).

Kimball counseled members to be liberal rather than conservative in calculating their fast offering donations: "Sometimes we have been a bit penurious and figure that we had for breakfast one egg and that cost so many cents and then we give that to the Lord. I think that when we are affluent, as many of us are, that we ought to be very, very generous."[4]

Since 1984, the Church also has been engaged in humanitarian efforts for short-term disaster relief in cases of hurricanes, earthquakes, tornadoes, or other natural events, and has provided non-disaster assistance, such as health education, medical equipment, measles vaccinations, and clean water, throughout the world. Unlike the Church Welfare System, humanitarian relief is not directed primarily to Church members. Over nearly a thirty-year period beginning in 1984, the Church provided approximately $1 billion for the temporal assistance of people in 167 nations around the world.[5]

Caring for the poor includes more than just providing immediate material needs. In 2001, the Church created the Perpetual Education Fund to help Latter-day Saints in poorer countries receive an education. This program has been instrumental in helping Latter-day Saints attend colleges and other training programs. Support from this fund was given to over 50,000 participants in fifty-one nations in its first ten years of operation.[6]

The Church's role regarding the poor and needy may take on even greater importance in the future as the task of caring for the poor and needy continues to grow. In the Book of Mormon, Alma recounted that missionary labors had more "success among the poor class of people" (Alma 32:2). The Church's growth is very similar today. As the Church adds missions across the world, most of them are in nations with greater poverty levels than exist in the historical LDS population centers of the United States and Canada. One estimate in 2000 was that by 2030, there would be an additional 30 million Church members who are poor.[7] Church members increasingly will be expected to play critical roles in aiding their brothers and sisters both spiritually and temporally.

---

4. Spencer W. Kimball, "Welfare Services: The Gospel in Action," LDS General Conference, October 1977, https://www.lds.org/general-conference/1977/10/welfare-services-the-gospel-in-action?lang=eng (accessed April 3, 2014).

5. "Humanitarian Aid," http://www.mormon.org/values/humanitarian-aid (accessed April 3, 2014).

6. Rebekah Atkin, "The Key to Opportunity: Celebrating 10 Years of the Perpetual Education Fund," *Liahona*, December 2011, http://www.lds.org/liahona/2011/12/the-key-to-opportunity-celebrating-10-years-of-the-perpetual-education-fund?lang=eng&query=perpetual+education+fund+statistics (accessed April 3, 2014).

7. Warner Woodworth, Joseph Grenny, and Todd Manwaring, *United for Zion: Principles for Uniting the Saints to Eliminate Poverty* (Orem, Utah: Unitus Publications, 2000), 3.

Government Welfare and Church Welfare

Presiding Bishop H. David Burton recounted in a general conference talk an experience of David O. McKay, as a young missionary in Stirling, Scotland, in 1897. Elder McKay offered a poorly dressed woman with sunken cheeks a missionary tract. The woman answered, "Will this buy me any bread?" Elder McKay realized this woman was not ready to hear the gospel. Instead she was "in need of temporal help, and there was no organization, so far as I could learn, in Stirling" that could give it to her.[8]

Our family spent a summer in Scotland exactly one century after Elder McKay was a missionary there. We toured exhibits that had been maintained to show tenements that poor people typically inhabited during the nineteenth century, the kinds of places that Elder McKay would have seen a century earlier. Fortunately, they were just exhibits. Scots now enjoyed the decent housing, adequate clothing, and sufficient food that woman, and many like her, had lacked in Elder McKay's time.

What made the difference? For nearly all Scottish people, it was not the Church of Jesus Christ of Latter-day Saints. Likely it was not a church at all. Rather, it was government policy. Great Britain, like most other industrialized nations of the world, had determined that the temporal welfare of its people was a priority, and government had a significant role in ameliorating the suffering of millions of people in poverty.

Of course, many members would argue that there is no resemblance between government welfare and the welfare mission of the Church. Because the most prominent Mormon perspectives on government have come from economic conservatives or libertarians, many Latter-day Saints would claim there is no relationship between what the government does and what the Church does in terms of welfare. For example, President Ezra Taft Benson proclaimed in 1986 that "government becomes primarily a mechanism for defense against bodily harm, theft, and involuntary servitude. It cannot claim the power to redistribute money or property nor to force reluctant citizens to perform acts of charity against their will."[9]

It is vital to note that this strong statement was President Benson's personal opinion. Even though he occupied the position of Church president, no prophet since then has repeated it. It is not Church doctrine. Yet many members likely assume it is.

---

8. Bishop H. David Burton, "The Sanctifying Work of Welfare," *Ensign*, May 2011, 81.

9. Ezra Taft Benson, "The Constitution—A Heavenly Banner," BYU Devotional Address, September 16, 1986, http://speeches.byu.edu/?act=viewitem&id=87 (accessed April 3, 2014).

As a result, if they think anything about the relationship between the gospel and welfare, they likely see the Church Welfare System, with its emphasis on first drawing on the resources of the extended family as the antidote to the government's welfare efforts. They see government welfare as designed to sustain a bloated, inefficient bureaucracy and blame its policies for contributing to a sense of entitlement for hand-outs, without demanding accompanying work projects that stress accountability or efforts at independence. They see government welfare as weakening not only self-respect, but also aspirations for financial independence and helping others. In contrast, they see the Church system as effective in connecting welfare to work and helping people rise out of poverty. Clearly, in their view, the Church's system is a substitute for reliance on government programs.

Who the Church Welfare System Does and Does Not Serve

Is the Church's welfare program a substitute for government? Or is it really a supplement? To answer this, one must first consider the purpose of the Church Welfare System. It was created to provide for the needs of active Latter-day Saints who are willing to work in return for the help they receive. It is primarily a short-term assistance program. Its fundamental assumption is that generally self-sufficient members who encounter a temporary difficulty simply need short-term assistance as they negotiate the crisis. This help, it is also assumed, is "earned" by the member's previous payment of fast offerings and contributions to work projects. It is not designed as a long-term program to handle extended, and perhaps even lifelong, needs. Because of this, it can only help a small and specific group—a minute fraction of the poor and needy around the world.

Latter-day Saints who oppose government welfare might also conclude that, since the Church has created a welfare system, other churches must also have their own systems people can rely on. Some other churches do, in fact, have organized welfare systems to serve their own members, although not as extensive as the Church's. However, like the Church, these other private efforts are usually limited to providing temporary help to a small segment of the poor. Even that responsibility stretches their resources in normal times. In economic recessions, the needs easily swamp the resources.

The Church has additional programs beyond the Welfare System. For example, humanitarian relief worldwide includes several programs: Helping Hands coordinates volunteer labor within a given geographical area to help beautify communities and clean up and rebuild after natural disasters. The Perpetual Education Fund focuses on preparing young men and women to learn useful trades and equipping them with the skills they need to acquire jobs in their local communities. LDS Charities provides immunizations, wheelchairs, neonatal care, and clean water projects around the world. These are all critical efforts to care for the poor and needy.

To be more efficient, the Church often unites its efforts with other non-profit relief agencies such as Catholic Charities, the Red Cross, or CARE to aid those who are needy throughout the world. Nevertheless, even when these non-profit organizations combine their efforts with the Church, the gap between resources and needs remains large. These agencies all coordinate with local governments in alleviating need. Indeed, government assistance does offer a significant complement to private help. For example, in the wake of the tsunami that hit southern Asia in December 2004, U.S. relief agencies, with the help of private donations, pledged approximately $200 million in aid. The U.S. government alone pledged $350 million.[10]

Who Receives Church and Government Welfare

Many Latter-day Saints probably assume that government welfare is only for those outside the Church. To the contrary, faithful members of the Church use these programs all the time. For example, many of us have lived, or will live, well beyond the age when our use of Social Security and Medicare funds match what we have contributed to those systems. At that point, our bills are paid with money from others. Every senior citizen who faces massive health-care bills and cannot pay them becomes a recipient of Medicaid, a government welfare program. Many college students, particularly those who are married with young families, use Pell Grants to pay for their education. WIC (Women, Infants, and Children) is designed to assist pregnant women, new mothers, and their young children, including those who are LDS. These are forms of government welfare. And most people are glad they exist.

Latter-day Saints who utilize these programs are rarely people who would rather live off others than work themselves. Typically, they include the elderly who are no longer able to work or young people who need help in obtaining the educations that will equip them to become productive, tax-paying members of society. Catastrophic medical emergencies or the sudden unemployment or underemployment of a family's primary bread-winner are emergencies that exceed most families' resources. The difference between people

---

10. "Tsunami Aid: Who's Giving What," BBC News, January 27, 2005, http://news.bbc.co.uk/2/hi/asia-pacific/4145259.stm (accessed April 4, 2014); and "Bush Aims to Boost U.S. Tsunami Aid," BBC News, February 10, 2005, http://news.bbc.co.uk/2/hi/americas/4252171.stm (accessed April 3, 2014).

who use government welfare and those who use Church welfare is not as stark as many might assume.

It is easy to express pride in the Church's welfare system and not even consider others who are outside of it. As one LDS scholar asked, "Are we guilty of blindly supposing that *our* poor are the unfortunate few who experience reversals creating temporary needs quickly resolved by an efficient Church program, while *their* poor are the masses of hopeless, helpless souls an undefined somebody will take care of?"[11] The reality is that the poor are similar—whether they are in the Church or not.

System Differences: The Church and Government

Assuming that the Church's welfare system is perfect because it is inspired and that it always "works" while assuming that the government's welfare system is fundamentally flawed in both conception and practice is unfair. These two programs do not and cannot operate in the same way. A quick comparison between the two systems illuminates the vast differences between them.

First, Church leaders completely control the Church's welfare plan. They do not answer to a public constituency in devising or implementing it. They can make decisions about what aspects to include, how much to spend, and where resources are allocated without much public transparency. They answer to the Lord, but that is quite different from having to respond to a citizenry.

On the other hand, government leaders do not exercise such control. Government welfare is the product of an open decision-making process that includes Congress, the White House, the bureaucracy, and the public, as well as state and local governments and even private sector agencies. The American people certainly want it that way. However, this puts the government at a severe disadvantage compared to the Church in terms of being able to make decisions quickly without the involvement of many players, each with their own agendas and standards of what constitutes "success."

Second, because of the Church's central control, its decision-makers can choose who to cover in the program, how much to assist them, and whether to change those standards at any time. Bishops have discretion over how to use Church welfare funds and control over whom they help and how. They can and do refuse funds based on their assessment of the worthiness of the potential recipient. Church membership alone does not guarantee qualification for receiving Church welfare.

---

11. James R. Christianson, "Humanity and Practical Christianity: Implications for a Worldwide Church," *BYU Studies* 29, no. 1 (1989): 42; emphasis mine.

The government has much less flexibility than the Church in terms of who can access welfare. Once legislation is passed to include a certain group of individuals based on certain formulas (such as low-income families, college students, and the elderly) everyone in that group is eligible to receive that benefit. There is little discretion; instead welfare programs are guided by a set of rules that limit a bureaucrat's ability to exercise subjectivity to include or exclude certain individuals in an idiosyncratic manner.

Third, the scope of the programs is vastly different. The Church's program applies to hundreds of thousands of individuals at any given time. That is a major contribution to the welfare of individuals, particularly in the intermountain West where Church membership is large and the program is well developed. Understandably, the Church's welfare efforts are applauded by many both in and outside of the Church. However, the number of persons that the Church is able to assist is insignificant compared to those on government welfare. Government programs affect billions of people throughout the world.

Fourth, not only is the scope of the Church's capabilities relatively small in terms of the number of persons it can help compared to government programs, but the Church generally concentrates on short-term aid for those it serves. Government programs, on the other hand, tend to provide both long-term and short-term assistance. In the United States, the federal government delivers that long-term assistance with programs such as Social Security, Medicaid, and Medicare.

Fifth, the Church relies heavily on volunteer work to implement its welfare program. Virtually every ward involves not only bishops and Relief Society presidents who receive no compensation for their work, but also full- and part-time missionaries and volunteers who give time in various capacities across the welfare system. The government, by contrast, relies largely on trained professionals and thus has higher overhead in the execution of programs.

To compare the Church's program with those run by government is unreasonable since each entity operates under vastly different constraints and expectations. The government operates more transparently to satisfy a broad, demanding constituency, while the Church does not. The Church's aid is intended primarily to serve short-term needs; the government handles primarily long-term assistance. The Church's recipients are a group the Church chooses to serve. Government cannot be so selective.

What Should Be Government's Role?

Even when many Latter-day Saints realize that a direct comparison between Church and government welfare is unreasonable and impossible, they must deal with questions about what the government's role should be.

Unfortunately, the scriptures do not provide explicit guidance in this area. The welfare state that exists today was not a feature of government when any of the canonized scriptures were written. However, the absence of a stated government role does not mean that such a role today violates gospel principles. The scriptures fail to mention many aspects of modern life—technology is one example—that we use to further the work of Christ.

At the same time, there are plenty of admonitions in the scriptures about our need to care for the poor and the needy. Who is responsible for that task? Is this only an individual or a Church responsibility? Does society as a whole have any role? Who should be doing this?

The answer is: "All of the above." Latter-day Saints should interpret and implement our scriptural admonitions to help the poor at multiple levels—individual, family, church or other charitable group or organization, and society as a whole. Scriptural passages on caring for the poor and needy are not only directed to individuals as individuals (such as sitting with a sick family member, providing financial assistance to fund a poor missionary or struggling college student, or taking bread to a neighbor)—they also allow for and direct activities that can be done at a larger level (such as by the Church and even society as a whole).

In fact, Church leaders have rejected the view that charitable work should be done only at the individual level. Instead, they have created an infrastructure that commits the institution of the Church to the care of the poor and needy. In 2010, Church leaders applied scriptural directives concerning the poor and the needy to the Church as a whole by adding the mission of caring for the poor and the needy to the already existing threefold purpose of the Church. Clearly, Church leaders believe that this mission has society-wide application and does not apply simply on an individual basis.

If our obligation to the poor should extend beyond our individual efforts and abilities, then why do so many Latter-day Saints oppose government's role in this important endeavor? One reason for the lack of support for government role among Church members may be due to the common perception that the government is grossly inefficient in comparison to the Church and that it benefits those who are able but unwilling to work.

Undoubtedly, there is waste and fraud in the government's handling of welfare, but the Church system experiences waste or fraud as well. The Church Welfare System suffers from many of the same difficulties of any large bureaucratic organization. That is not to say that these problems are rampant. The reliance on volunteers reduces overhead costs. Moreover, volunteers likely share the concern of Church leaders that members' financial contributions should be used wisely. That alone helps minimize waste. But a problem of waste or fraud would not be widely reported because, unlike government systems that function under outside scrutiny through Congressional oversight, legally mandated public reports, and press coverage, the Church's system is not transparent to the public or even to the Church's membership.

At the same time, government administration of entitlement benefits is not necessarily inefficient. For example, tens of millions of Americans who qualify for them receive veterans' benefits, Pell Grants, unemployment compensation, disability payments, and Social Security checks on a timely basis. The few who do not get such checks on time, are denied them wrongfully, or do not deserve them in the first place are those the news media focus on. Understandably, such an emphasis gives the impression that the exceptions constitute the rule.

There are also similarities in who benefits from both systems. Not all those who receive Church welfare assistance also receive government help, but it is likely that many do in some form or another. If they have lost a job, for example, they are probably getting Church assistance as well as unemployment compensation. A poor young family struggling to make ends meet while one or both parents strives to get an education might receive Church welfare help as well as Pell Grants for tuition and books. A young mother could be on a government program to assist new mothers and their children while also getting some support from the bishop's storehouse. To suggest that people who receive Church welfare are deserving of it while those who receive government welfare are not is to imply that these are two distinct groups of people. Instead, they are basically the same people who are seeking assistance for themselves and their families in any way they can. And in most cases, whether they receive government assistance, Church welfare, or both, they make an effort to go off welfare as soon as they can.

Should People Be Compelled to Do Good?

If society has an obligation to care for the poor and the needy, what is the vehicle for doing so? Is it government? From a libertarian or conservative perspective, many would suggest that government cannot be considered a legitimate means of caring for the poor and needy because it coerces people to do good by taking their money for social welfare through taxes. Opponents of government's role also point to a perceived contrast between the Church's approach to caring for the poor and needy and the government's. In the Church, they say, individuals voluntarily give of their means to pay tithing, fast offerings, or make other donations to assist others. Therefore, individuals reserve the right to not assist the poor, if they choose to do so. But citizens cannot choose to withhold taxes that underwrite social welfare programs if they disagree with those programs, find them inadequate, or judge the recipients as unworthy.

The comparison, however, is not entirely correct. Technically the government cannot compel anyone to comply. Rather, it can only punish people for non-compliance. For example, tax evaders who claim that the government has no authority to tax for the food stamp program can choose not to pay, risking a fine or jail sentence as a consequence. In an analogous manner, the Church also does not compel compliance with charitable programs; but like government, there are consequences for not doing what the Lord requires. Indeed, from a gospel perspective, those consequences for non-participation are much greater than those imposed by government. The Savior told his disciples that, if they did not feed the hungry, clothe the naked, and take in the stranger, they would end up in "everlasting fire, prepared for the devil and his angels" (Matt. 25:41). Furthermore, by refusing to pay a full tithe and fast offering, a Latter-day Saint can be restricted from participating in the temple. The Church can affect one's eternal state. And it is not quite as easy to escape the Lord's penalty as it is the government's, which misses some tax evaders.

So, if anything, there is a stronger incentive to follow the Lord's commandments to avoid long-term, rather than just temporary, punishment. The Lord's justice is sure. The consequences are eternal and not just earthly. Again, the choice to obey the Lord's admonition is a voluntary one, but the consequences are not.

Of course, the liberal soul does not provide compassionate care to the poor and the needy for the purposes of avoiding eternal punishment. Similarly, the liberal soul does not look primarily at the coercion of a tax system. Rather, the liberal soul focuses on the good that comes from helping others in need. When the emphasis is on making sure that senior citizens live decent lives, that children have enough to eat, and that families have adequate shelter, the liberal soul accepts the sacrifice that comes with that service to those in need.

Indeed, the decision of citizens in a democratic society to voluntarily tax themselves to help others is a mark of a charitable people. The society's choice to do so assures that others' temporal needs are met. It helps build a just and decent society for all. A struggling college student with several small children and a wife who stayed home to care for them once remarked to me how great the United States was—that it would help them with various government programs so they could live while he obtained an education to eventually support his family. It speaks highly of a society of people willing to help others they do not know. We should all be grateful to live in a society where the many are willing to give some of their own income to help others in need.

Being compelled to do certain things, such as pay taxes for social welfare programs, is a standard feature of a governed society. We are all compelled to certain behaviors when we live in a society with government. When I drive to work every day, I am stopped by several traffic lights. If I run those lights, I will be fined and perhaps jailed, even if I have not put on-coming or cross traffic at risk by driving through red lights. The purpose of that law with its associated penalties, of course, is to make the safety of others a higher priority than my personal convenience. I am compelled to be considerate of other drivers. It is true that I might be considerate even without those laws; unfortunately, many of us are not. I admit to exasperation when I wait at a red light, even though there is no cross traffic and I am in a hurry. Through laws, government elicits good behavior from us that we might not otherwise give.

Similarly, contributions to social welfare programs come through government taxation. Taxes are collected from citizens to help meet the needs of others regardless of the personal preferences of the taxpayers. Without that taxation, we all might be tempted to just be selfish. Obviously, the line determining how much taxation is good is an individual perception; but the law requiring tax payment, even a small amount, offers each individual the opportunity to participate in a public good, i.e., offering assistance to others in need.

Government plays an important role in the society's decision to carry out its goals; and while it is not the only means to do so, it is the most capable vehicle when society believes an aim is critical to its own good. Indeed, even politically conservative Latter-day Saints approve of some of those aims. For example, society abhors the sexual exploitation of children. Where do we turn to make policy that protects innocent children? Do we politely ask child pornographers to cease and desist? Of course not! We turn to government, calling for laws that ban child pornography and punish violators of those laws.

We, of course, also take other actions such as morally condemning it and boycotting companies that portray children sexually in advertising. However, because of the gravity or scope of some issues, we insist on including government policy as well. We do this because we know that government's actions can cover the whole society and not just part. We know that all will benefit from such laws and that no one should be harmed because the application of a vital societal policy is not universal. These laws are a signal of the priorities of a society. A society that wishes to take care of its children does not rely solely on the good will of those who have a desire to hurt those children. It is society as a whole, through its government, that takes necessary action.

Care for the poor and needy is the same. Much of what we do to alleviate the problem is done on an individual basis. Candy stripers volunteer in hospitals. People donate to a wide range of organizations intent on helping the poor, such as Sub for Santa, Toys for Tots, food banks, homeless shelters, and so on. Kind people often spontaneously help their neighbors in time of need with food, clothing, and shelter.

Government is an additional means for helping the poor and needy. In fact, government makes the most sense as a universal program that covers costs that cannot effectively be carried by smaller entities such as individuals, families, churches, and other charitable groups. During an economic recession, charitable organizations typically are overwhelmed by the need to provide assistance to so many who are suffering. Job creation, health care, employee retooling, food, and shelter are needs that become daunting for local communities to meet alone.

While some individual Church leaders in the past have attempted to discourage members from receiving government assistance when they are in need, it was never Church policy to prohibit members from doing so.[12] During recent economic recessions, the Church has not urged members to forego participation in government programs. If the Church was philosophically opposed to members receiving such benefits and wanted to provide for these individuals instead of government doing so, then it would have said so. To the contrary, the Church has counseled bishops to "help members receive assistance through community and government agencies."[13] Thus, after a devastating tornado hit Joplin, Missouri, local Church leaders there cooperated with government agencies to aid residents. "We don't want to get ahead of local agencies," a stake leader said. "We want to work with them. We respect and commend them for what they're doing, and we want to build important relationships because we know that disasters will indeed happen again. . . . [O]ur association with these agencies is essential."[14]

The objective of the Church's system to help those in need is not to replace government. Indeed, that is not even a task the Church would contemplate. Rather, it is to cooperate with government to provide the best and quickest assistance to people in need when they need it.

---

12. President J. Reuben Clark was a strong opponent of members taking governmental assistance, and President Ezra Taft Benson also urged Church members not to take food stamps. Thomas G. Alexander, *Mormonism in Transition: A History of the Latter-day Saints, 1890–1930* (Urbana: University of Illinois, Press, 1986), 192; Ezra Taft Benson, "A Vision and a Hope for the Youth of Zion," BYU Speeches, April 12, 1977, http://speeches.byu.edu/?act=viewitem&id=85 (accessed April 3, 2014).

13. Church of Jesus Christ of Latter-day Saints, "Welfare Leadership in the Ward," *Handbook 2: Administering the Church,* http://www.lds.org/handbook/handbook-2-administering-the-church/welfare-principles-and-leadership/6.2?lang=eng#62 (accessed April 3, 2014).

14. Melissa Merrill, "In the Aftermath of the Tornado," *Ensign,* July 2012, https://www.lds.org/ensign/2012/07/in-the-aftermath-of-the-tornado?lang=eng (accessed April 3, 2014).

The Intersection of Church and Government

The symbiosis of Church and government in social welfare is a highly practical approach to caring for the poor and needy. The Church and other charitable organizations simply cannot handle the massive demand for welfare assistance in economic hard times. Without government aid to the poor and needy, charitable organizations would be faced with the daunting task of providing services currently given, in the United States alone, through Social Security, Medicaid, Medicare, Temporary Assistance for Needy Families (TANF), Supplemental Nutrition Assistance (SNAP), WIC (Women, Infants, and Children), and CHIP (Children's Health Insurance Program).

Where an industrialized society exists, the Church can focus on short-term needs rather than attempting to accomplish what government agencies currently do in those countries. Where the nation possesses adequate health-care coverage, educational opportunities, or employment, the Church can fill remaining gaps. For example, an elderly sister living on an old age pension may still need Church assistance in supplementing that monthly check to purchase food, pay the rent, and buy medications. A family hit by a sudden job loss can receive Church welfare beyond what unemployment compensation offers. In the United States, for example, the family can get CHIP for the children, WIC for the wife and newborn child, and food commodities from the Church's storehouse. All of these entities can work together to help get these people through difficult times in their lives.

A government role in caring for the poor and the needy also involves easing the burdens on individuals and families hit with medical catastrophes. By taxing all and redistributing those resources to those in need, the government program assures that the family does not bear the total burden of overwhelming health-care costs alone. A family with a suffering parent or child can receive the needed health care but not become indebted for life. For example, a neighbor family of ours faced huge medical bills because of the sudden mental illness of a child. They risked losing their house and going into bankruptcy. At the same time, the father lost his job. A combination of government and Church assistance helped them through this temporary hardship in their lives. The burden on their immediate family or local ward would have been overwhelming had it not been for both Church and government role in aiding them.

Through government, society can meet common problems that are not unique to particular individuals or groups. These are universal needs that government can predict individuals will need and therefore provide services for. Senior citizens who retire on fixed incomes, for example, have a common need for a financial cushion that enables them to live decently when they are no longer capable of working. Pregnant mothers need adequate prenatal health care. Children require medical and dental check-ups and care to assure that their bodies and minds are healthy as they grow. These are predictable necessities—not unique circumstances. Many people in poverty will need these services just as much as well-off people. Those needs can be met through the government role.

Why not rely on charitable institutions solely? History has shown that this approach has not worked. When societies have excluded government in favor of private sector charities, needs too often remain unmet. The result is massive, needless suffering. For example, in the United States during the nineteenth century and the early twentieth century, charitable organizations provided the bulk of help for individuals in need. However, many people fell between the cracks. In a time of economic catastrophe, those charities were inundated with demands they could not meet. The Great Depression in the 1930s spurred the creation of a national social safety net through Social Security and government works programs, because so many people, particularly the elderly and families with children, suffered. Many European nations instituted social services in the first half of the twentieth century in recognition of the massive social needs left unfulfilled by the private sector alone.

An economic disaster like the Great Depression has not hit the United States since, although economic recessions have been common occurrences. However, when recessions happen today, the effects on individuals and families are mitigated by the existence of a social safety net. The most vulnerable in society are less vulnerable today because society, through government, offers more care for the poor and needy.

Nevertheless, it is a societal choice. Government role is not the only means for caring for the poor and needy nor is excluding government involvement the Lord's preferred means. Instead, the society can decide how to undertake this task. Any society that steps up to the task is beginning to take seriously the Lord's admonition to remember the poor.

When a society, through government, seeks to fulfill its role to care for the poor, inevitably some individuals will object. They are bothered because their money (in any amount) is being taxed by the government for social welfare. Often, Church members fall into this category. One reason some object is that they fail to see some problems as societal and systematic rather than individual and idiosyncratic. They will gladly help the widow across the street, the homeless person in the park, or a weeping preschooler who has become separated from his mother. They do not lack compassion for the individual in front of them, but they often fail to see that many others in similar need may not be so fortunate as to have a compassionate neighbor or stranger willing to help.

Others who object are perhaps simply uninformed or neglectful about the needs of the poor in society. Perhaps they have not encountered difficulties in their own lives or have simply forgotten what it is like to be poor. Because of this, they may condemn the needy as being slothful and dependent. The experience of financial setbacks—losing a job, a medical emergency, being the victim of a crime that seriously damages the family home—can be humbling and increase empathy for others in similar situations. Many, however, have not yet developed that empathy. I once had a student who questioned the need for social welfare programs such as Social Security. He suggested that, since he was majoring in finance, he could manage his own investments more effectively than Social Security. He could not understand why he had no right to opt out of that government program.

To a certain extent, this student was probably correct in claiming that he could manage his investments more effectively than the government. However, Social Security was not designed for those who could successfully plan for their retirement. It is designed for those who do not have the skills, means, or money to make those investments for themselves. And, even with smart investments, a sudden downturn in the stock market or an unexpected tragedy could wipe away this student's savings. Then, he would have little or nothing to live on, despite his experience in money management and his best efforts to live a financially independent life. I hope that this student someday becomes a home teacher, elders' quorum president, or bishop responsible for helping a family who is poor, unemployed, and on the verge of homelessness despite their efforts to work hard and play by all the rules. I hope he learned that these government programs, including Social Security, Medicare, and Medicaid, reflect the reality of our existence as human beings rather than the theoretical models of economic conservatism or libertarianism.

Isn't Government Social Welfare Wasteful?

When Ronald Reagan ran for president, he liked to talk about welfare queens who drive their Cadillacs to the welfare office to pick up a government check. His rhetorical point was to portray government social welfare programs as wasteful because recipients do not really need the assistance. At the same time Reagan was making such claims, the U.S. Census Bureau analyzed who was receiving welfare assistance. They found that 52 percent of welfare recipients who were continually on welfare were children and teenagers under age eighteen. They also discovered that the popular perception of lifelong welfare recipients was a myth. Fifty seven percent of welfare recipients received aid for two years or less. More than one in three remained on welfare for no more than a year.[15]

Certainly there is waste in government welfare programs. It occurs in any operation, including in the business sector and our own Church. Such waste could be as small as a few cents on wasted printer paper to millions spent on an unsuccessful marketing campaign. Of course, the fact that waste occurs almost everywhere does not mean that it is acceptable. In fact, waste in social welfare is particularly bad because it means that resources meant for caring for the poor and the needy are being diverted from their assigned purpose. When waste in welfare occurs because of fraud, it is particularly reprehensible because individuals' needs are at stake. Society, through its government, should target those who commit such fraud. For example, in 2012 the U.S. government arrested ninety-one medical professionals, including doctors and nurses, for $430 million in false Medicare claims.[16] Such actions must be prosecuted because they rob both the taxpayers and those who are in real need.

However, the inevitable existence of some waste and fraud is not sufficient reason for abandoning a mission to assist others. Politicians such as Ronald Reagan have perpetuated a myth of rampant welfare fraud to gain votes and support for his anti-government positions. Reagan's rhetoric was a good example of the saying, "the perfect is the enemy of good." By demanding perfection (when perfection is impossible for any organization), they would withhold good—much needed help for many.

What Government Can Do

As emphasized in this chapter, government can and does play important roles in caring for the poor and the needy. Government can help individuals better their lives, particularly individuals who are the most vulnerable in our society. These are not abstract or remote concepts. They are realities that matter in people's lives and make the key difference between fulfilling our potential on earth instead of being hampered in carrying out what the Lord has sent us to do. Access to education, health care, and the basics of food, shelter, and clothing are not luxuries in life's journey. Rather, we cannot function on this earth without them, including the tasks the Lord has given us to do.

---

15. U.S. Department of Commerce, Bureau of the Census, "A Look at the Welfare Dependency Using the 1984 SIPP Panel File," Paper presented at the annual meeting of the Population Association of America, New Orleans, Louisiana, April 21–23, 1988, http://www.census.gov/sipp/workpapr/wp75.pdf (accessed April 3, 2014).

16. "91 Are Charged with Fraud, Billing Millions to Medicare," *New York Times*, October 4, 2012, http://www.nytimes.com/2012/10/05/business/medicare-fraud-charged-against-91.html?_r=0 (accessed April 3, 2014).

Education

"The glory of God is intelligence" (D&C 93:36). This revelatory proclamation suggests a critical linkage between divinity and intelligence. Intelligence is knowledge, and one of the most efficient ways to acquire that knowledge comes from education. Education is critical to our ability to succeed in this life and the life to come.

How most of us receive an education today is quite different than it was two hundred years ago. In the United States, for example, education was a private commercial transaction until the 1800s. Private schools and tutors educated the children of the affluent. Other children received little education, perhaps only enough to read, write, and do basic arithmetic. Not only did the poor not have the money for educating children, but they usually did not have the time either. A struggling farm family needed everyone capable of handling a shovel, an axe, or a hoe to contribute to the management and functioning of the farm. This is why Joseph Smith had the equivalent of only a third-grade education.

For many people in the world today, the poor still lack the means of obtaining an education, even if laws mandating schools are on the books. In Nigeria, 42 percent of children never go to school. In Sub-Saharan Africa, the average household pays 25 percent of the cost of an education, which is an enormous and often impossible burden for many poor families. Governments in that area of the world pay, on average, less than $100 per year per child to educate a child.[17]

Today, the vast majority of citizens in industrialized nations receive public educations, which are paid for by taxpayers and administered by government. Thus, ability to pay does not determine whether a child receives an education. Government serves all by providing universal access to education regardless of household income.

The poor and needy benefit the most in such situations because they are least likely to be able to pay for an education. Although the number of years of mandated attendance, the availability of supplies, and the level of a teacher's training, vary widely, even a modest education provides opportunities for individuals to acquire the skills necessary to get a job, to participate in the economy, and to support themselves and their families. Education, therefore, plays a vital role in caring for the poor and needy because it can

---

17. UNESCO, "Reaching Out-of-School Children," http://www.uis.unesco. org/Education/Pages/reaching-oosc.aspx (accessed April 3, 2014); and Karen MacGregor, "AFRICA: More Fees, Private Tertiary Education: UNESCO," May 22, 2011, *University World News,* http://www.universityworldnews.com/article. php?story=20110520183741986 (accessed April 3, 2014).

help prevent poverty in the first place. It lifts the poor out of poverty when they acquire the proficiency necessary to survive economically in their society.

In many cases, education is carried out by private institutions. For example, the Church sponsors three universities and a college, which are supported by members' tithes to help young Latter-day Saints prepare for a variety of careers. Additionally, the Church's Perpetual Education Fund helps Latter-day Saints outside the United States to gain access to occupational training. Other churches also devote enormous resources to education. The Roman Catholic Church has parochial K–12 school systems across the world. Protestant denominations, Muslims, Orthodox Judaism, and other religions are dedicated to educating the young. Various churches also sponsor higher educational institutions such as Notre Dame, Baylor, and Southern Methodist University, to name a few. Non-religious private universities also play similar roles.

Despite these private initiatives, government is the major force in education today. The vast majority of K–12 students in the United States attend public schools. Government also runs state universities and colleges that educate millions of students. If publicly funded higher education institutions did not exist, far fewer people would hold degrees and possess the skills essential for the technological age of the twentieth century.

Since the public school movement in the United States was started by Horace Mann in the 1830s, public schools have become the great equalizer of a population, bringing together students from various walks of life. They have offered universal public education to assure that even the poor have the opportunity to gain the knowledge and skills essential to pursue a successful vocation. Public education is particularly important for children and teenagers who lack parental support; in many such cases, teachers and administrators can challenge and inspire children to achieve their greatest potential.

Many other nations do not have developed public education systems that serve that purpose. For example, an exchange student from Brazil who stayed with us for several months described the school system in his city as shoddy and ineffective. He explained that his parents sent him to a private school because the public schools were poorly run. He was lucky to be in an affluent family that could afford to send him to a private school, which the vast majority of families in his country could not do. Mormon discusses the problems with such a situation among the Nephites: "And the people began to be distinguished by ranks, according to their riches and their chances for learning; yea, some were ignorant because of their poverty, and others did receive great learning because of their riches" (3 Ne. 6:12).

The liberal soul supports the implementation of a public education system that is both inclusive and effective in providing education for all. That is a system run by government. It requires all in society to pay into the system in the form of taxes. On the other end, society as a whole benefits from a well-educated population capable of serving in the various roles essential for civilization. An educated individual also feels a sense of self-worth and can face the temporal challenges of life with considerable confidence. An educated person is better able to fulfill his or her God-given mission on earth. In developed nations, government, through its management of this system, is society's tool for carrying out this role.

Health

Not only do all human beings need an education, but they also need to be healthy. Poor physical health limits our ability to serve each other. When our physical needs—food, shelter, clothing, and health—are not met, it is difficult to concentrate on other things beyond those needs. The Word of Wisdom is an example of the Lord's concern for our individual health and our ability to have strength to carry out our respective missions on earth.

Are there any admonitions regarding the individual's responsibility toward society or, vice versa, in terms of health? Yes, indeed. Church leaders have viewed health care as an issue that goes beyond the Word of Wisdom. For example, early Church leaders in Utah sponsored training in medicine. Brigham Young encouraged women such as Ellis Reynolds Shipp and Romania Bunnell Pratt to receive medical training in the East. Additionally, the Church started and maintained a network of hospitals in Utah designed to provide health care for citizens, whether they were Latter-day Saints or not. Early Church leaders knew that individuals should not be left on their own for medical care. The community needed qualified health professionals and facilities, and Church leaders sought to fill that need.

Today, although the Church has divested itself of hospitals and clinics, it still assists in providing medical care for the community. The Church sponsors nursing and medical assistant programs, as well as pre-med emphases, at Church universities to provide trained health-care professionals for society. Church-owned institutions and companies use wellness programs to encourage individuals to engage in healthy lifestyles designed to promote physical well-being.

Of course, some will argue that the government should play no role in providing its citizens with health care. For example, in 1979, President Benson condemned national health insurance as "a euphemism for socialized medicine."[18] However, the Church as an institution has taken no position on how health care should be delivered in a society, despite its being a

---

18. Ezra Taft Benson, "A Vision and a Hope for the Youth of Zion," *BYU Speeches*, April 12, 1977, http://speeches.byu.edu/?act=viewitem&id=85 (accessed April 3, 2014).

recurring discussion in American politics for more than half a century. In 1993–94, a debate ensued about universal health care as the White House tried to institute a comprehensive health-care system. Again in 2009–10, the issue was hotly debated when Congress considered and finally passed health-care reform legislation. During all that time, the Church issued no statements telling members to support or oppose health-care reform.

Since the Church has taken no position on this issue, the individual member can make his or her choice about health-care insurance, access, and delivery. Under debate is whether health care, like other issues discussed previously, is solely an issue for the individual, family, and private group, or whether government should play a significant role. In making that call, the liberal soul sees clear advantages for health-care access and delivery going beyond the confines of individual or private organizational efforts.

Some advantages to the government's playing an important role in health care begin with the fact that the health-care system affects everyone in a society. Nearly every individual uses the services of medical professionals' and hospitals or clinics at some point in their lives. Indeed, many people have chronic illnesses and spend much of their lives under medical supervision. Therefore, the physical well-being of nearly everyone is connected to the quality of the health care delivery system in a society. How well doctors and nurses are trained, how high the standards of medicine are, and how much services cost, are all issues that affect the whole population. And that effect is not minimal. Poor health care or lack of health care access can lead many people to become or remain dangerously sick. While the most serious effects are damage to the quality or length of an individual's life, other consequences include low productivity for workers, massive costs to the economy, and the inability of many to participate fully in society, including the fulfillment of their God-given missions.

The facilities of modern medicine are miracles of our age that we can appropriately regard as blessings from the Lord. We live in a marvelous time when people live longer, fuller, and more productive lives than ever before. This is not only true in industrialized nations like the United States and Europe, but it is also true across much of the world.

Government already has played a central role in helping produce that miracle. For example, the cost of medical research to cure diseases such as AIDS, Alzheimers, muscular dystrophy, and others is enormous. Governments assist in funding essential medical research to find cures to crippling or even life-threatening diseases. For example, in the United States, the National Institutes of Health alone devotes billions of dollars to assist medical research. Government also sets standards for health-care access that assure such access to nearly all. Those regulations include limits on how insurance companies can treat individuals who need care. Without those regulations, more people would be denied health care coverage, be cut off from health care because of preexisting conditions, or be left wondering if they would receive the care they need when they entered a hospital or a doctor's office.

In the United States, government also insures many people who would not be able to afford their needed care. Through Medicare and Medicaid, government programs for health-care insurance, tens of millions of Americans receive access to needed health care. Such a provision is particularly true of the poor and the needy. They are least able to meet the medical bills they incur due to illnesses—either large or small. Without these programs that ensure basic health-care access, their children would more likely be malnourished, they would be more susceptible to life-threatening or disabling diseases, and they would die earlier because they lacked access to regular medical care.

Without health-care insurance, medical problems can become much more serious. Before health insurance was expanded to include nearly all in the United States through legislation in 2010, the uninsured faced difficult dilemmas during a medical emergency. In the early 1990s, I remember going on a Boy Scout troop campout with one of my sons. One of the other boys fell on a log and tore open his leg. I took him back home. His father was at work, and I asked his mother if she would like me to drive her and her son to the emergency room. She replied that since they had no insurance, they could not go to the hospital and that she would stitch up the wound on her own. I admired the woman's courage and pluck, and I knew she was doing the best she could under the circumstances; but I worried that her medical skills were not up to those of professionals, particularly since she had no training.

This family's situation was shared by millions of Americans. They faced the dilemma of having medical needs but not having the ability to pay for health care that would meet those needs. Hundreds of millions of people still encounter this problem on a regular basis in many nations.

This mother's experience would be foreign to citizens of most industrialized nations outside the United States. In many of these nations, government delivers health care through its own hospitals and clinics staffed by government-paid doctors and nurses. The ability to pay has nothing to do with access to decent health care. Private systems may also exist, but they are generally reserved for the rich who can afford them for extra or elective care. Several other industrialized nations have highly regulated private hospitals and physicians but heavily subsidize health insurance so that all can have access to it. Such systems ensure that the poor and needy can receive care when they need it.

Several societies, such as the United States, have attempted to come up with private solutions. However, even those private solutions require extensive government regulation to assure that citizens are adequately covered by privately owned health insurance companies. The problem is that there is no financial benefit for private for-profit insurers to help chronically sick patients or those suffering catastrophic diseases or injuries requiring multiple surgeries, for instance. Therefore, if they had their choice, they would not cover such people. If the government did not require coverage for such individuals, the corporate bottom line typically would win out over providing expensive care for the poor and the needy who often require it the most.

Let me make clear that this is not a discussion primarily about other people. It is about nearly everyone in society. When a medical disaster strikes in our family, what is meant by "the poor and needy" can quickly turn from other people to ourselves. That is why affordable health-care access is so crucial in providing the proper and best care for the poor and needy; indeed, it is key to that task. The liberal soul favors such access and realizes that government can make the difference between society caring for the poor and needy and society neglecting them. "The righteous considereth the cause of the poor; but the wicked regardeth not to know it" (Prov. 29:7).

Economic Opportunity

When I was a newly returned missionary, a friend of mine gave me a job with his landscaping business. I spent that summer digging ditches, moving rocks, installing pipe, and performing other strenuous, physical tasks. It was hard work, but I was glad to have a full-time job until I started school again.

Most people want to work. They want to support themselves. When they have a spouse and children, they feel a sense of responsibility to provide for their families. It is a drive that leads all of us to contribute to society in order to receive that paycheck. That, in turn, allows us to pay the bills and improve ourselves financially.

Those who are poor and needy in society are usually that way because they lack sufficient employment. Some have jobs but are underemployed, work part-time, or have jobs that pay wages below their families' basic needs. Especially during recessions, this may be because no other jobs are available. Whatever the reason, the lack of adequate employment may contribute to their situation. This is why economic opportunity is so crucial to caring for the poor and needy.

The Church places a priority on helping to provide economic opportunity. President Gordon B. Hinckley expressly linked employment and education when he said to the youth of the Church: "It is so important that you young men and you young women get all of the education that you can. . . . Education is the key which will unlock the door of opportunity for you. . . . [Y]ou will be able to make a great contribution to the society of which you are a part."[19] To help address the needs of the under-employed, the Church's LDS Employment Services manages a network of employment helps, including training for those searching for jobs, employment resource centers for finding work, and employment specialists in each ward who have expertise in linking Church members to available job opportunities. The Church is not alone in offering resources for economic opportunity. Other community service organizations, such as the United Way, Goodwill Industries, and the Salvation Army, also assist with employment opportunities.

At the heart of the issue, though, is that economic opportunity depends on employers hiring employees. The primary task is the arrangement between privately owned companies and their employees. A rich supply of jobs in a community offers the opportunity for all to be employed and give back to the society in which we live.

Is there a role for government in providing economic opportunity, or is this an area really only handled by private businesses? Government is important in at least three ways, besides the obvious observation that government at all levels (local, state or province, and national or federal) is also an employer. These include providing the general climate for economic opportunity, helping people to find jobs, and protecting their rights once they are in the workplace.

As economic relations between individuals have evolved over time, the government's role has become increasingly important in economic matters. For most of the history of the world, a business traded with those who were geographically nearby. For example, a cobbler's clients were those who lived within the town or in a certain section of a larger city. So it was with the butcher, the milliner, or the baker. As transportation improved, the circle of business expanded to include broader swaths of territory, perhaps even whole nations.

Today, the business climate is global. A bicycle shop in China sells its product to a dealer in Melbourne, a factory in Malaysia makes shirts sold in Chicago, and a website designer in the Czech Republic works for a company in New York. Economic interactions take place across the globe between people who are distant and never actually meet in person. Government can facilitate or inhibit such trade. It can impose barriers that limit trade—either generally or for specific products—or it can minimize or eliminate barriers to promote international commerce. Government controls the extent to which business can grow beyond national borders and international commerce can blossom.

Government can also spur or shrink business activity. Regulations or taxes that inhibit businesses can stifle economic opportunity, while deregulation

---

19. Gordon B. Hinckley, "Inspirational Thoughts," *Ensign*, June 1999, 4.

can allow the growth of monopolies that eliminate competition and strangle new businesses.

How does all this economic dynamic affect care for the poor and the needy? Government can help create an environment where economic growth is possible. Such a climate increases the likelihood that full employment will occur and that all who can work will be able to do so. Such a condition does not happen without planning. That is where government can serve as a traffic cop who, rather than stopping business traffic, works to facilitate it for the benefit of all—business owner, consumer, laborer, and the society in general.

Government also enlarges economic opportunity by creating rules that open the door to make it available to all, including the poor who need it the most. The poor most likely fail to get hired, sometimes because they belong to a particular group that employers find undesirable, such as the disabled, women, the middle-aged or elderly, or racial minorities. Government regulations that forbid discrimination and require business to actively counter it are intended to help the needy be as eligible for employment as others who have less trouble getting jobs or being promoted within a workplace.

Government also can protect workers after they have been hired. Workers are at the mercy of their employers in a variety of ways. They should not lose their rights when they enter the workplace. For example, an employee should not be subject to harassment by an employer nor should an employer be able to make promotions based on criteria that are unrelated to the job or that violate the workers' privacy. This protection against the employer also can take the form of workplace safety regulations. For example, when workers are injured at an unsafe workplace, they lose the ability to make an income because they are injured. That means they have lost economic opportunity. If they are killed on the job, their families suffer financially as well as emotionally.

Although sometimes an employee can self-terminate and find another job, this solution cannot be relied on. Without restrictions being placed on them, employers can demand that their employees work extreme hours in unnecessarily dangerous conditions. Think of little children working twelve-hour shifts in weaving factories that had no shielding on the moving parts of equipment and that made no attempt to control the lint that free-floated in the air, and which the children could not avoid breathing, thus causing respiratory ailments.

Why can't the employee seek improvement at his or her job? Many can, but others who seek better working conditions face the risk of being fired or demoted at will. In times of recession when jobs are at a premium, employees may feel helpless because they cannot simply move to different work. Government rules minimizing safety hazards are intended to take people out of the pool of those who could otherwise be exploited.

Government can regulate the way businesses treat workers to assure economic opportunity. We can all hope that individual businesses would not discriminate against people in certain groups and rob them of economic opportunity. We can hope that private companies would make their workers' health and safety an important priority. And we can hope that customers would demand higher standards from the businesses they frequent. Unfortunately, while many businesses and customers meet such exemplary standards, many others do not. Leaving the decision on how to treat prospective or current employees solely up to the employer means that many people will suffer. This is not caring for the poor and needy.

Government Is "the Enemy"—Until You Need a Friend

William Cohen, a former Secretary of Defense and Republican U.S. Senator from Maine, once commented that government is the enemy until you need a friend. I saw that principle vividly demonstrated once while attending a local "meet the candidates" night. Most of the evening was spent with the participants attacking government for its intrusion into people's affairs. They complained that government was too big and powerful and should be curtailed. Then, one man who had joined in the expression of these grievances told the candidates for public office that there was a problem with a sewer line in his backyard and asked the candidates what they could do for him. I chuckled at the fact that this man was happy to denounce the government generally or when others used its services but at the same time wanted government to help him when he had a need.

In life, we never know when we will need a friend. We never know when we will be sick, lose a job, care for a child with special needs, and so on. Having a government that can be a friend in need is a wise policy for a society and for individuals. The liberal soul recognizes that and sees the individual, the group, and society, through government, as all playing important roles in caring for the poor and the needy.

The liberal soul understands the importance of caring for the poor and needy. Most of that care of others comes in the form of person-to-person assistance. Much of the rest is delivered by groups and organizations, such as the Church. Those acts are essential. The liberal soul encourages them and participates in them.

But the liberal soul also realizes that some ways in which the poor and needy are cared for cannot be administered exclusively on an individual basis or even by groups or organizations. The liberal soul understands that society as a whole carries an obligation for the poor and the needy. Indeed, there are some aspects of such care—including education or health-care access—that are best handled by society as a whole. The burden on the individual, the family, or a personally known group is too heavy to bear when catastrophe strikes. When the society bands together to offer assistance that is difficult for an individual or family alone to provide, that is a good thing. Far from being contrary to the gospel of Jesus Christ, it is a fulfillment of the gospel commandment to be our brothers' and sisters' keepers.

CHAPTER 4

MINGLING RELIGIOUS INFLUENCE WITH CIVIL GOVERNMENT

In the early years of the Church, leaders worried that their views on government were being misconstrued by others. To clarify the Church's position on the role of governments, they set out a declaration of principles regarding government. In 1835, Oliver Cowdery wrote the document now known as Doctrine and Covenants 134. Even though that section was not written by Joseph Smith and does not include the revelatory wording of "thus saith the Lord" present in other sections, it is included in canonized LDS scripture as a "declaration of belief regarding governments and laws."

As someone who was interested in the law and who later studied law, Oliver should have been familiar with the legal discussion about the role of religion and the state, as well as constitutional provisions concerning religion. He also would have been acutely aware of the incongruity between the spirit of what the First Amendment of the U.S. Constitution dictated about government's role in religion and what Missouri officials were doing to persecute believers of a minority religion.

Section 134 strongly supports the government's role in protecting freedom of conscience and predicts that governments that do not hold the rights of conscience inviolate will not enjoy peace. Therefore, it decries any attempt to use government to force religious beliefs or practices on citizens. That includes any laws "prescribing rules of worship to bind the consciences of men." Nor should government be in the business of dictating "forms for public or private devotion" (D&C 134:2, 4, 5).

Section 134 takes an overarching position on the role of government and religion that is wise to remember today when many, including some Latter-day Saints, assert that the United States should be a "Christian nation." Verse 9 says that Latter-day Saints "do not believe it just to mingle religious influence with civil government, whereby one religious society is fostered and another proscribed in its spiritual privileges, and the individual rights of its members, as citizens, denied."

Despite this verse in the Doctrine and Covenants, the debate still rages about how much government and religion should be entangled. And the social and demographic changes that have occurred in American society have made the question about the relationship between the two even more potent. In response to U.S. Supreme Court decisions on the establishment of religion (such as school prayer, display of Christian symbols on public property, and whether religious schools are eligible for government funding), many Church members contend that the United States needs to return to its historical status as an explicitly religious nation. In other words, they argue that government should take a position in favor of religion favored by the government and that the religion should be Christianity.

Indeed, the United States was, at one time, a more religiously homogenous nation that explicitly acknowledged a particular religious connection. For example, in 1892, the majority of U.S. Supreme Court justices declared that America "is a Christian nation."[1] The Court pointed to the opening and closing of legislative bodies' deliberations with prayer, various laws excluding many activities on the Sabbath day, and the multitude of Christian churches in the nation as evidence of Christianity's influence on society in general as well as the government and the law specifically.

However, the United States today is a vastly different nation in religious terms. The percentage of Americans who consider themselves Protestants has fallen precipitously. Today, only 51 percent of Americans self-identify as Protestants. Another 24 percent are Catholic. Religions that are neither Protestant nor Catholic, a category which includes the Church of Jesus Christ of Latter-day Saints, constitute 6 percent of the population. Sixteen percent of Americans say they are not affiliated with any religion.[2] The changes in U.S. religious affiliation are indicated in a statement in 2009 by President Barack Obama that, even though the United States has a large population of Christians, "we do not consider ourselves a Christian nation or a Jewish nation or a Muslim nation; we consider ourselves a nation of citizens who are bound by ideals and a set of values."[3]

---

1. *Church of the Holy Trinity v. United States*, 143 U.S. 457 (1892).

2. The Pew Forum on Religion & Public Life, "U.S. Religious Landscape Survey," 2007, http://religions.pewforum.org/reports (accessed April 2, 2014).

3. The White House, "Joint Press Availability with President Obama and President Gul of Turkey," Ankara Turkey, April 6, 2009, http://www.whitehouse.gov/the-press-office/joint-press-availability-with-president-obama-and-president-gul-turkey (accessed April 3, 2014).

Nor is the United States alone in these trends. Great Britain once viewed its role as "Christianizing" a heathen world, but today about one-quarter of the population of the United Kingdom is non-Christian.[4] Canada once was almost exclusively Protestant or Catholic. Today, about 5 percent of Canadians are Muslim, Hindu, or Sikh. Between 1971 and 2001, the percentage of Canadians having no religious affiliation increased from less than 1 percent to 16 percent.[5]

Today, many Americans would side with the Supreme Court justices' 1892 statement that the United States should be considered a Christian nation. Therefore, they claim that Christianity, as the dominant religion, should enjoy a special status. Many Latter-day Saints would join in that opinion despite the fact that many Christians do not consider the LDS Church as a Christian denomination and might exclude Mormons from the Christian majority. Ironically, the rise in the number of Mormons would likely be considered by some evangelical Christians to be evidence of a weakening of traditional Christianity occurring over the past century, both in the United States and other nations.

Given the ongoing debate about the role of religion in government, the intersection of religion and government is a matter of apprehension for the liberal soul as well. The liberal soul is concerned because this topic strikes at the heart of the relationship between the believer and the government he or she is expected to uphold. The role of government in religion fundamentally affects how that believer is able to express his or her beliefs verbally and practice publicly what he or she believes. That is why the extent of separation between church and state is an issue that the liberal soul cannot avoid.

Religion and the U.S. Constitution

No other written constitution has had such a singular impact on other constitutions in the world as the U.S. Constitution. This is particularly true in the area of religious freedom. The First Amendment to the U.S. Constitution states succinctly: "Congress shall make no law respecting an establishment

---

4. "We Believe, But Not in Church," *BBC News*, May 18, 2004, http://news.bbc.co.uk/2/hi/uk_news/3725801.stm (accessed April 4, 2014).

5. The Pew Forum on Religion & Public Life, "Global Religious Landscape," December 18, 2012, http://features.pewforum.org/grl/population-number.php (accessed April 2, 2014); "Overview: Canada Still Predominantly Roman Catholic and Protestant," (accessed April 3, 2014); Statistics Canada, http://www12.statcan.ca/english/census01/Products/Analytic/companion/rel/canada.cfm (accessed April 3, 2014); and "Population by Religion, by Province, and Territory (2001 Census)," in *Statistics Canada*, http://www.statcan.gc.ca/tables-tableaux/sum-som/l01/cst01/demo30a-eng.htm (accessed April 3, 2014).

of religion, or prohibiting the free exercise thereof." With the exception of a clause forbidding a religious test for public office, this is the sum total of what the U.S. Constitution says regarding religion. There is no mention of God in the U.S. Constitution. The national motto "In God We Trust" is not there. Nor is the wording of the Pledge of Allegiance or specifically the phrase: "One nation under God."

This may come as a surprise to many Latter-day Saints in the United States. They assume that the Constitution explicitly endorses religion and are positive it mentions God. Some tell me that the delegates at the Constitutional Convention in 1787 started each day of their proceedings with a prayer. (That is not true. The Continental Congress that wrote the Declaration of Independence did so, but not the Constitutional Convention.)

These Latter-day Saints in the United States, like so many Americans, are simply misinformed about what the Constitution says about religion. They don't realize that, instead of promoting religion in the Constitution, the Framers actually did the opposite. They kept religion out of the Constitution and therefore out of the new federal government they were creating.

Through the Constitution, the Framers established the first secular national government in the world. In this context, "secular" does not mean anti-religious. The Soviet Union was anti-religious. North Korea is still anti-religious. The U.S. Constitution and government are not anti-religious. They are just secular.

How is the U.S. government both secular and not anti-religious? It is not anti-religious because the First Amendment prevents Congress from prohibiting freedom of religion. That means Congress cannot stop people from believing and practicing the religion of their choice, unless there is a compelling governmental interest to do so.

That phrase, "compelling governmental interest," sounds like a big loophole. But it is not. Today, religious freedom enjoys the highest level of scrutiny—strict scrutiny—that the U.S. Supreme Court applies to federal laws regarding religious practice. That means the Court looks suspiciously at any law that limits religious freedom. Such scrutiny would include, for example, a law barring missionaries from proselytizing door-to-door. As a result, the burden of proof for the government is high in arguing that such a law should be upheld by the Court.

In nearly all cases, the Supreme Court has extended that prohibition on Congressional action to state and municipal governments as well. Unfortunately, the Court did not take this position until the twentieth century, which was too late for the early Latter-day Saints living in Missouri or Illinois. Had the justices applied the First Amendment to the states at that time, perhaps the suffering of the Mormons would have been lessened. At least, the vigilante groups could not have been designated as formally authorized militia units.

The First Amendment's protection of religious freedom, as well as the Court's application of that protection beyond Congress to all governmental levels, is an indication that the U.S. government is not anti-religious. This distinction between secular and anti-religious is an important one. So many people misunderstand the concept that a government that is neutral on religion and provides no official place for religion is not necessarily the same as an anti-religious government. Obviously, anti-religious governments do not protect religious freedom. Instead, they ban religion or place severe limitations on religious activity.

At the same time, the Constitution made the U.S. government a secular one by offering no role in government for an established church or official religion. There was no constitutional preference for a particular religion or even religion at all built into the Constitution. Unlike other governments of that day and many governments at present, the U.S. government was unusual in the sense that it was purposely detached from any religion.

What did this mean in practical terms? It meant that clergy were not paid by the federal government, a common practice in the colonies and states early in American history. Also, believers in minority religions—such as Quakers, Jews, and Catholics—were not excluded from the provisions of the Constitution. Previously, minority religious adherents were subject to harassment and persecution, even by government. Incidents such as destroying the property of dissenters, interrupting their meetings, and whipping their preachers to drive them away were common in colonial America. Colonies (and later states) passed laws forbidding non-Christians from serving in government office.

Under the Constitution, the U.S. federal government did not require that a person hold a certain religious affiliation to serve in government. In fact, it did the opposite: Article VI of the Constitution declared that "no religious test shall ever be required as a qualification to any office or public trust under the United States." It prohibited making any law saying that being a member of a certain religion, such as Christianity, was a prerequisite for holding office in the United States.

This lack of an explicit role for religion was a radical departure from the governmental systems of the day. All of those elements of the intersection of church and state just mentioned—a dominant state church, state control of the church, a religious test for holding public office, persecution of those not belonging to the dominant church by the government, and policies that supported the maintenance of that single church—were common in Europe, the Middle East, and Asia at the time the U.S. Constitution was written.

The Framers intentionally rejected a model of state-church relations that was virtually universal at the time.

The creation of a government without an official state church or any role for religion in the government meant the United States federal government would be the first secular government in the world. Bluntly put, no religion would receive an official government mandate, no religion would get any governmental preference, and religion itself would carry no official standing as part of government under the Constitution. Those were all signs of a secular government, and the U.S. government was a modern pioneer.

The U.S. Constitution's secularism is still remarkable compared to many contemporary national constitutions. For example, the Lutheran Church is constitutionally recognized as the official state church in Denmark and Norway. The Church of England has the same status in Great Britain. The Philippines Constitution seeks "the aid of Almighty God." And most Arab nations recognize Islam as the official religion of the nation and follow Islamic law.

However, the U.S. Constitution, and its lack of an official role for religion in the government, helped the spread of secular governments throughout the world. Many other nations now have constitutions that do not provide for an established church. Nations like France, Ireland, Spain, and Italy that formerly had strong ties to the Roman Catholic Church have downplayed a religious role in government and disestablished an official church. Many democratic nations founded since 1787 have followed the Unites States' example by not including a role for an established church in their constitutions. These include, for example, Brazil, India, South Korea, and South Africa.

The Framers and Religion

The Framers' failure to incorporate any religious role in the government was not due to neglect on their part. They did not merely forget to include an established church or specific mention of the role of religion in government. Rather, it was completely intentional. Early American political leaders purposely sought to separate church and state at the national level. They wanted to avoid a repetition of the religious establishments that governed other nations with all the incumbent problems of a state religion.

Nor did the Framers do this because they were hostile to religion. While atheists have created secular governments that are hostile to religion, the Framers had no intent to harm religion. It was not their wish to use government to encourage people to become agnostics or atheists, as was the case in Communist countries. Early American political leaders were unusual precisely because they did not use their public position to promote their private religious beliefs.

The Framers did not create the first secular government because they were atheists or even agnostics. To the contrary, they believed in God and considered themselves Christians. Most were church-goers, and their affiliations included Anglican, Methodist, Congregational, and Catholic, as well as others. The writings of political leaders such as George Washington, John Adams, Benjamin Franklin, and Thomas Jefferson document their belief in God. They made reference to the Almighty in their writings, and some of them attributed America's success explicitly to God's hand.

Like many Americans today, they differed among themselves in their level of religiosity. Franklin did not attend church regularly. Washington attended church but did not partake of holy communion (the sacrament) as most church-goers did. Adams, on the other hand, frequently attended and participated in church services.

However, their approach to religion generally conformed to the social expectations of the day. For example, ministers delivered the sermons and offered the prayers in church. Indeed, it was the ministers who performed religious acts in all other public settings. Lay people did not pray in public meetings. Images of the Framers kneeling together in public prayer stem from the imagination of the artist, rather than historical fact.

Their private worship probably varied considerably. Whether George Washington actually knelt in an open field in prayer next to his horse at Valley Forge, as Arnold Friberg portrayed in his famous illustration, is something we may never know. (The originator of the Valley Forge story was the same person who started the story about the youthful Washington and the cherry tree, which has been found to lack contemporary documentary support.) On the other hand, close aides of Washington recorded that they interrupted him during morning devotions when he was kneeling in prayer in private in his tent.[6]

Washington is a good example of the contrast between private morality and governmental power. He used his farewell address in 1797 to argue that "religion and morality are indispensable supports" to the welfare of a nation. Yet at the same time, in keeping with his role as supporter of a constitution that banned religious tests for public office, he declared that "no man's sentiments are more opposed to any kind of restraint upon religious principles than mine are."[7]

---

6. Steven Waldman, *Founding Faith: Providence, Politics, and the Birth of Religious Freedom in America* (New York: Random House, 2008), 56–57; Ron Chernow, *Washington: A Life* (New York: Penguin Press, 2010), 132.

7. Chernow, *Washington,* 132–33.

The irony of the Framers as religious people and the government they created as a secular one is confusing for many Americans, including Latter-day Saints. It has led to two false conclusions. One is that the government these political leaders established was not secular, but actually religious. It must have been because they themselves were religious. The other mistake is to assume that the government was secular because early American political leaders were secular.

Neither is true. The beauty, and irony, of the American government's founding is the fact that religious people created a secular or religiously distant and neutral government. Why did they do that? Why would they not do what is so much expected today, which is to use their power to further their own religious views?

The approach of early American political leaders to religion and government grew out of their own experiences as well as their understanding of history. They were aware of the persecution of minority religions that led the Puritans to come to the United States in 1620. They knew the Massachusetts Bay Colony had become a religiously intolerant society, a development which led Roger Williams and others to leave Massachusetts and form their own colony in today's Rhode Island. They knew that established churches were common in the states in the 1600s and 1700s; the Anglican Church enjoyed the status of being the official state church in the mid-Atlantic colonies while the Congregationalists held the same power in New England.

More than that, the power of government was used to coerce religious compliance and punish religious dissent. People were forced to pay taxes to support churches to which they did not belong. Catholics were banned in many colonies, and Jews were persecuted in most colonies. For example, Connecticut allowed all Christian denominations but banned those that were non-Christian.[8]

Nor was such intolerance limited to isolated colonies early in the colonial period. In fact, intolerance became national policy at the time of the Revolutionary War. Even the Continental Congress joined in the religious discrimination; in 1774, it issued a proclamation against Catholics. Three years later, a committee of the Continental Congress urged the states to raid Quaker meetinghouses to determine if they were treasonous.[9]

In light of all of those experiences, early American leaders wanted something different. They did not want a United States where religion was a cause

---

8. Leonard Levy, *The Establishment Clause*, 2nd ed. (Chapel Hill: University of North Carolina Press, 1994), 1–51.

9. Steven Waldman, *Founding Faith: Providence, Politics, and the Birth of Religious Freedom in America* (New York: Random House, 2008), 8, 9, 14, 51, 109.

of controversy in the operation of the government. They also thought about the immediate consequences of imposing a national religion. How popular would this new constitution be across the states if it played favorites in terms of religion? If a national religion was built into the Constitution, would that hinder ratification of the Constitution?

But primarily they realized that this religiously diverse nation was propelled forward only by a fragile political consensus. Injecting religion, especially determining the status of state churches that would give special status and access to tax-based funding, could tear the political consensus apart. The new nation consisted of Anglicans, Congregationalists, Baptists, Catholics, Quakers, Methodists, Jews, and other religious groups. How could the United States support one of them? And how could the United States even support Christianity as an official religion without squabbling over who was and was not a Christian. Jews clearly were excluded, but mainstream Christian denominations were even suspicious of the Baptists and the Quakers.

The inability of government to use its power to promote religion among the populace was an important point for some of the Framers. James Madison was particularly devoted to this cause. He had spent much of his public life fighting established religion in the state of Virginia. He viewed the First Amendment's religious clauses as vital because it meant "congress should not establish a religion, and enforce the legal observation of it by law, nor compel men to worship God in any manner contrary to their conscience."[10]

It is interesting how quickly American public opinion changed on the subject of government and religion at this time. While established churches were common in the late 1700s, they had disappeared almost completely by the early 1800s. Indeed, the secular approach the Constitution took that made government neutral toward religion became a source of pride for many Americans. In his first presidential inaugural speech, Thomas Jefferson expressed his satisfaction that the United States had "banished from our land that religious intolerance under which mankind so long bled and suffered."[11] In later life, Jefferson felt that one of his greatest achievements was his role in disestablishing a state church in Virginia in the 1770s. Jefferson also was the originator of the phrase, the "wall of separation between Church and State," which he felt was the intent of the First Amendment's prohibition of "the establishment of religion."[12]

---

10. Richard Labunski, *James Madison and the Struggle for the Bill of Rights* (New York: Oxford University Press, 2006), 224.

11. Adrienne Koch and William Peden, eds., *The Life and Selected Writings of Thomas Jefferson* (New York: Random House, 1944), 322.

12. Jefferson's Letter to the Danbury Baptists, January 1, 1802, Library of Congress, http://loc.gov/loc/lcib/9806/danpre.html (accessed March 26, 2014).

Early American political leaders generally believed that separation was beneficial for both the church and the state. In a letter to a friend, Edward Livingston, in 1822, James Madison wrote about religion and government that "every new and successful example . . . of a perfect separation between the ecclesiastical and civil matters, is of importance; and I have no doubt that every new example will succeed, as every past one has done, in showing that religion and Government will both exist in greater purity the less they are mixed together."[13]

The Liberal Soul and Separation of Church and State

Early American political leaders' approach to the role of religion in government is a model for the liberal soul. They were personally religious but did not attempt to use the power of government to impose certain religious views and practices on the whole society. The liberal soul knows the difference between being personally religious and seeking to create a believing society through personal conversion, and employing the power of government to bring about faith and religiosity. It is the former that matches the approach of Doctrine and Covenants 134 as well.

The liberal soul knows that religion is too important a part of each individual's personal life to compel belief. The individual choice to believe or not to believe and what, exactly, to believe is not one for government to make. The Eleventh Article of Faith is clear: "We claim the privilege of worshiping Almighty God according to the dictates of our own conscience, and allow all men the same privilege, let them worship how, where, or what they may." That should be the motto of the liberal soul regarding freedom of religion. All should be allowed to worship as they wish or not to worship if that is their choice. With that as our guide, then government's role is clear: It does not play a role in taking sides or making decisions about religious faith or practice.

This position includes not using government to promote a belief in divinity or prayer or religious activities. It also means not allowing government-sponsored prayers in schools or in other government settings. It forbids the government's promotion of religious activities or the display of religious symbols on government property. Such use would contradict the freedom embodied in the Eleventh Article of Faith.

This is not an anti-religious position. It is not an attempt to ban religion or proscribe religious activity. In fact, it is the opposite. The neutrality of the

---

13. James Madison, Letter to Edward Livingston, July 10, 1822, James Madison Papers, Library of Congress, http://memory.loc.gov/cgi-bin/query/r?ammem/ mjmtext:@field(DOCID+@lit(jm090033)) (accessed April 3, 2014).

government regarding religion allows all religions the opportunity to flourish without advantage given to anyone. It also means that religion must operate on its own rather than being propped up by government regulations.

It is no coincidence that the best breeding ground for the restoration of the gospel was in an environment where government could not kill a new religion because it challenged existing religious orthodoxies. The secular nature of the U.S. government allowed the Church of Jesus Christ of Latter-day Saints to take root and grow. Even in the United States, the Church faced opposition from state governments not subject to federal constitutional provisions banning religious discrimination. But it is vital to remember that such discrimination did not originate from the central government, which was constitutionally mandated to be religiously neutral.

This does not mean that government is forbidden to help charitable organizations, a category that includes the support of many religious groups. Organizations that do good works for a society should be encouraged. These include organizations that provide food for the hungry, clothes for the needy, shelter for the homeless, and mentoring to help the unemployed to get jobs. Churches, synagogues, and mosques, as well as other religious organizations, are a large part of that effort. So an effort to exclude religious organizations from the tax-exempt status intended to facilitate such good works would be counterproductive and antireligious. On the other hand, religious organizations are not the only organizations that do good things in society. So they should not be singled out for such status. But the good that religions do, among other groups, should be encouraged by government in a way that neither harms nor helps religion through government power.

The liberal soul understands that the separation of church and state is a difficult position politically. Many people are concerned about declining moral values and associate this deterioration with explicit judicial decisions forbidding prayer in public schools or displaying the Ten Commandments or Christian symbols such as crosses or nativity scenes on a city hall lawn at Christmas. Fears about moral decline are real, but Supreme Court decisions are not the cause. Instead, they are easy scapegoats for wider and deeper societal changes.

Separation: Benefits for Government

Separation of church and state does not hurt a society. On the contrary, it actually helps it. The separation of church and state benefits the government as well as religion. Separation aids government by removing it from many issues regarding religion. When government begins to take sides regarding religion—for example, by declaring that a country is a Christian nation—then it is an easy step to privilege Christianity over other beliefs. It becomes logical to begin to impose religious tests: If Christianity is the national religion, it follows that leaders ought to share those beliefs. It is a short distance to the assumption that Christian churches should receive government support. Before long, a nation moving in that direction has an established church connected to government.

At that point, the questions begin: If Christianity is the national religion, which brand of Christianity enjoys that privilege? Even if no one church is privileged, how can this be implemented in terms of preferences?

If public prayer is said jointly in the classroom by teachers and students, what kind of prayer can be said? Must it be non-denominational? In that case, the prayer must conform to the government's rules about what a prayer should sound like rather than the teachers' and students' own conscience or religious beliefs.

On the other hand, if all are able to say the prayer they wish, will parents find it acceptable to have their children participate in prayers of faiths they don't believe in? For example, can a Wiccan prayer be said by public school children? For many Christians, a Mormon prayer would be suspect. And many Mormons would be hesitant to participate in many conventional Christian prayers.

Or if the state supports religious schools, how does it do so? For example, the state of Rhode Island at one time provided money to school districts to help pay parochial school teachers as long as they did not teach religion or "any subject matter expressing religious teaching, or the morals or forms of worship of any sect."[14] It then became the job of the state to examine the curriculum of parochial school classes to determine whether religion was being taught. Is that the business of the state?

For much of the twentieth century, the state of Utah provided credit toward graduation for released-time seminary classes that studied the Old and New Testaments (though not the Book of Mormon or the Doctrine and Covenants). Because of this differentiation, the state was responsible for certifying the curriculum of LDS seminaries. Again, should the state be doing that?

Many city councils begin their sessions with prayer, often by a citizen in attendance or, in other places, clergy who have congregations in the city. But such a practice raises serious questions as well. For example, when one resident attempted to use his prayer to make a statement against government-sponsored religious activity (such as city council prayers), the city council

---

14. Richard Davis, "Should There Be a Strict Separation between Church and State? Yes," in Daniel K. Judd, ed., *Taking Sides: Clashing Views on Controversial Issues in Religion* (Guilford, Conn.: McGraw-Hill/Dushkin, 2003), 302–9.

debated whether his prayer was really a prayer. Should a city council be ruling on the content of an individual's prayer?[15]

When there is separation between church and government, the government need not make such decisions. It does not become enmeshed in religious belief and practice. That is why the U.S. Supreme Court has ruled that the Constitution requires the government to be neutral regarding religion and remain aloof from decisions about religion. For the most part, the U.S. Supreme Court has taken this position, not because the justices are anti-God, but because that is what is required of them by the U.S. Constitution and is the best way to secure continued religious freedom.

Some Latter-day Saints interpret the Supreme Court's decisions upholding the secular government created by the Constitution as anti-religious. For example, President Ezra Taft Benson declared that Americans had "allowed our courts, through their anti-prayer, anti-God decisions, to outlaw in the schools the positive belief of the truths contained in the Declaration of Independence, the very foundation of our nation."[16]

However, it is not that the Supreme Court was anti-God or anti-prayer. Instead, the justices recognized that the Framers created a secular government where church and state are distant rather than entangled. Imagine how much more the justices would be drawn into religion, as well as government agencies and legislatures, if there were not such separation. The enforcement of separation protects the government from being sucked into debates over religious beliefs and practices—a position where government clearly does not belong.

Separation: Benefits for the Believer

Separation of church and state also benefits religious believers and the churches to which they belong. Establishment of religion harms a church that is an "established" church because, historically, such churches have become intertwined with government and lost much of their autonomy as governmental power is used to direct the church. For example, the injection of political considerations colors the appointment of cardinals or bishops, the determination of church policy, and even statements of doctrine. When the government begins taking an interest in the affairs of the church, then decision-making on church policy invariably becomes affected by political considerations rather than spiritual ones. The church suffers as a result.

---

15. Joe Costanzo, "Decision Stems from a Suit over a Prayer to 'Mother in Heaven,'" *Deseret News*, September 12, 1997, A1.

16. Ezra Taft Benson, "This Nation Shall Endure," BYU Devotional Address, December 4, 1973, http://speeches.byu.edu/?act=viewitem&id=1004 (accessed April 3, 2014).

But separation particularly benefits believers of minority faiths, including Latter-day Saints. The minority believer is most vulnerable to the state's role in religion because the state follows the majority will. In a society where most people belong to one religion, that majority will reflect the views of those in that majority religion. If the majority does not approve of minority religious beliefs and practices, then suppression of minority religions may follow. Therefore, separation preserves the rights of people even when their beliefs are unpopular with the majority.

In no country does the joining of church and state benefit Latter-day Saints. First, the official church will not be the LDS Church. Even if it is a nation where Christianity is the official religion, the LDS Church will not benefit since traditional Christian denominations have a long history of rejecting Latter-day Saints as Christians. Therefore, it is highly likely that an official church will not be favorable toward the LDS Church. Government suspicion of the LDS Church could range from a mild rejection to outright hostility. At any level, Latter-day Saints are not better off in such a society.

We only need look at current examples to see the problem. Certainly, Islamic states, which have high levels of state-religion association, are not sympathetic to LDS missionaries or even to Christian missionaries at all. The Russian Orthodox Church has sought to use government power to limit missionary work by other Christian churches in Russia. And Israel, the only official Jewish state, does not allow LDS missionaries to proselytize. Missionary work does not thrive where church and state are joined, and it is virtually axiomatic that an established religion will use state resources to prevent the spread of the restored gospel of Jesus Christ. This condition has historically prevailed in the United Kingdom, Scandinavia, and most European countries, and such laws are still on the books, although they are no longer enforced.

However, a member of a religious minority, including a Latter-day Saint, is much more protected in a nation where church and state are distinct and separate. In those cases, government power cannot be used to restrict religious practice. In a nation where church and state are distant and the power of the state is not employed in behalf of the church, the minority believer—be he or she a Mormon, Jehovah's Witness, Muslim, or Jew—need not fear government-sanctioned persecution as long as the believer observes the laws of the land.

Of course, some argue that decisions about religious values and practices should be determined by majority rule. If the majority wants banners in school that assert religious slogans or quote scriptures, currency that includes the name of God, pledges of allegiance that assert religion, or prayer in schools that affirm the presence of God, then that should be the policy. Moreover, if that majority is of a particular religion, then that majority should be able to use government resources and policies to further its beliefs in line with the majority's preferences. Nativity scenes or creches should be allowed on government property at Christmas. Statues of Jesus should stand on public property. Such majorities see no reason not to place monuments listing the Ten Commandments in public parks and engraving scriptural statements on the walls of government buildings. All of this should be done to support the beliefs of the majority religion.

The liberal soul disagrees. That disagreement is rooted in the liberal soul's magnanimity toward and concern for others, which includes recognition of the right of each individual to believe as he or she wishes and to practice those beliefs without intrusion from others, particularly government representatives. The liberal soul is more concerned about protecting individuals' rights to apply their religious precepts and practices to their lives than the right of a majority to impose their religion beliefs and behaviors because they *are* the majority.

Undoubtedly, in most areas of public policy, majority rule is the guide for making decisions that satisfy the most people. But right of conscience does not fall in that category. As Doctrine and Covenants 134 makes clear, freedom of conscience is an individual right; it is not determined by the majority in a society. Therefore, a society of liberal souls does not use government to violate conscience by forcing anyone to accept religious views, especially a particular religion to which an individual dissenter does not subscribe.

For the liberal soul, the right of a minority not to believe in the same way as the majority, or not to believe at all, is sacrosanct. This is a vital protection for Church members, since minority status is the rule for Latter-day Saints around the world, and ostracism and even persecution are common for Latter-day Saints in many nations. But it also is a protection for all who constitute the religious minority wherever they live.

Even when the liberal soul is part of a religious majority, that same respect must be given to the minority. Many Latter-day Saints in Utah, for example, may believe that majority rule should govern in Utah and, therefore, LDS policy can be enforced on such issues as prayer in school, religious decorations associated with holidays displayed on government property, and regulations governing access to alcohol. However, majority rule in such matters can be a double-edged sword. One never knows when the majority will become the minority, and suddenly what was a power to enforce a religious policy with which Latter-day Saints might agree becomes a weapon to coerce Church members to practice what they do not believe or not allow them to practice what they do believe. An example is when a Latter-day Saint living in Utah moves to another part of the United States where a dominant religion gets to make the rules about religion because its members are the majority there.

All should be allowed to believe as they wish and practice their religion in accordance with those beliefs or be allowed to have no religion at all. A believer or nonbeliever should not be required to support religious beliefs or practices of which he or she does not approve. It is easy to say that a nonbeliever should not be forced to attend church or pay tithing. We all understand that. However, what if a nonbeliever is expected to listen to a prayer at a city council meeting or if his or her child is expected to recite a prayer in a school classroom? What if the non-believer's taxes are used to support the erection of a religious symbol on public property?

Or how about a believer who simply does not believe the same way the majority does? This could include students who object to a school teacher using classroom time to promote a religious text they do not believe in or to condemn a religious text they do believe in. Should a non-Christian be expected to join in a Christian prayer every time he attends a sports event or a high school graduation?

Perhaps the issue becomes more powerful for Latter-day Saints if put this way: How many Latter-day Saint parents who say they approve of prayers in schools would feel the same way if their children were exposed to a steady barrage of evangelical Christian (and sometimes anti-Mormon) propaganda in school at their expense as taxpayers? How many would want their children joining a classroom prayer to Allah or Lord Shiva on a daily basis? How many Latter-day Saints would enjoy being compelled to participate in a Hindu, Muslim, or Buddhist ritual before they could speak at a city council meeting? How many would want their children giving a pledge each day that includes a reference to Confucius or Zoroaster? In those cases, how many Latter-day Saint parents would be appeased by the argument of the majority that the minority should go along because the majority has the right to impose its will? Most Latter-day Saints would not like any of these scenarios.

Some who favor a government role in promulgating religion will reply that the person in the minority—the minority religion member or the non-believer—should not be so concerned about religious symbols and practices by the majority through government. The response goes: Why is it they cannot just sit respectfully through city council prayers? Why are they so upset when some of their government money goes to government expression of religion? Why not just accept the majority's religious practices?

Latter-day Saints should be perplexed by that argument. We are taught over and over that we should not compromise our religious beliefs and practices. Instead, we should hold firm to them even in the face of majority pressure to abandon them. We should find it easy to understand why someone else is determined not to compromise his or her principles either.

The liberal soul understands that conscience is such a powerful force that it should not be subject to government control. The freedom to worship is fundamental to the liberal soul, not only for his or her spiritual enrichment, but for the edification of others as well. Allying government with a certain set of religious beliefs and compelling objectors to participate (either through tax money or joining in a form of worship that is hollow for them) is a violation of that freedom of conscience.

Latter-day Saints also should favor separation because it has furthered the missionary work of the Church and the ability of Church members to worship freely. The history of the early days of the Church is a tale of persecution. What the Framers sought in terms of religious establishment and religious freedom was not achieved—either immediately or for many years afterward. The persecution that Latter-day Saints endured in Missouri and Illinois based on religion was exactly the kind of intolerance early American political leaders like Washington, Jefferson, and Madison wanted banished from the United States. However, many people before the Civil War considered the United States a nation that could not tolerate Mormons and the governor of Missouri actually authorized their "extermination" in 1838.

The First Amendment prohibited Congress from impinging on the free exercise of religion, but initially that did not apply to the states. As a result of this failure to extend these protections to states, religious minorities were subject to state power. In the case of the Latter-day Saints, the states of Missouri and Illinois were unwilling to offer protection for minority religious practices. The result was intense persecution that was ignored by the state or, in the case of Missouri, even officially sanctioned by the governor with the infamous 1838 extermination order of Mormons from Missouri.

Joseph Smith bemoaned this inability of the federal government to intervene to protect religious minorities when he criticized the U.S. Constitution for failing to "provide the manner by which that freedom can be preserved, nor for the punishment of Government officers who refuse to protect the people in their religious rights, or to punish those mobs, states, or communities who interfere with the rights of the people on account of their religion."[17]

The application of the provisions of the First Amendment to the states that occurred in the early twentieth century, and the change in attitudes towards religions, particularly minority religions, has meant that the Church of Jesus Christ of Latter-day Saints can flourish in the United States. The early Saints were driven to the Rocky Mountains because they were persecuted elsewhere. As Church members spread out from Utah during the twentieth century, they encountered changing attitudes, particularly in the latter half of the twentieth century. Official discrimination was no longer tolerated. Americans began to accept the reality of minority religions and that acceptance of such religions on an equal basis with majority religions became a quintessentially American

---

17. *History of the Church,* 6:56–57.

cherished concept. The Supreme Court's decisions upholding separation of church and state helped bring about those changing attitudes. It is no coincidence that the enforcement of the "established church" provision of the First Amendment, and its application to the states, occurred not long before LDS Church growth throughout the United States. Nor is it any coincidence that the end of established churches in various nations and the resulting separation of church and state have facilitated missionary work and the growth of the Church there as well.

Separation and Religious Influence in Government

At the same time, the separation of church and state does not mean that religion is excluded from the public square. Some secularists believe that religious voices have no place in the public forum. Indeed, that is their objective. They advocate for separation of church and state to prevent religious organizations from influencing public policy. In that sense, they are just as intolerant as religious extremists.

The liberal soul no more agrees with them than it sides with those who object to the separation of church and state. They are as exclusive as their polar opposites on this issue. Both sides wish to dominate the other. Neither should be allowed to do so.

The liberal soul knows that religious groups have a right to lobby to affect policy. That right is not diminished because churches, synagogues, and mosques are religiously based rather than founded on a secular philosophy. Religious organizations also have the right to mobilize members to lobby as well. Church leaders, regardless of their faith, have the right to urge their members to vote in certain ways or support certain legislation, as they see fit. In the United States, if such advocacy relates to candidates or political parties, that religious organization can lose its tax-exempt status. It is not that a church is constitutionally prohibited from engaging in support of specific candidates and political parties. Rather, like any other charity, they are simply no longer considered a tax-exempt organization.

Nor does separation of church and state mean that religious believers must check their beliefs when they enter the door of government. Religion can be part of the rationale someone uses for supporting or opposing a particular public policy. Advocacy of policy need not be based on non-religious supports to enter the public square. A public official can be motivated by religious beliefs to sponsor certain legislation or oppose other bills.

However, religious believers need to recognize that a rationale for public policy based on religious belief may not persuade others who do not share that particular religious belief. And it would be least persuasive for those who have no religious belief at all. For example, Church members who use prophetic statements to promote some policy position should not be surprised when others who are not LDS are not convinced by the appeal to the authority of a leader of a religious organization to which they do not belong. However, the use of such logic is certainly up to the individual and should not be banned by government.

The Challenge for the Liberal Soul

The balancing act required by religious freedom and expression on the one hand and the need on the other that government refrains from being entangled in religion is not an easy one at times. The liberal soul can be tempted to use government power to enforce religious practices because those religious practices are so much a part of the liberal soul. It is easy to forget that Latter-day Saints in the early days of the Church suffered under governments that were religiously intolerant and that many governments today still act that way toward the Church and its members. It is tempting to ignore the history of persecution of the Church and its application to all minority faiths and, instead, insist on a Christian-based government. After all, will not a theocratic state exist in the Millennium anyway?

However, the Lord has given us earthly governments for the moment, not theocratic ones. And the divinely inspired U.S. Constitution established a religion-neutral government that banned intolerance rather than enabled it. That is the kind of government we are expected to live under today. We need to make the best of it by creating a society where all can believe and practice without government interference or favoritism.

The goal of a society where government keeps its distance from religion, and vice versa, is a worthy one. It is even vital to the continuance of the preaching of the gospel. At the same time, such a society must protect religious freedom and the right of religion to operate in the public sphere. This society is achievable, despite the efforts of both extremes to undermine it. The liberal soul seeks to bring about and maintain such a society because, for our day and time, it is the closest we come to our ultimate goal of becoming a Zion people.

CHAPTER 5

"THE EARTH IS THE LORD'S, AND THE FULNESS THEREOF"

When God placed Adam and Eve in the Garden of Eden, He gave them a living area that included "every tree that is pleasant to the sight and good for food" (Gen. 2:9). He provided a space for them that would serve their physical needs. He even made the garden an aesthetically pleasing environment for them.

It is in and through these settings that we can appreciate God and become closer to Him. Moses climbed a mountain to talk to God. Joseph Smith sought wisdom in a grove of trees. And, most importantly of all, Jesus retired to a garden to become the atoner of all humans.

But He did more than that. God gave Adam and Eve dominion over the earth. He made them and all their descendants the rulers over the fish, the fowl, and every animal on the earth. Everything God made was in the hands of man: "Thou madest him to have dominion over the works of thy hands" (Ps. 8:6).

How far did that dominion go? Did it give Adam and all his descendants the right to do whatever they wished with God's creations? Could they destroy what God gave them and still fulfill God's commands?

That dominion was not given to Adam on a personal whim. God put Adam in charge for a specific purpose. Adam and Eve were expected to respect the garden, to care for it, "to dress it and to keep it" (Gen. 2:15).

That responsibility to dress and keep the earth has belonged to each succeeding generation. Today, it has fallen to us, the earth's current occupants. However, no previous generation has held as much dominion over the earth as we do. With the advent of nuclear war, our generation possesses the ability to decimate the earth and everything on it. But even short of that, humans today hold enormous power over the future of the earth on which we live. We can change the course of rivers, flood vast land areas, and create acid rain pouring over thousands of square miles. We can destroy vast spaces of land, water, and air quickly.

That is why the concept of stewardship over our environment is so vital. The Doctrine and Covenants reminds us that:

> All things which come of the earth, in the season thereof, are made for the benefit and use of man, both to please the eye and to gladden the heart. . . . And it pleaseth God that he hath given all these things unto man, for unto this end were they made to be used, with judgment, not to excess, neither by extortion. (D&C 59:18, 20)

What is judgment? How do we avoid excess? How do we not use extortion? What does it mean to "dress and keep" the earth the Lord has given us? How do we act as wise stewards in respect to this awesome responsibility we have been given? What, exactly, is our job?

Some of our recent and current practices in environmental care can make us wonder whether we are fulfilling our God-given task. For example, can we be stewards and destroy the natural beauty of our land? What about carving large holes into mountains? What about polluting rivers and streams? How about fouling the air we breathe? If we kill off plants and animals that are part of the ecosystem the Lord created for our "benefit and use," are we still keeping God's command? These are questions the liberal soul asks.

The War over the Environment

In recent years, the concept of stewardship over the earth has been lost in the midst of nasty partisan rhetoric about the environment. Many Latter-day Saints in the United States have heard the views of certain talk show hosts who label those who support environmentalism as radical tree huggers. Environmental concern is derided as fantasy in the midst of ad hominem labels. For example, radio commentator Rush Limbaugh calls environmentalists "wackos," while another talk show host, Glenn Beck, asserts that people who believe that global warming is occurring are socialists.[1]

The issue of climate change has become a political football. Is climate change man-made or a natural phenomenon? The question should be answerable by facts. Instead, the reply too often is based on a person's partisanship; Democrats are certain of one position and Republicans the other. According to a recent Pew Research Center survey, 53 percent of Democrats believe global warming is occurring and humans are the cause, while only 16 percent of

---

1. "Rush Limbaugh, the 'Obnoxious Anti-Environmentalist' Was Right," *The Rush Limbaugh Show*, July 29, 2010, at http://www.rushlimbaugh.com/daily/2010/07/29/rush_limbaugh_the_obnoxious_anti_environmentalist_was_right (accessed April 3, 2014); and "Glenn Beck: Obama's Socialist Climate Czar," *Glenn Beck Show*, January 12, 2009, http://www.glennbeck.com/content/articles/article/198/20024/ (accessed April 3, 2014).

Republicans think that way.[2] Not surprisingly, this debate generates more heat than light. The objective is to score points, win elections, and protect particular interests rather than to find solutions to environmental problems.

Church Leaders' Calls for Stewardship

For Latter-day Saints, however, concern for our environment should not be just a political issue. Instead, it should be viewed as a God-given command. The repetition of that command can be found in scriptural declarations, Church history, and modern prophetic actions and admonitions.

Psalm 24 reminds us that "the earth is the Lord's, and the fulness thereof" (Ps. 24:1). In Doctrine and Covenants 104, that message is repeated: "I, the Lord, stretched out the heavens, and built the earth, my very handiwork; and all things therein are mine" (D&C 104:14). We are in the Lord's hands. He is the master "in whose hand is the soul of every living thing, and the breath of all mankind" (Job 12:10).

We are not the owners of this earth, including the property we may claim during our lifetime. Rather, we are merely its temporary custodians. Heavenly Father entrusts us with the responsibility to care for His creations. Each generation has the responsibility to remember that. Rather than adopting an attitude that God has given us carte blanche, we must realize that we have a sacred responsibility to pass on to the next generation the world which we inherited and which God gave us to "dress and keep."

All of us are accountable for how we treat those earthly things God has given us. This includes the physical environment in which we live: "For it is expedient that I, the Lord, should make every man accountable, as a steward over earthly blessings, which I have made and prepared for my creatures" (D&C 104:13).

Environmental stewardship has been a facet of the Church of Jesus Christ of Latter-day Saints since the days of Brigham Young. When Mormon pioneers first arrived in Utah in 1847, they faced a land that had been nearly untouched by human presence. The Native American tribes had made little impact on their environment. The pioneers had the opportunity to use this land, a promised land, for their benefit. President Brigham Young urged these pioneers to respect what they had been given. "We should love the earth—we should love the works which God has made."[3]

---

2. Pew Research Center for the People & the Press, "Little Change in Opinions about Global Warming," October 27, 2010, http://www.people-press.org/2010/10/27/little-change-in-opinions-about-global-warming/ (accessed April 3, 2014).

3. Brigham Young, June and July 1865, *Journal of Discourses,* 27 vols. (Liverpool and London: LDS Booksellers Depot, 1855–56), 11:112, http://journalofdiscourses.com/11/18 (accessed April 3, 2014).

President Young urged Latter-day Saints to develop the land the Lord had given them: "Progress, and improve upon, and make beautiful everything around you. Cultivate the earth and cultivate your minds. Build cities, adorn your habitations, make gardens, orchards, and vineyards, and render the earth so pleasant that when you look upon your labours you may do so with pleasure."[4]

However, almost immediately, the search for economic gain overrode prophetic counsel. Some of the pioneers considered their own economic interests above their stewardship responsibilities. Entrepreneurs overgrazed lands, stripped the timber from forests, and polluted the air.

Despite prophetic counsel, concepts of environmental stewardship among Church members during the nineteenth century and early twentieth century seemed to fade as time passed. In its place, according to historian Thomas G. Alexander, came a secular entrepreneurism on the part of some Latter-day Saints. That approach considered the land and its resources as a tool for greed. In the quest for material wealth, the impact on the environment was ignored and the Lord's command to be stewards was discarded.[5]

However, Church leaders were still concerned about the environment in Utah. President Heber J. Grant endorsed the creation of national parks in Utah, including Bryce and Zion's National Parks and Cedar Breaks National Monument.[6] In the 1970s, President Spencer W. Kimball urged Latter-day Saints to take better care of their physical environment. He admonished Latter-day Saints "to dress and keep in a beautiful state the property that is in your hands." This beautification campaign included razing broken-down homes and other buildings, clearing weeds out of ditches, repairing sheds and corrals, and repainting old barns.[7]

In more recent years, the Church has gone "green." It has become dedicated to "green" meetinghouses across the world, including use of solar panels, recycled building materials, and xeriscaped landscaping. Presiding Bishop David Burton explained that "there is something very doctrinally sound when we talk about conservation of resources. . . . This aspect of our culture has become a vital part of our DNA."[8]

---

4. Brigham Young, June 12, 1860, ibid., 8:83, http://journalofdiscourses.com/8 (accessed April 3, 2014).

5. For a discussion of early Utahns' attitudes and behavior concerning the environment, see Thomas G. Alexander, "Stewardship and Enterprise: The LDS Church and the Wasatch Oasis Environment, 1847–1930," *Western Historical Quarterly* 25 (Autumn 1994): 340–64.

6. Thomas G. Alexander, *Mormonism in Transition: A History of the Latter-day Saints, 1890–1930* (Urbana: University of Illinois Press, 1986), 194.

7. Spencer W. Kimball, "God Will Not Be Mocked," *Ensign*, November 1974, 4.

8. Paul Beebe, "Mormon Who Led Salt Lake City Makeover Steps Aside," *Salt Lake Tribune*, April 1, 2012, http://www.sltrib.com/sltrib/money/53826007-79/

Yet, among many Church members there is an opposite approach. It is an ecotheology that states that our physical surroundings are not very important and the earth will be destroyed anyway. Indeed, the destruction of the earth is God's form of punishment and the fulfillment of prophecy.[9] Why should we try to prevent it since it is God's will?

What Should the Liberal Soul Do?

The liberal soul understands the importance of stewardship and that the earth is not ours to do with just as we wish. Zoology Professor Clayton White summarized the questions the liberal soul asks: "The Lord loaned us the earth and all therein. In a very real sense we are merely borrowing it. It is the apple of his eye, for it is through this earth and our mortality here that he can bring to pass our eternal life. . . . Are we going to return the earth in as good a shape as we received it? Or are we carelessly destroying it and the things therein, contaminating it for our own short-term material and personal gain?"[10]

Some Latter-day Saints hold a couple of fallacies regarding our stewardship over the environment. One is that since the Second Coming will occur within our lifetime, we need not worry about using up precious resources. All this talk about depletion of resources, they argue, is useless because that will never happen before Christ's return. Since many assume the millennium is right around the corner, why worry about environmental degradation? We will be saved from it by the Second Coming.

The scriptures tell us that no one knows when the Second Coming will occur. Therefore, to waste the resources of the Earth with the expectation the Second Coming will occur by a certain time is foolhardy. What if resources are depleted before the Second Coming? Then what?

Of course, the conclusion that millennialism solves all current problems, including environmental ones, is not new. Several groups in the United States alone—from the Millerites in the 1840s to the California minister who predicted the end of the world on May 21, 2011—have made this claim. They all have been wrong because they base their prophecies on speculation, not knowledge. Latter-day Saints should avoid the trap of following those who do not know, but instead merely speculate.

---

burton-church-lds-lake.html.csp?page=1 (accessed April 3, 2014).

9. For a description of this school of thought, see George Handley, "Heaven and Earth: Thinking Through Environmentalism," in Justin F. White and James E. Faulconer, eds., *Common Ground, Different Opinions: Latter-day Saints and Contemporary Issues* (Salt Lake City, Utah: Greg Kofford Books, 2013), 275.

10. Clayton M. White, "The Cry of the Falcon," *New Era*, November 1979, 43.

Since we do not know when the end of the world is and we are still here on the earth right now, we should assume that our stewardship responsibility has not been abrogated. The Lord's command to care for the earth applies until He rescinds it. Only then are we free from that obligation. Actually, since the earth we dwell on will become the celestial kingdom, that day may never come.

Another false assumption is that God gave us these resources precisely to use up as we see fit. We are supposed to exploit them because we have "dominion" over everything. However, President Young explained that our purpose is not to use up the earth, but actually to multiply our natural resources: "The very object of our existence here is to handle the temporal elements of this world and subdue the earth, multiplying those organisms of plants and animals God has designed shall dwell upon it."[11]

Each Person's Task

Stewardship for the liberal soul exists at three levels. One is the individual. Regardless of what others do, each of us has his or her individual stewardship over the natural resources within our control. This includes whatever the Lord has given us of His earth for our individual use. That means water, land, energy, and any other natural resource within our control.

As stewards over our own resources, we can take individual steps to use those resources wisely. These may be small steps and they may appear insignificant. For example, in terms of water usage, we could reduce the length of our showers, minimize how much water we use when we brush our teeth, limit watering lawns to avoid waste, etc. For energy, we can avoid leaving on lights when no one is present in a room, lowering the thermostat in winter as much as possible, and raising the temperatures in summer so our air conditioners run less frequently. We can avoid needless car trips that waste gas and take positive long-term actions such as recycling or installing energy-efficient windows and doors. These are all decisions that we can make individually to lessen our impact on natural resources and help preserve them for generations to come.

These seemingly small actions, done individually, do not constitute dramatic lifestyle changes. But taken collectively, they can make a major contribution to the conservation of our natural resources and the fulfillment of the Lord's command that each of us individually "dress and keep" the garden the Lord has given us.

---

11. Brigham Young, January 26, 1862, *Journal of Discourses*, 9:169, http://journalofdiscourses.com/9 (accessed April 3, 2014).

We can teach our children about the need to husband resources and respect the creations of God. Humanities Professor George Handley has put this succinctly:

> I believe that the Lord cares more about what kind of children we are raising rather than how many, but I also emphatically believe that the kind he wants are not merely morally clean non-smokers and non-drinkers but also morally modest consumers, respectful toward all life and grateful users of His resources, and generous in their willingness to sacrifice so that others might have the same opportunities they enjoy.[12]

What People Can Do in Groups

The next level is what people can do within groups and organizations, including corporations. Corporations and non-profit organizations can make those same decisions that individuals do in regards to their own uses of natural resources. Doing so reflects the understanding on the part of groups that they, too, hold a stewardship over environmental resources within their control. For example, these organizations can add to environmental stewardship by conserving water, reducing electricity use when rooms are not in use, and opting for tele-conferencing over traveling whenever possible. They also can convert their manufacturing facilities into more environmentally friendly factories, thus reducing the level of greenhouse gases they emit into the atmosphere.

Moreover, some companies already are joining in the effort to recycle or make new products that minimize environmental harm. They range from grocery stores that recycle cans and bottles to automobile manufacturers turning to natural gas or electric cars and reducing the emission of carbon dioxide. These companies are taking seriously their stewardship obligations.

The Role of Government

Unfortunately, not all individuals are conscious of environmental stewardships. And many corporations today are not good environmental stewards. That's why a third level of action is necessary—government. Voluntary restraint simply does not work for everyone. Government intervention should be a last resort. Obviously, it would be better if everyone cooperated voluntarily. Sadly, that does not happen.

Government action is the reflection of society's values and preferences. Taking care of the environment should be one of those values. Reducing harmful elements that destroy animal and plant life and conserving the land

---

12. Handley, "Heaven and Earth," 278.

for agricultural production as well as recreation and aesthetic enjoyment should be a society-wide goal. Through government's role in maintaining, preserving, and regulating our natural assets, those resources can be maintained for generations to come.

At the same time, failure to act wisely in environmental stewardship affects all, not just a few or even one. If, for example, a factory is dumping raw sewage into a river, that decision is hardly an individual one. It affects everyone downstream, including boaters, swimmers, those who fish, as well as people whose water needs for bathing, drinking, and cooking are drawn from that river. If a factory's smokestack emits pollutants into the atmosphere, people for miles around are subjected to polluted air. That leads to ill health and, for certain groups of people, potential death.

One individual holds the power to damage many others through environmental neglect. For example, in a dry climate, it may seem like a harmless prank for a teenager to set the brush near a housing subdivision on fire. But the potential effect on many people—the public cost to put out the fire, the danger to people's homes, the possibility of injury or even death—is enormous.

That is why government plays an essential role in protecting the environment, thereby safeguarding all who are affected by that environment. Fire regulations are imposed by governments. Pollution controls also are imposed by government. Land use policies are imposed as well. Again, if government does not enforce stiff penalties for violation, then the selfish acts of one can affect the whole. Government must play a role to limit individual action when the society as a whole is damaged or even threatened by large-scale environmental irresponsibility.

There are extremists who believe that government has little or no role in these matters. They argue that individuals and corporations should be allowed to make decisions about how to use their property without government intervention. For them, the statements above by conservative political commentators are right on the mark. Unfortunately, this anti-government view is held by some Latter-day Saints whose visceral opposition to government role blinds them to the need for joint environmental stewardship. It also is shared by Latter-day Saints with the millennialist views described above. Whatever the rationale, it is a perspective that prevents society from acting in the interest of the whole and blocks society-level actions necessary to fulfill the Lord's command to "dress and keep" the living space God has provided.

And the danger is real, not philosophical. For example, Lake Erie was severely polluted by continual factory dumping of waste products over many years. The lake became so polluted that swimming was no longer allowed and fish died. The lake even caught fire. A lake that was intended to meet the material and aesthetic needs of humans and act as a home for many species of plants and animals became a vast wasteland of human pollution.

Near upstate New York, a neighborhood called Love Canal had been the dumping ground for a chemical company's toxic waste before a housing subdivision was built. Residents began to experience severe health problems. Pregnant women had a higher than normal number of miscarriages and their children were more likely to be born with birth defects. Residents were diagnosed with cancer at a higher rate than typical.

Ideally, if government is involved, it can be local and state government that solves the problems. But that often is not the case. Too often, these governments are closely connected to local business interests, some of whom seek profit over environmental protection. Local and state elected officials rely on such business interests for campaign contributions and, necessarily, reflect their concerns. This sad situation is demonstrated in the two cases just mentioned. Local and state governments were slow to act to prevent these disasters.

Another reason local and state governments may not resolve these issues is that natural resources do not necessarily stay within certain political boundaries—local or state. For example, air and water transcend these boundaries, causing the effects of environmental decisions in one state to be felt in other states. This was true in the case of Lake Erie. Pollutants dumped from a factory in one state resulted in pollution touching four states. The acid rain that was created by emissions from a factory in one state affects several states in the northeastern United States.

This explains why government's role typically occurs at a larger level—the national level. It also can happen through intergovernmental agreements among states, but that, too, requires coordinated action above the state and local levels. Since state and local governments lacked the authority to solve problems outside their own boundaries and often did not cooperate among themselves to resolve issues, the Environmental Protection Agency (EPA) was created by Congress in 1970. The EPA regulates industries that were quick to sacrifice the environment for their own interests in order to further bottom-line profits. Interestingly, while some companies were willing to impose pollution controls, they did not want to do so unilaterally for fear they would no longer be competitive with those companies that did not do so. The EPA role assured that all companies operated under the same standards and therefore did not place environmentally conscious companies at an economic disadvantage.

The EPA has been heavily criticized by economic conservatives as strongly intrusive into their affairs. These concerns can be real in some circumstances. However, overall, the EPA reflects society's concern that environmental conservation ranks as a national priority. Since the creation of the EPA, as well as subsequent legislative and executive actions by the federal government, air and water pollution standards have been enacted and the nation's air and water supply are cleaner today than they were forty years ago.

Government has the obligation to take action to stop individual and corporate decisions that harm the land, water, and air that our Heavenly Father has given us. Anti-pollution regulations by government agencies are one example of essential government action. In addition, government can encourage responsible stewardship behavior. Using the taxing power to encourage energy efficiency is one means for rewarding those who decide that natural resources are not unlimited.

Governmental action can be more than just regulatory. It also can stimulate industry in more eco-friendly directions. Government can provide seed money for research and development of alternative energy sources such as wind and solar energy and the use of hydrogen fuel and natural gas. The costs of business investment in new energy forms can be high, and government can provide incentives for industry to explore new energy sources.

Government also can be educational. For example, public schools can teach children about the importance of caring for our environment and taking individual actions to further that objective. Government-sponsored public information campaigns, through public service ads, can help enlighten the public about ways to save the environment. Government is not the only educational tool; the private sector plays a critical role. But government is one contributor to greater public appreciation of the value of environmental stewardship.

Conclusion

For the liberal soul, stewardship over the earth is a sacred responsibility given by God. All inhabitants of the earth have been granted this stewardship responsibility. All are accountable to God for how we carry out this stewardship. The liberal soul understands that and seeks to be the kind of steward the Lord is proud of.

Most of that stewardship obligation rests at the individual level. If each individual takes action to conserve and preserve rather than waste, then environmental resources can be maintained for generations to come. With billions of people each taking responsibility for his or her own individual sphere of influence over the environment, the effect would be enormous in producing a usage of the earth's natural resources in line with the concept of stewardship.

However, that stewardship obligation goes beyond acting individually. It also includes encouraging corporations and organizations in taking steps to act as wise stewards as well. Corporations and organizations hold enormous power today over resources. No longer does the world live in a feudal age when organizations were nearly non-existent and corporations did not exist at all. Because they are present and hold power over natural resources, they too must acquire a sense of environmental stewardship.

Since individuals and organizations do not always act in the public's interest, government policies are necessary to enforce compliance. And since environmental problems do not respect private property or political boundaries, those problems need to be addressed at the level of government that can best address them. That is why society through government also holds a stewardship role as well.

The liberal soul should support government policies that help fulfill that stewardship role, particularly when compliance does not occur voluntarily and the effects of neglect have far-reaching consequences for society as a whole. Individually and collectively (as groups and as society as a whole), we all share the God-given obligation to "dress and keep" the beautiful world He has given us.

CHAPTER 6

THOU SHALT NOT KILL

Despite the fact that the twentieth century began with the "war to end all wars," war has been a constant in recent years. I have lived through several wars my country has waged with other nations—Vietnam, Afghanistan, and two with Iraq. In addition, the United States military has been involved in short-term conflicts in far-flung places such as Grenada, Panama, Haiti, Somalia, Bosnia, and Libya.

My own family has been affected by these military actions. My father was in the Navy during the Korean and Vietnam Wars. Two brothers-in-law fought in Vietnam. I have nephews who have served in Iraq and Afghanistan. Chances are that more of my relatives will be engaged in war in the future.

Beyond wars between nations, civil wars are constantly being fought across the globe. Factions within a nation declare war on each other and battle for months, years, or even decades. Tens of thousands of people die in these conflicts each year.

Throughout the history of the world, war has been the rule and not the exception. The Hundred Years War between England and France in the fourteenth and fifteenth centuries dragged on through successive generations and created the current concept of a standing army. The Seven Years War in the middle of the 1700s involved several European nations of the day including England, France, Prussia, Austria, Spain, Portugal, and Russia. One of the most brutal conflicts was the Civil War in the United States in the 1860s, which took the lives of an estimated 750,000 soldiers.[1] Ghastly casualties characterized World War I and World War II where millions of people, both among soldiers and civilians, lost their lives. People were driven from their homes, men were conscripted into military service, women were raped, and children were killed by bombs falling on their homes.

---

1. J. David Hacker, "Recounting the Dead," *New York Times*, September 20, 2011, http://opinionator.blogs.nytimes.com/2011/09/20/recounting-the-dead/ (accessed April 3, 2014).

President Gordon B. Hinckley chastised people who celebrate the great empires of the past, explaining that each of them had a dark side consisting of a "grim and tragic overlay of brutal conquest, of subjugation, of repression, and an astronomical cost in life and treasure." He then observed that "our Father in Heaven must have wept as He has looked down upon His children through the centuries as they have squandered their divine birthright in ruthlessly destroying one another."[2]

Why War?

Why has there been so much war in the history of the human race? James, an apostle and the brother of Jesus, provided a simple explanation in his epistle: "From whence come wars and fightings among you? Come they not hence, even of your lusts. . . . Ye lust, and have not: ye kill, and desire to have, and cannot obtain" (James 4:1–2).

Lust, greed, and pride are all reasons why individuals fight with each other. They also explain why nations rise up against one another. History is replete with examples of nations going to war because they sought selfish aims—either by the people generally or their leaders specifically, or both. For example, the Japanese bombed Pearl Harbor on December 7, 1941, to assert their claim of unchallenged dominance over the Pacific Ocean. Saddam Hussein invaded Iran in 1980 to redirect public unrest away from his brutal rule and toward an external enemy.

Sometimes war easily can be identified as a conflict involving a clear aggressor. The Napoleonic Wars in the first decade of the nineteenth century stemmed from Napoleon's desire to rule Europe. Similarly, World War II was an example of aggression by Adolf Hitler, Benito Mussolini, and Japanese generals bent on controlling the world. Again, Saddam Hussein invaded Kuwait in 1990 to rule a nation that he felt belonged to Iraq but which was also endowed with oil reserves that would enrich Hussein and his regime.

In other cases, blame is shared by both sides when the urge to wage war rages. For example, in the Seven Years War of the 1750s and 1760s, Britain and France fought over who controlled North American colonies, both seeking dominance and both willing to fight to gain it. In 1914, the Austro-Hungarians, Russians, Germans, and French all stumbled into war through national pride and miscommunication. Government leaders were reluctant to seek peace and understanding in the face of perceived insults.[3]

---

2. President Gordon B. Hinckley, "War and Peace," *Ensign*, May 2003, 78.

3. See, for example, Barbara Tuchman, *The Guns of August* (New York: Macmillan, 1962).

Nations initiating a war typically assert that they hold some moral right to fight. A nation may do so to claim territory considered theirs, forestall a predicted invasion by an enemy, right a wrong to their national pride, or some other similar reason. Argentina declared war on Britain to recover islands off its coast that it said were part of its territory, not Britain's. The United States declared war on Spain when national pride was wounded by the sinking of an American battleship supposedly destroyed by the Spanish. The United States went to war in Afghanistan and Iraq to defeat terrorism.

In wartime, both sides usually claim that God is on their side. Religious leaders often provide theological support for the war and encourage their followers to fight evil by participating in the war. President Abraham Lincoln described this phenomenon during the Civil War between the North and the South: "Both read the same Bible, and pray to the same God; and each invokes His aid against the other. . . . The prayers of both could not be answered; that of neither has been answered fully."[4]

The claim of divine approval rarely is accompanied by evidence beyond wishful thinking or an attempt to legitimate less noble aims. The bottom line is that people cause wars, not God. People may consider themselves fighting in God's name, but Heavenly Father is not the instigator of wars nor does He condone war, except in unusual situations.

The Liberal Soul and War

The thirst for war, even for the most benign of reasons, should not characterize the liberal soul. The liberal soul views war as evil; it is the fullness of Satan let loose upon the world. The liberal soul values each individual as a child of God and seeks to serve others and help improve their lives, but war is the opposite of these qualities. In war, people are targets, not human beings. Life is cheap, not precious. Violent death is a constant companion, not a rarity.

What differentiates the liberal soul from others is charitableness toward all. It is impossible to be charitable to others while you are killing them in a war. A warped rationale might be that LDS soldiers are sending enemy troops to spirit prison where they can hear the gospel, something that might not happen to them on earth. A sister in one ward even joked to a Vietnam veteran that he had done just that. He was not amused by the humor. Such thinking does not conform to Church doctrine.

---

4. "Transcript of President Abraham Lincoln's Second Inaugural Address (1865)," National Archives, http://www.ourdocuments.gov/doc.php?flash=true&doc=38&page=transcript (accessed April 3, 2014).

Occasionally there are silver linings in war. Noble acts do emerge, such as the soldier who risks his own life to save that of his comrade, or better yet an opponent's. Or the soldier who places civilians out of harm's way during a battle or gives food to starving children whose fathers still fight against him or her. Nor are noble acts performed only by soldiers. For example, during World War II, non-Jewish civilians hid Jews in their attics, despite the risk of imprisonment or death.

But these acts compete with an array of evil deeds that characterize war. These deeds not only are done constantly by human beings during wartime, but many justify them as moral during a time of war. Satan must be pleased when faith, hope, and morals held by good and righteous people are swept away in moments of despair over the disaster surrounding them.

War often leads to questioning the very existence of God. Participants in war wonder why a loving God could allow such horror to be perpetrated. In the midst of war, it is easy to conclude there is no God. How could there be? How could He beget such awful children who seek to destroy each other?

In war, where people carry weapons and hatred, morals are often thrown to the wayside. Soldiers assume that, with the power of the weapon, they can intimidate, abuse, and destroy without consequence. Those who make war assume God is not watching or that there is no God to watch.

War unleashes a sense of vengeance as violence begets violence and atrocity calls for an even greater atrocity. A soldier who sees a buddy shot down may seek revenge—not so much on the enemy soldier who fired the shot or hurled the grenade, but on everyone who wears that uniform or fights for that side. Civilians can become surrogates for enemy soldiers and be made to suffer punishment for supporting the enemy.

Even those who do not engage intentionally in such atrocities nevertheless may still participate in war's horrors. For example, in modern warfare, civilians are as much targets as soldiers. During World War II, both the Allied and Axis forces dropped thousands of bombs on civilian populations in Germany and Britain. Some of those men who firebombed people from hundreds of feet in the air would have helped any of those people had they seen them in need on the street. Or today, a soldier at a base or a sailor in a submarine can launch a missile that devastates a community hundreds of miles away. In warfare today, thousands of human lives can be ended by the push of a button. We may consider ourselves more advanced today, but warfare is more pernicious. Not only can so many lives be snuffed out within minutes in a nuclear war, but even waging a conventional war can be so mechanical and sterile that war's deadly consequences can seem remote and unreal.

The liberal soul takes seriously the admonition to "renounce war and proclaim peace" (D&C 98:16). Yet the Israelites proclaimed the Lord to be "a man of war" because He had fought for them against Pharoah's armies, and David, king of Israel, believed that the Lord helped to prepare for war (Exod. 15:3; 2 Sam. 22:35). Is the Lord a prince of peace or a man of war? Does the Lord seek peace or war? What should be the liberal soul's choice—war or peace?

Justifications for War

Of course, the decision about whether to go to war is not an easy one. That is true whether it is made by a government or by an individual. Indeed, the decision to go to war is a personal one, not just one made by governments. Individuals, regardless of what nation they are citizen of, cannot abdicate responsibility of whether to go to war. Despite social, political, or even legal pressure, each individual must make a personal decision about whether to wage war. Nevertheless, the consequences of any choice are serious.

One reason this decision is difficult is the issue of patriotism. As individuals, Latter-day Saints are caught between loyalty to nation and abhorrence to war. When considering this dilemma, Latter-day Saints may remember those LDS soldiers in Germany in the 1940s who opposed the war but were still expected to fight for Nazi Germany, or others who are drawn into some other conflict where they believe their country is in the wrong.

However, the problem really is closer to home for many Latter-day Saints because so many live within the United States. Since the United States has acquired the role of global police officer and intervenes in conflicts around the world, U.S. soldiers are ordered to fight in diverse places such as Iraq, Afghanistan, Bosnia, Somalia, and Panama. Often these conflicts do not affect the national security of the United States directly, but occur because of expectations of American military leadership around the world. These attitudes often originate with Americans who perceive the United States as the world's leader and therefore, naturally, as the world's enforcer.

When considering the United States' military role, the following questions should be continually in the minds of Latter-day Saints, particularly those who serve in the military: Are there times when a nation is justified in going to war? Is it ever moral to wage war? What constitutes Christ-like attitudes and behavior in wartime?

Two extreme positions are not satisfactory. One extreme is that the Latter-day Saint should participate in war on others whenever war fever takes over. It is more than just a sense of loyalty to the nation; it is a desire to do battle with others in support of national pride.

Usually, this haste to war is accompanied by disdain for those who are more hesitant about war. During the Vietnam War, I heard references to opponents to the war as the equivalent of the unrighteous who opposed Captain

Moroni in the Book of Mormon. In other words, disagreement on national war policy was tantamount to unfaithfulness to the Church.

War fever—a desire to engage in war to satisfy national pride or loyalty—spurs war rather than a search for peace. Too often it gives carte blanche to a government to wage war instead of finding diplomatic solutions to conflicts. Too often it can lead to hasty religious justification for unjustified war. That extreme is unacceptable.

But so is the other—pacifism. Christian pacifism is a deeply entrenched belief, although not one commonly practiced. Mormonism does not have a policy of established pacifism, in theory. In practice, LDS leaders embraced pacifism during much of the nineteenth century, as it applied to national conflicts. Brigham Young and Latter-day Saints solicited participation among pioneers in the Mormon Battalion during the Mexican War, but Church leaders and members generally avoided the Civil War as well as the Spanish-American War. That pacifism ended by World War I, when Church members participated in American military units fighting in France and B. H. Roberts of the First Council of the Seventy even served as a chaplain. Pacifism is not a Church doctrine today, although some individual members adopt such a practice.

Yet a universal pacifism does not include provision for times when war may need to be waged. It does not allow exceptions to the general rule of avoiding war and proclaiming peace. Yet such exceptions can exist. Sometimes war is the solution to right a wrong and undo an injustice.

If not militarism or pacifism, then what should be the stance of the liberal soul? There is a middle way that allows war in rare circumstances. Those circumstances center on two necessary conditions that may justify war. Those are national self-defense and defense of others in other nations where citizens are in physical danger.

National Self-Defense

Self-defense is a natural reaction to a personal threat. When someone is attacking us, our instinct is to take the weapon from their hands and restrain them so they do not harm us. Self-defense on an individual basis is similar to national self-defense. A nation that is attacked is justified in defending itself against an aggressor nation.

But the self-defense claim can be abused when an individual perceives a non-existent threat. If your neighbor owns a gun or even has a past criminal history, that does not mean he or she currently is a threat. Nevertheless, you may believe a threat exists and feel justified in invading your neighbor's house or attempting to forcibly evict him or her. Those actions would be unacceptable in the absence of a real threat. In fact, they may even be facades for some other objective such as stealing the neighbor's gun or buying the neighbor's land cheaply.

Similarly, the threat to national self-defense also must be real. Adolf Hitler invaded nations when he claimed they were threatening him. Of course, his assertions were hollow. Hitler's vast military strength and the neighboring nations' lack of armed forces gave the lie to Hitler's claims.

In 2003, President George W. Bush declared a preemptive war doctrine, which justified a first strike against a nation that was a serious threat to the United States. That doctrine was directed at Iraq, a nation the Bush administration considered a threat to the safety and security of the United States. In fact, Iraq was not a threat to the United States. Indeed, it was not really even a threat to its neighbors since it had disarmed itself by destroying chemical and biological weapons before the war began. The most recent time Iraq's military had gone to war (the Persian Gulf War in 1991), it had proven to be an ineffective army easily routed by the United States and other allied nations. The application of that doctrine to a nation that was not a threat to the United States demonstrated how the self-defense claim can be misused.

Moreover, the defense must be proportional to the threat. If someone is robbing your home and pointing a gun at you, you want to take the gun away from him or her if you can. Your objective is to disarm the intruder and then turn him or her over to the police. A disproportional reaction is to kill the intruder when it is unnecessary or, even more extreme, to track down his or her relatives so each can be executed as a means of punishing the robber for that crime. It is one thing to block an attack in self-defense; it is another to seek revenge and destroy the attacker rather than dismantling his or her ability to attack again.

The same logic applies to national self-defense. When the goal is to disarm the aggressor nation and prevent it from waging future attacks—the approach the United States followed with Germany and Japan following World War II—then the response is appropriate. But when it goes beyond that level to unleash acts of revenge that lead to destruction of a people, then the objective no longer is national self-defense. An example is the treatment by Russian soldiers of German prisoners of war and civilians during World War II, which was characterized by mass shootings, rapes, looting, and destruction of property.

Defense of Others in Physical Danger

If you saw an elderly woman robbed by a teen, would you intervene to save her? Would you at least call 911 to summon the police? Our instinct is to help when we see someone in danger. I believe that this individual instinct also applies to society and to government.

If a defenseless or militarily inferior nation is attacked by a militarily strong and aggressive nation, then war can be justified to stop the attack and protect those who are vulnerable. Similarly, when a brutal dictator is killing his own people through mass executions, indiscriminate bombings, or military brutality, then military intervention is justified to stop those assaults. Our joint humanity justifies attempts to save others when it is in our power to do so.

Caveats to these Conditions

However, war is not automatic, even in these conditions. First, the events must be real and not merely assertions. Claims alone cannot justify war. A country must be in danger or others within a nation must be in actual physical danger before military intervention should be sanctioned.

Plus, saving those people must be the actual reason for the war. It cannot be a pretense that a government employs to wage war for other reasons. Underneath the interventionist rhetoric, the real reason could be achieving economic gain or exacting revenge for a past offense. If the real reason is something other than the defense of others, then the war is wrong.

Too often in the history of the world, conflicts have occurred not because of national self-defense or the actual physical defense of others. Instead, a host of other factors constitute the real reasons for war. In those cases, the two conditions mentioned above become mere smokescreens.

One example of a real reason for waging war is national pride. Too often, when the people of one nation believe they have been insulted by the people of some other nation, then the first resort is war. For example, in 1914, the assassination of Archduke Ferdinand, the heir to the Austrian Empire, by a Serbian nationalist sparked World War I. The reaction to that incident by various nations resulted in the needless deaths of millions of soldiers and civilians. The heads of governments in Europe may have felt justified in going to war because they were fearful of other nations or felt justified in protecting a weaker nation, but war was unnecessary at that time to accomplish national defense or protection of another set of people in actual danger.

Even when the latter condition—defense of others in danger—exists, war is not necessarily justified. All other means should be used first to determine whether war can be avoided and whether the aim of providing defense can be achieved through peaceful means. Other means such as negotiation, sanctions, or blockades avoid bloodshed and, in many cases, can bring war-bound nations together to find peaceful solutions. War should be the last resort, not the first.

Unfortunately, the presence of these elements—a justifiable war and the exhaustion of other means of resolution—still does not necessarily mean war should follow. For three reasons, war still should not be undertaken:

First, a nation may lack the resources to oust a dictator abusing his or her own people in another nation, even if the will existed to do so. In practical terms, protecting the defenseless is an overwhelming task in a brutal world. Dictators who oppress their people are common occurrences. It is not feasible for every wrong to be righted, every dictator to be removed from power, even by the combined forces of the world, through war.

Second, the costs of war may well outweigh the benefits. Indeed, the act of going to war could result in worse atrocities and more lives lost than allowing the dictator's rule to continue. Many people could die in the effort to save citizens of a nation from dictatorial rule. Even if that were to happen, there is no guarantee that the resulting situation would not be worse. Instability that arises from sudden, violent regime change can breed anarchy and then another dictatorship.

Third, a homegrown revolution can be encouraged that avoids a larger conflagration. In that case, the people of a regime can be encouraged to rise up and depose their own dictator with limited assistance from others. This goal is not impossible to achieve. It happened during the Revolutionary War when American patriots fought their own battles, albeit with limited assistance from other nations. The Arab revolutions in 2011 and 2012 arose internally, yet some succeeded in toppling dictatorships.

Even when all the conditions for war exist, it must be widely acknowledged that going to war is a sign of failure and not success. Rather than a demonstration of glory and pride, it should be recognition of the inability to settle issues without war. Avoidance of even justifiable wars wherever and whenever possible should be the objective of the liberal soul. Eugene England, a well-respected LDS thinker, considered self-defense as well as national defense to be warrants for waging war but added that "the highest ethic would call me to do everything else possible" to create a society where the problems that led to war were resolved peacefully before war occurred.[5]

The Liberal Soul at War

But what happens when, despite all efforts to avoid war, a nation goes to war? What does that mean for the liberal soul who, as a citizen, is expected to go to war as well? How does the liberal soul remain true to that calling while surrounded by the evils of war—both on the battlefield and in the minds of those peoples who are at war?

---

5. Eugene England, "A Case for Mormon Christian Pacifism," in *Moral Perspectives on U.S. Security Policy: Views from the LDS Community*, edited by Valerie M. Hudson and Kerry M. Kartchner (Provo, Utah: BYU David M. Kennedy Center for International Studies, 1995), 100.

This dilemma is not easily resolved for the liberal soul. On the one hand, he or she seeks to follow the Lord's admonition to be a peacemaker even when called upon to fight and kill others. Whether the call to war exists because of a national policy of military service or the individual's genuine conclusion that the conditions for a just war exist, the question still remains of whether the individual should join in the war effort.

The liberal soul probably will ask the question: Why not become a conscientious objector? Should the liberal soul automatically refuse to participate, despite the consequences of disobedience to the government? There may be times when conscientious objection is the only choice for the liberal soul because of the evil nature of the government or the wickedness of the particular war. Conscientious objection may be the product of a careful consideration that a current war is not justified. Those who make such a choice are not cowards but typically brave individuals who are willing to face the social and legal consequences of such a decision. In many nations, such a choice can lead to imprisonment or, in some dictatorial regimes, even death.

Yet there are times when participating in war could be the right choice for the liberal soul. In those cases, the liberal soul is justified in wearing a uniform and carrying a lethal weapon. Then the liberal soul would be faced with combat situations in which his or her objective is to take the life of the enemy. In such situations, how does the liberal soul at war act? How does the liberal soul remain true to the admonitions of the Savior to love and be a peacemaker?

The liberal soul can have attitudes and take actions in the midst of war that conform to the expectations of a disciple of Christ. Such attitudes and actions are not easy. Many others in uniform may not understand. They will express contrary attitudes and engage in opposite actions, and, indeed, they may ridicule the liberal soul for not doing the same. But the attitudes of the liberal soul toward war are too important to leave to popular opinion. Here are four approaches to handling the demands of war.

Avoiding Total War

"All things are fair in love and war." The total war approach suggested by this common phrase seems to justify any and all actions as part of a war environment. This attitude captures the concept of total war. In total war, the enemy is not just defeated; the enemy is humbled. And whatever actions are necessary to accomplish that end are considered legitimate. Total war means employing any means or breaking any rule of conduct to defeat the enemy and win the war. Total war imposes no limits on what occurs during combat or in support of combatants to achieve the objective of victory. It justifies physical brutality, psychological harassment, torture, and so on.

I am not sure about love, but all things are not fair (or legitimate) in war. The liberal soul approaches war differently than others. The liberal soul eschews total war. To the liberal soul, war is not an opportunity to obliterate an enemy. Rather, the objective is to end war and restore a just peace.

But what if the war is justified? Is not total war legitimate when the cause is right? Not to the liberal soul. Even a just war cannot be waged as total war. A just war quickly becomes unjust when waged as total war.

Fortunately, most nations have agreed on the boundaries of justifiable combat. In 1949, the major nations of the world signed the Geneva Conventions agreeing to respect human rights, especially in wartime. Not all nations abide by their own agreement. However, most nations have seen the wisdom of collective abandonment of the total war concept, at least in theory. Additionally, the specter of punishment by the world community, as exemplified by the Nuremberg trials of Nazi leaders following World War II, can reinforce that commitment.

But the liberal soul must make individual decisions regarding total war. For example, is it acceptable to destroy a civilian's home as part of a mission, even though that act is not essential to the mission? Should a wounded enemy soldier be rescued or left for dead?

It would be tempting to conclude that such actions are justified in wartime. After all, is it not the objective to destroy the enemy? Have enemies not caused much grief and pain to soldiers, to their comrades, and to their families? Should not they be treated as they would treat the liberal soul?

The answer must be no. The liberal soul knows that those who are on the other side in a conflict—uniformed or civilian—are also children of God and deserve to be considered as such, even if those "enemies" do not see themselves or others in that light. In a justifiable war, the liberal soul supports national government policy that prevents the enemy from conducting war any more but preserves that enemy for a life after the war.

Once I had an interview with Elder Enzio Busche, a member of the First Quorum of the Seventy who was from Germany. He had fought in World War II as a Hitler Youth. I marveled at the irony that, nearly fifty years later, he was serving in the leadership of the Church with other men who had been soldiers on the other side in World War II. Had they been in the same battle and in hand-to-hand combat, one of them would have been expected to kill the other. Or one of his fellow General Authorities may have bombed his home in Germany. Now, they worked together to further the gospel of Jesus Christ.

Total war would not have permitted the post-war life that enriched all of them. It would have prevented soldiers from returning to their homes and families, when that is really all they want to do and which they should be allowed to do. There would have been no homecoming and no opportunity to contribute to society in peaceful and productive ways. Total war robs everyone's future.

Loving Your Enemies

War is not a natural state for an individual or a society. Most of us seek to avoid conflict with others. In normal circumstances, we have no desire to leave our homes and families and go to a foreign place to fight other people we do not even know. Given a choice, not many of us would do that voluntarily.

In order to persuade ordinary people to go to war, a government uses coercion or propaganda, or some combination of the two. Government forces citizens to serve in the military through involuntary induction. Propaganda means creating a psychological will to go to war. Nations do that through building up national pride, demeaning other nations, and creating a rationale for attacking some other nation or joining an ongoing war among other nations.

The term "propaganda" has negative connotations, suggesting the image of governments feeding the public false information. That is true in some cases. But propaganda is not necessarily false. For example, information a government distributes to its citizens may accurately convey conditions in another nation. Indeed, those conditions may justify going to war. In such cases, it can be a valuable tool.

However, propaganda often rests on half-truths. For example, proponents of going to war against Iraq in 2003 were confident that Saddam Hussein possessed weapons of mass destruction and some even suggested that nuclear weapons were soon to be part of the Iraqi weapons arsenal. These statements were made even though a United Nations-sponsored investigative team searching Iraq before the war could find no such weapons. Those who wanted war dismissed the truth as a barrier in their rush to war.

One particular feature of propaganda is exaggeration. Facts are often embellished to make people feel justified in waging war on others against whom they have no legitimate grievance. Governments routinely attempt to whip up war fervor to gain public support for going to war.

But the liberal soul must resist the temptation to join the chorus of war. Instead, the liberal soul realizes that the objects of national wrath are really people much like us. They are not the enemy, but real people with hopes, dreams, and families who love them.

The liberal soul remembers that the soldier opposite has a family and primarily wants to live life undisturbed by war and violence. The death of a loved one in combat or related conditions (such as disease, starvation in a prison camp, etc.) will leave a hole in the lives of innocent people for years to come. Also, the house that is underneath the bomber's wings holds a family that does not want to die; the long-range missile fired by pushing a button could kill people whose only crime is living near a military target. The liberal soul refuses to replace a love for others that the Savior taught with a hatred of certain peoples with whom the nation is at war.

One way to build animosity among people is to demean others of a different nationality with undesirable adjectives, characterizing them as, for example, evil, dirty, unscrupulous, or fanatic. A caricature of ordinary human beings is necessary to make the enemy appear other than human. Germans in World War I were portrayed in U.S. propaganda posters as gorillas while the Japanese in World War II had pointed ears, sharp teeth, and menacing stares. A related tactic is to coin derogatory nicknames. In World War II, Americans called Germans "Krauts" while Japanese were "Japs."

The liberal soul must question the propaganda leading up to war to assure that it is accurate and not manipulative. Despite the popular drive to promote hate before and during wartime, the liberal soul must resist those efforts. At the beginning of World War II, the First Presidency issued a message concerning the war advising members caught up in that war that "hate can have no place in the souls of the righteous. . . . Hate is born of Satan; love is the offspring of God."[6]

Seeing Innocents Caught in War

A soldier with a gun has power over human life, and the temptation is strong to use that power to destroy, particularly when the soldier is filled with anger, frustration, and fear for his or her own life. Perhaps the soldier's close friend has just been killed, or the soldier comes across some atrocity committed by enemy soldiers. At that moment the soldier is placed in the middle of a hostile population who resents the presence of foreign troops. That powder keg of resentment can be ignited, and innocent civilians are easy targets.

War often harms civilians more than those in uniform because civilians lack the ability to defend themselves. While civilians should be immune from danger because they are non-combatants, the history of war is replete with cases of civilians being bombed, raped, pillaged, and brutally murdered and being termed "collateral damage."

Preserving those who are innocent is also a selfish act. The memory of violent acts, even carried out under orders, is nearly impossible to erase. Former Senator Bob Kerrey, a Medal of Honor recipient who lost a leg while fighting in Vietnam, recounted attacking a village in Vietnam where a Viet Cong

---

6. President Heber J. Grant, "First Presidency Message," *Conference Report*, April 1942, 88–97.

leader was supposed to be hiding. Kerrey's unit attacked, killing all of those present, but afterward they found the bodies only of women and children. Many years later he related his feelings about that day: "You can never, can never get away from it. It darkens your day. I thought dying for your country was the worst thing that could happen to you, and I don't think it is. I think killing for your country can be a lot worse. Because the memory haunts."[7]

Facing the Ethics of Torture

One of the current debates over war is whether torture—physical or psychological—is ethical. Torture is a tactic used to extract information about the enemy that could be valuable in wartime. However, the specific types of torture—waterboarding, sexual humiliation, extreme sleep deprivation, physical beatings—would be considered clearly inhumane in other settings. Should the liberal soul oppose torture, even if it could glean information that saved lives?

Legally, torture is a violation of international treaties and therefore it breaches international law. The Geneva Conventions ban cruel treatment of prisoners of war, including the use of torture. Yet nations still use torture, even those who signed the Geneva Conventions. Since the beginning of the "war on terror," the United States has employed torture to attempt to gain information from enemy prisoners.

Even putting aside the question of ethics, there are practical reasons for a nation not to employ torture. One is the fact that torture is not as effective as is sometimes claimed. Those who are tortured can manufacture information to stop the torture.

Moreover, use of torture encourages more use of torture. A nation that tortures its prisoners legitimates torture. Other nations will feel justified in using torture as well, when given the opportunity. Even though many nations of the earth have signed treaties to limit torture, there is strong pressure today to match torture used by one nation with more torture used by other nations. And that usage doesn't just apply to authoritarian systems. While still claiming they are somehow different and morally superior, some democratic nations have copied the tactics of dictatorships.

But torture has moral difficulties as well. Clearly, it is the abuse of a human being by another human being. The intent may be noble, such as acquiring information to save others' lives, or it can simply be cruelty. The line between the two may be indistinguishable. And that is why torture harms the

---

7. Gregory L. Vistica, "One Awful Night in Thanh Phong," *New York Times Magazine*, April 25, 2001, http://www.nytimes.com/2001/04/25/magazine/25KERREY.html (accessed April 3, 2014).

torturer as well as the tortured. The person who tortures becomes a torturer. It does not matter that he or she was following someone else's orders. The moral consequences rest with the individual and not just with the superior who orders the torture.

The liberal soul urges governments to ban torture as an instrument of national policy. For example, just as torture is banned for the punishment of domestic crimes or even as a means of extracting information about crimes, so torture should be prohibited in wartime against enemy combatants. Torture has no place in a society based on the teachings of Jesus Christ, the example for the liberal soul.

The Liberal Soul, Globalization, and the Role of the United States

Church leaders often have admonished members to pray for peace among nations. At the beginning of the Iraq War, President Gordon B. Hinckley urged members to "call upon the Lord, whose strength is mighty and whose powers are infinite, to bring an end to the conflict, an end that will result in a better life for all concerned."[8] But the First Presidency also has recognized that peace between nations does not come just from individuals acting separately. When President Barack Obama was reelected in November 2012, the First Presidency and the Quorum of the Twelve congratulated him and also expressed the hope that "our national leaders reflect the best in wisdom and judgment as they fulfill the great trust afforded to them by the American people."[9] Government is important in setting national policy regarding war and peace.

Individuals can and should urge national governments to choose peace. Indeed, it is the obligation of the liberal soul to support government policies that will produce peace. That includes electing candidates who are not quick to begin wars or consider national pride more important than the lives of individuals, particularly men and women in uniform who are put in harm's way by their policies. It also means working for public policies that seek diplomatic solutions to international problems and supporting the creation of arbitrating bodies that seek peace between peoples.

One current issue for the liberal soul is globalization. Globalization is the integration of economy and culture beyond national boundaries. While some may fear globalization because of the cultural change it produces, it is not a fearful thing for the liberal soul. Rather it is positive because it holds

---

8. President Gordon B. Hinckley, "War and Peace," *Ensign*, May 2003, 78.

9. "First Presidency and Quorum of the Twelve Congratulate President on Election Win," Newsroom: The Official Resource for News Media, Opinion Leaders, and the Public, November 6, 2012, http://www.mormonnewsroom.org/article/statement-on-election-result (accessed April 3, 2014).

the potential of reducing the tendencies of nations to choose war over peace. Because the world is more connected today than it has ever been, goods move much more freely across national borders. Economic interdependence which comes with globalization reduces the likelihood of war since nations become reluctant to cut off trade that sustains their economies. For example, in 2011, the United States imported $400 billion in goods from China and exported over $100 billion to China.[10] If China and the United States went to war, over $500 billion in products would stop moving across these two national borders. The effect on each nation's economy would be severe. That single relationship is a microcosm of the global trade that characterizes our time and helps minimize the tendency to go to war.

Not only do goods move across borders, but so do people and ideas. Beyond economic interaction, peoples of various nations have become better acquainted with each other through travel and cultural exchange. As a result, we come to recognize our commonality rather than emphasizing our differences. As ideas travel from nation to nation, we come to see that the problems of one nation—such as air and water pollution, hunger, gross economic inequalities, and finite natural resources—are shared by many other nations. That expanded knowledge leads us to seek to create solutions to world problems together rather than attempting to do so separately.

Globalization creates a shrinking world where individuals across the globe see themselves as they really are—i.e., interconnected physically as well as spiritually. Innovations in communication and transportation have made our human condition—as sons and daughters of a loving Heavenly Father—more apparent to us. Whether we are a tourist traveling to some other land or a person watching a television set practically anywhere in the world, we are exposed to others beyond our own neighborhood, community, or nation. Through Facebook, email, texting, and other media, we can keep in touch with people all over the world and forge friendships that cross national boundaries.

Greater international interaction means that nations have incentives to find mutually beneficial solutions to problems rather than choosing war. Globalization has fostered the sense that the world, not just an individual nation, is our home. Therefore, those who occupy it with us are fellow human beings created in the image of God. All of us have the responsibility to work together to improve our home—the world. The liberal soul recognizes that reality and promotes more international interaction to achieve that end. Given our status as brothers and sisters who occupy a shared planet, cooperation across national boundaries makes sense.

---

10. "Trade in Goods with China," U.S. Census Bureau, http://www.census.gov/foreign-trade/balance/c5700.html (accessed April 3, 2014).

One way to do that is to support international organizations that arbitrate conflicts and work for peace. And yet such a concept is lost on many Latter-day Saints. When I first moved to Utah, I saw billboards and yard signs proclaiming "Get the U.S. Out of the U.N." Such sentiments are not unique to Utah. I've seen such signs elsewhere in the United States. But these signs in LDS-dominant areas suggest that many Latter-day Saints believe the United Nations is bad. I wondered why they thought that.

The United Nations is not a perfect institution. The U.N. General Assembly and the adjoining U.N. agencies often fail to preserve human rights. But since its inception in 1945, no world war has occurred. In the previous thirty years, two world wars involved dozens of nations. Repeatedly, nations have solved their problems through the United Nations rather than through war. Internal conflicts within nations have also been settled through the United Nations. In other cases, it has not been successful in ending conflict. However, given the record of the world moving toward a third worldwide war in 1945, the United Nations has been a significant force in mitigating conflict among nations.

Through its affiliated agencies, such as the World Health Organization (WHO), the World Food Programme, and the U.N. High Commissioner for Refugees (UNHCR), the United Nations has played a role in improving the world. It has helped in fighting communicable diseases, giving food assistance to tens of millions of people who are starving, and offering relief to those forced to leave their homes to avoid famine or war.

These governmental organizations are not antithetical to the gospel. Indeed, the desire to help others and the willingness to commit resources to do so are in accordance with gospel principles. For example, at a recent conference of non-governmental organizations, a top UNHCR official said he wanted the UNHCR and these organizations "to urge together here a renewed focus on self-reliance activities in our camps, in our settlements, in our urban situations." Such self-sufficiency will help empower those who have been displaced.[11]

Again, a defense of the concept of international cooperation does not imply that these organizations always do what they should or perform their tasks without problems. Some U.N. agencies have been subject to corruption, incompetence, and bias. There is no question that the United Nations can be vastly improved.

Nor does it mean that governmental organizations are the only ones who can resolve world problems. Non-governmental organizations play vital

---

11. "UNHCR Promotes Innovation and Self Sufficiency at Annual NGO Meet," July 3, 2012, UNHCR News, http://www.unhcr.org/4ff300320.html (accessed April 3, 2014).

roles as well in finding solutions to global problems such as ending poverty, eradicating disease, and offering emergency assistance to those in need. The Church has cooperated with such non-governmental organizations to handle temporal needs of millions of people, most of whom are not Latter-day Saints.

The Church itself also enhances international interaction and understanding. As the Church spreads across the globe, increasingly Church members everywhere have come to perceive the Church as a much more diverse place. As a BYU professor, I have seen the growth of the Church in the representation of various nations in the student body. Unlike when I was a student or even when I began teaching at BYU, students today are more likely than before to come from nations in Africa, Asia, and Eastern Europe.

This change has occurred among Church leaders as well. The General Authorities today are drawn from a wide array of nationalities and cultures. Many of the Seventy are from Asia, South America, Africa, and Europe. Those who applaud these changes were pleased when a European was called to be a member of the First Presidency in 2008.

Church leaders today stress that they preside over a worldwide church rather than one limited to a particular U.S. or Intermountain West culture. President Hinckley told a BBC radio interviewer that the Church is "not an American church. We are not an English church. We are not a Japanese church. We are a world church with a world message and a world program."[12]

The missionary program alone has fostered international understanding. Hundreds of thousands of Church members have served as missionaries in other nations and gained an appreciation for varying cultures beyond their own. Students in my classes have recounted how their respective missions to places such as Latin America or Asia have changed their perspectives on the connection between wealth and righteousness. Those experiences also enhanced their desire to serve others both spiritually and temporally. That is one reason they want to study government; they want to use government service to make the world a better place.

As Americans we frequently pride ourselves on being citizens of the best nation in the world. We believe we are superior to other nations militarily, politically, and economically. Church members often share that view that the United States is the nation God created and the one that God particularly blesses above other nations. The Book of Mormon's reference to America as the promised land, along with repeated Church leader statements, as well as books and other writings by various Church members, have fostered the perception that the United States is exceptional not only in our eyes, but also in the Lord's.

---

12. "Excerpts from Recent Addresses of President Gordon B. Hinckley," *Ensign*, August 1996, 60.

However, the liberal soul is cautious about confusing patriotism with jingoism. Because the liberal soul understands that all peoples are brothers and sisters, he or she views Americans as one people among many across the globe and the United States as one nation among many in the world. Americans should love and be loyal to America but should realize that national loyalty is not unique for Americans. Therefore, love of nation should be a means of recognizing yet another similarity with peoples across many nations rather than as a tool for feeling pride and superiority toward other nations.

Among nations, the United States does possess unusual characteristics. Historically, it has been a vocal advocate of democracy and has been more willing than any other nation to devote the lives of its citizens and the surplus of its wealth in assisting peoples of other nations temporally and politically. It has had a long history of national stability. Americans are broadly united in acceptance of national political, social, and economic institutions.

Nevertheless, other nations are not inferior to the United States because they possess different characteristics. Nor should American exceptionalism be a rationale for giving the United States greater power over other nations. Instead, all nations are worthy of respect, as are all peoples within those nations. Fortunately, as Latter-day Saints travel to other nations to serve as missionaries, most come to love the peoples of those nations and gain greater respect for those cultures and nations.

The liberal soul appreciates the value of other cultures, nationalities, and peoples. That respect means that other nations are not expected to play a subservient role vis-à-vis the United States. Rather, the United States should be a partner with other nations in seeking the good of all—a good that is defined by all and not just one. International cooperation, whatever the organizational form, is a principle that furthers peace and prevents war. It reduces resentment toward one nation as the dominant player. It encourages all nations to participate in joint endeavors to solve world problems.

"Nor Do Anything like Unto It"

In Doctrine and Covenants 59, the Lord commanded the Saints to refrain from committing serious sins. "Thou shalt not steal; neither commit adultery, nor kill, nor do anything like unto it" (D&C 59:6). That command is violated continually by those who do something like unto killing. This includes not only the physical taking of life through abortion, but also the theft of emotional and spiritual life through neglect and abuse, particularly of children.

Abortion has become legal in most industrialized nations of the world. However, the Church has opposed the practice. The Church's website states that the Church "believes in the sanctity of human life. Therefore, the Church opposes elective abortion for personal or social convenience."[13] President Spencer W. Kimball noted the similarity between this command not to "do anything like unto" killing and the practice of abortion when he declared that "abortion must be considered one of the most revolting and sinful practices in this day."[14] Similarly, Elder Dallin H. Oaks said that "many laws permit or even promote abortion, but to us this is a great evil."[15]

The liberal soul sees life as inherently precious because it comes from God. Each child is a son or daughter of Heavenly Father and our brother or sister; every individual on earth has come from our Heavenly Father's presence. Such life is not sent to earth to be discarded by others, particularly for personal convenience.

Abortion allows an individual to make life-and-death decisions about another human being. It is a terrible and final act. The application of that decision-making power today is inherently unjust. One child born prematurely at twenty-three weeks is placed in an incubator and hooked up to tubes to sustain life. Prayers are said to keep that child alive so that he or she can grow to be an adult. Another child at that same gestational age, however, is either killed in the womb or is taken from the womb violently and allowed to die immediately after being taken out of the mother's body.

What is the difference between the two? It is the will of the mother. One mother wants her unborn child while the other does not. Should someone else decide when a person can live or die? Similarly, if an unborn child is potentially viable to live outside the womb on his or her own, should that child be protected from the decision on the part of someone else, even that child's mother, to put him or her to death?

According to advocates for abortion rights, the difference is a woman's control over her body. Indeed, the Lord did give each of us control over our own body. We can use it as we wish. Nevertheless, there are consequences for how we use it. As a result, we cannot use it in a way that harms others. For example, I do not have the right to swing my leg in the middle of a jam-packed sidewalk. I do not have the right to use my mouth to yell "fire" in a crowded theater. I have no right to use my fists to assault another person. The law prevents me from walking down a city street with no clothes on, even though I may wish to display my body in that way.

---

13. "Abortion," Official Statement, Newsroom: The Official Resource for News Media, Opinion Leaders, and the Public, http://www.mormonnewsroom.org/official-statement/abortion (accessed April 3, 2014).

14. Spencer W. Kimball, "Why Call Me Lord, Lord, and Do Not the Things Which I Say?" *Ensign*, May 1975, 4.

15. Dallin H. Oaks, "Protect the Children," *Ensign*, November 2012, 43.

So it is with pregnancy, except even more so. Pregnancy is unique. In no other situation is one person wholly within another person. In pregnancy, two people are so physically intertwined that the condition of one directly affects the other. As a result, both are affected by decisions made by the mother about her body. Such decisions are not limited to the choice of whether to abort a child. They also include physical exercise, proper nutrition and care for medical conditions, or the use of drugs, alcohol, or cigarettes. These actions of the mother affect the child not only in the womb but also potentially throughout the life of the child.

Mothers have a responsibility to care for their children, to love and nurture them, and to watch over them to see that they grow. This is true both for the already-born child and the as-yet-unborn child. Children are the most vulnerable humans in society. They survive because of the care of others, whether in the womb or outside it.

The Church's position is that abortion in most cases is wrong and that a member who has or performs an abortion can be subject to Church discipline. Some may consider the Church pro-choice because Church policy provides some exceptions for abortions, such as in cases of incest or rape or when a "competent physician determines that the life or health of the mother is in serious jeopardy."[16] But the Church is not pro-choice in the sense that the difference between the two choices has no moral overtones or ecclesiastical consequences.

However, the liberal soul as a citizen must approach abortion not only from a personal standpoint, but also as a policy issue. There, the Church does not provide formal guidance. Individual Church leaders have urged public policy leaders to limit abortion. For example, in 2012, Elder Dallin H. Oaks spoke about the importance of protecting children and on the evils of abortion as well as denouncing other abuses and neglect of children. He also urged "politicians, policy makers, and officials to increase their attention to what is best for children." Similarly, Elder Russell M. Nelson in 2008 expressed concern that governments that legalized abortion were not obeying God's commandments.[17] But the Church itself "has not favored or opposed legislative proposals" on abortion policy.[18]

The Church's position has been situated much more closely to the "pro-life" position in the sense that abortion is considered sinful except in a certain limited set of circumstances. At the same time, if enacted into public policy, the Church's position would allow more choice than a complete ban on abortion advocated by many abortion opponents. It is safe to say Church leaders generally would prefer public policy on abortion that places more limits on

---

16. "Abortion," in *Handbook 1: Stake Presidents and Bishops* (Salt Lake City: Church of Jesus Christ of Latter-day Saints, 2010), 17.3.1.

17. Oaks, "Protect the Children," 43; and Russell M. Nelson, "Abortion: An Assault on the Defenseless," *Ensign*, October 2008, 32.

18. "Abortion," Official Statement, Newsroom.

the practice than currently exists in most industrialized nations, including the United States. Statements directed at national governments that decry abortion move in that direction.

Nevertheless, it is significant that the Church has avoided the extremes of the abortion debate by taking neither the absolute pro-choice position nor the absolute pro-life position on this issue. Those extremes have dominated the policy discussion over abortion, and people easily get the impression they must join one camp or the other. The Church institutionally has not done so. Nor must members feel that they must do so in order to be good members of the Church.

A major flaw in the debate over abortion is the fact that both sides address only part of the problem. On the "pro-choice" side, the priority is given to the rights of one person (the mother) with little or no attention to the rights of the other (the child). Even in the face of growing medical evidence of fetal heartbeats and physical and mental development, the pro-choice side generally refuses to view the issue as anything but a woman's right over her own body. Therefore, this side rejects adjustments to abortion laws intended to reflect scientific advances in understanding fetal development. Even though medical science knows more today about fetal development (such as the fact that a fetus looks and acts like a human being even in the early stages of a woman's pregnancy and has the capability to survive outside the womb at an earlier stage than previously thought possible), many pro-choice advocates are unmoved by such evidence.

Many on the other side seek to ban all or nearly all abortions regardless of the reason. At the extremes, this camp views law enforcement as the weapon for assuring compliance without concern for the situation of the woman. The goal is to ban abortions either by constitutional amendment or judicial decision.

The liberal soul sees the women who struggle with the decision whether to have an abortion as daughters of God. Similarly, their unborn children, who are the potential victims of that decision, also are sons and daughters of God. Laws that allow abortion on demand through most of a pregnancy damage society by allowing people to choose to end another's life for whatever reason they wish. Yet laws that restrict all abortions are neither feasible nor morally defensible.

Whether greater restrictions will be placed on abortion in the future is unknown. That decision will be left to future generations of individuals and policymakers, both in the United States and in other nations of the world where abortion is legalized, at least at some stages of pregnancy. However, there are immediate ways to reduce the number of abortions and address the root causes of many abortions. Providing incentives for adoption rather than abortion, for example, may help reduce the temptation to use abortion as a way to avoid child-rearing. These could include financial rewards for placing a child for adoption rather than aborting the child. Given the demand for adoptive children, a pool of funds might make adoption a financially attractive option for a pregnant woman, particularly a poor one facing the costs of child support. This possibility could be particularly applicable to women who had not had abortions previously. In the United States, over half of all women who have abortions have not had an earlier abortion.[19]

For the liberal soul, abortion is a tragedy since it involves the taking of a life and the initial decision to take a life, both of which are heart-wrenching for those involved. The liberal soul seeks solutions that affirm life and help women and men value human life, particularly at its most vulnerable stages. Those solutions include viewing children as gifts from God and not nuisances or burdens.

Not only is abortion detrimental to children, but so is much of what happens after birth. Children, the most vulnerable people in any society, are too often subject to abuse and neglect by adults. In many nations, adult behavior causes literal harm to children. At an individual level, such harm includes physical and psychological abuse directed at children by thoughtless or troubled adults. But it also comprises societal acts that endanger the safety of children, such as civil violence where children are raped, mutilated, and killed. Child slavery is a growing problem in the world, as well.

Less dramatic, but no less compelling is the fact that so many children are denied fundamental needs. Many go hungry day after day because adults who should be their caregivers neglect them and fail to provide adequately for them. Also, many lack adequate educational opportunities and face a life of ignorance and continued poverty.

The cause of this abuse is not just individual behavior; it also is bad government. Government leaders who enrich themselves at the expense of their citizens, leaders who fight wars and impoverish their populations through armed conflict, and governments that recruit child soldiers (children who grow up with machine guns over their shoulders, as well as blood on their hands) are all to blame for the abuse of children rampant in the world.

The neglect or deliberate abuse of children by adults results in the widespread destruction of a generation of the world's children. The responsibility to turn this situation around rests with individuals, groups, and governments. Public policy measures to increase educational opportunities, end armed conflicts, provide adequate health care, reconsider abortion at will, and punish abuse are essential to ending the mistreatment of children across the globe.

---

19. U.S. Census Bureau, "Births, Deaths, Marriages, & Divorces: Family Planning, Abortions," *The 2012 Statistical Abstract: The National Data Book*, http://www.census. gov/compendia/statab/cats/births_deaths_marriages_divorces/family_planning_ abortions.html (accessed April 3, 2014).

Conclusion

The liberal soul seeks to follow the Savior, the Prince of Peace, in advocating peace. The peace the Savior brings does not come through international treaties or armistices. It comes through understanding and following the path of Christ. That does not mean that peace agreements should not be pursued, but it is the attitude of love for others rather than a desire for conflict that is at the essence of the gospel of Jesus Christ. When that love is present, the desire for violence against others is absent. Elder Dallin Oaks once explained that the "peace the gospel brings is not just the absence of war. It is the opposite of war. Gospel peace is the opposite of any conflict, armed or unarmed. It is the opposite of national or ethnic hostilities, of civil or family strife."[20]

What can the liberal soul do to promote peace? One way is to love others—both those close to home and those far away. It is often difficult to love both. Some find it easier to love people far away than it is to love those in one's own family or neighborhood. In other words, humanity in the abstract is more appealing than humans in the flesh. Others, however, have no difficulty loving those who are around them and whom they know personally but find it hard to extend similar feelings toward humans out of their sight or sound. It may be because people far away are different in terms of religion, ethnicity, income level, or nationality. Coupled with a lack of proximity to others who are different, it is easy for some to impugn the motives of "foreigners" or imagine characteristics that make people in other nations and cultures too different, too alien to be loved.

The liberal soul must do both—love those nearby as well as those who live in nations far away. The Savior's parable of the Good Samaritan was such a call to love the foreigner and stranger as well as the close neighbor. Similarly, we cannot love God and keep the commandments and at the same time hold hateful feelings or even be suspicious of people of some other religion, ethnicity, or nationality that may be different or seem strange to us.

Another way to bring peace is to encourage others to love as well. This can be accomplished by deed as well as by word. It is difficult when both sides in a conflict seek to demonize the other, such as in the abortion debate. And it is often hard to love when the other person is unseen—be it an unborn child, a person who lives far away, or the individual on the other end of a text message or email.

It also is particularly challenging to show love when the pressure for war builds. For example, immediately following the attacks of September 11, 2011, many Americans experienced an urgent desire to take action. If such action were to bring the perpetrators of this hideous act to justice, then it would be in

---

20. Dallin H. Oaks, "World Peace," *Ensign*, May 1990, 71.

accordance with gospel principles. If the action was to strike out at whoever was available, regardless of their guilt in causing the airplane hijacking plot, then it was not the Lord's way. The war in Iraq, which was billed as a continuation of the "war on terror," was such an example since Saddam Hussein's regime had nothing to do with 9/11 nor did it even have any alliances with the instigator of the terrorist attacks, Al Qaeda. But it was a convenient, familiar target upon which to vent Americans' frustration about the 9/11 attack.

Objecting to unnecessary war is a responsibility of the liberal soul. Seeking to calm the forces of public sentiment, rather than inflame them, follows the example of the Savior. Seeing peace as a way to accomplish the Savior's goals, rather than through the horrors of war, is not necessarily the most popular position at times, but it should be the liberal soul's position at all times.

When war drums start beating in a society, it is the obligation of the liberal soul to refrain from joining in a war chant but instead to advocate peace, to suggest alternatives to war, and to ask whether other measures—diplomatic, economic, and moral—have been sufficiently applied to solve the problem. This is not easy when many people, including other Church members, begin waving the flag and calling for the mobilization of armies and navies to go out and fight for the nation in some foreign land.

The consequences of working for peace over war are not necessarily pleasant. The liberal soul may be accused of being unpatriotic for urging peace rather than war. Others will accuse the liberal soul of cowardice or even treason. Other Church members, particularly, can hurl charges of being on the devil's side. War challenges the liberal soul, not just because it is the antithesis of the gospel of Jesus Christ, but also because of the possible social opprobrium of those sitting in the next pew. However, social popularity was never the objective of the Savior during His mortal ministry. Nor should it be the goal of the liberal soul.

Another goal, however, should also propel the liberal soul. It is teaching by following the Savior's example. The liberal soul cannot solve the problems of the world. But he or she can make small contributions to the resolutions of those problems. Particularly, in times of heated debate, conflict, and war, the liberal soul can be the "leaven" in the loaf that eventually leads others to draw closer to the Savior and away from conflict and strife.

CHAPTER 7

IF YE ARE NOT ONE
YE ARE NOT MINE

While traveling on business to Philadelphia once, I attended church at a ward downtown. The sacrament meeting that day was devoted to the annual Primary program. As is true in most wards, the children were lined up in the front while the choir director led them through a medley of Primary songs.

Of course, that isn't unusual; I've seen that scene annually for as long as I can remember. What was unusual was the array of races represented. This group of children was highly racially and ethnically diverse, consisting of varying nationalities and accents. Faces of various colors looked up at their director, who was African American. In their diversity, they made a wonderful chorus singing in unison.

I wondered if that is not what the Church should be all about. These children were a microcosm of a worldwide Church that stretches through hundreds of countries and territories. It includes people of varying backgrounds, races, and nationalities. The gospel net "gathered of every kind" (Matt. 13:47).

The obvious skin-deep differences are not the only ones that distinguish us and potentially divide us. Any group of people, even with outward similarities such as gender or race, is diverse. We all differ in personality due to a variety of factors, including our life experiences. We have varying mental capacities, emotional difficulties, and physical limitations, none of which may be apparent by looking at us as part of an otherwise similar group.

Just as the differences among people generally are not always obvious, so the dissimilarities among Church members also may be hidden. From the perspective of someone wandering into one of our meetings, Latter-day Saints may seem uniform and devoid of individualism. Indeed, we do place an undue emphasis on outward dress and grooming as a measure of our conformity to the norms of LDS culture. For men, for example, the preference for white shirts, conservative suits and ties, and clean-shaven faces, which also is the picture seen at general conference, suggests a definite lack of individuality. But within any congregation, the differences below the surface are stark—marital difficulties, emotional concerns, financial woes, and, of course, varying levels of spiritual growth are all represented.

One of those disparities is the view of society, government, and the individual. Church members across the globe actually vary significantly in their approach to politics. Many European members believe in socialism, while some in the Intermountain West in the United States are ardent libertarians. Even within the United States, there are members who are Republicans and others who are Democrats. Diversity in the Church is not just racial, ethnic, and national; it also is political.

Becoming One

In the midst of this diversity, Latter-day Saints are continually admonished to become one. The Lord warned the Saints at a conference of the Church in Fayette, New York that "if ye are not one ye are not mine" (D&C 38:27). Similarly, the Saints in Corinth were counseled that "there be no divisions among you, but that ye be perfectly joined in the same mind and in the same judgment" (1 Cor. 1:10).

How do we square our diversity with that counsel? Do we ignore diversity and pretend we are one? Do we maintain our diversity and abandon the attempt to become "one?" Do we simply acknowledge that members are too diverse to be united?

Our "oneness" is not a unity based on uniformity. We need not be the same to be one. When Jesus prayed in the Garden of Gethsemane and spoke of being one with Heavenly Father and imploring that His disciples be one with him, clearly he was not referring to a physical oneness. They were separate physical beings. Instead, he spoke of oneness of purpose, a unity of cause.

Before the U.S. Congress adopted the national motto of "In God We Trust," the national motto was "E Pluribus Unum." That is Latin for "out of many, one." That motto referred to the melting pot that was the United States of America, drawing immigrants from Ireland in the early 1800s to southern and eastern Europe in the late 1800s and early 1900s to central and South America through the twentieth century. Those immigrants became Americans, even though their national backgrounds, skin color, ethnicity, and religion were different from the Americans of Protestant northern European ancestry who had preceded them.

This "unity from diversity" can apply to Latter-day Saints as well. We can be diverse in many ways but still be united in our common cause of seeking to be followers of Christ and keeping His commandments. We can be joined in that shared purpose without losing the individual and group identities and peculiarities which distinguish us from each other.

This "unity from diversity" strengthens any organization, including the Church. Paul refers to it in 1 Corinthians 12 when he talks about varying gifts of the Spirit and the role of each member in the Lord's church. Each of us has different gifts we give to the Church as a whole, said Paul:

> For to one is given by the Spirit the word of wisdom; to another the word of knowledge by the same Spirit; To another faith by the same Spirit; to another the gifts of healing by the same Spirit. (1 Cor. 12:8–9)

Paul went on to describe the Church as a body and that the "body is not one member, but many." Just as one part of someone's body—the foot or the ear—cannot say that another part doesn't belong to the body, so no member can decide that someone else, who is politically different, does not belong in the Church. In fact, the body is whole because of its diversity, according to Paul: "And if they were all one member, where were the body?" (1 Cor. 12:14, 19).

This means that everyone belongs in the Church and should not be excluded because of political differences. Indeed, no one has the authority to write someone out of the Church because of contrasting political views. Such an act is a tragedy when it occurs. The variety that each of us brings to the Church—even in political differences—enriches the Church as a whole. Paul went even further in showing how we should treat each other in the Church:

> Nay, much more those members of the body, which seem to be more feeble, are necessary: And those members of the body, which we think to be less honorable, upon these we bestow more abundant honor; and our uncomely parts have more abundant comeliness. For our comely parts have no need: but God hath tempered the body together, having given more abundant honor to that part which lacked: That there should be no schism in the body; but that the members should have the same care one for another. (1 Cor. 12:22–25)

What is Paul saying? That the members of the Church who are "more feeble" and less honored are even more necessary for the Church? Who are these people? These members are those who may be neglected or abused by others. They are those who are discriminated against and made to feel they do not belong.

Prejudice can be attributed to many factors—such as race, educational level (in both directions), or income—but it can also occur because of politics. For example, I have heard people say they cannot understand how a member of the Church can be a Democrat. The message, though perhaps unintended, is that, if someone is a Democrat, he or she does not belong in the Church. It is a message that some members have interpreted as an invitation to leave the Church, which they have done.

For some members, viewing politics as another form of diversity within the Church is difficult, perhaps impossible, for them to fathom. They are so wedded to their conception of politics and the gospel that they do not understand how other members with differing views can be unified with them. For those people, diversity within the Church, as it applies to politics, is a tolerance of evil.

Forming Political Parties among Members

Most Church members today may be unaware that Church leaders at one time encouraged and even embodied such diversity. By the late 1800s, the national parties were not really organized in Utah. Few Utahns belonged to either one of them. That national two-party system was late in coming to the Utah Territory.

That changed in the early 1890s, as Church leaders sought to help Utah achieve statehood. Even though the Utah Territory had been formed in 1850 and statehood was expected not long thereafter, more than forty years passed in territorial status. Surrounding territories such as Wyoming, Idaho, Colorado, and Nevada already had joined the Union as states.

The reason for Utah's delay was a fear on the part of national political leaders and the American public generally that Utah was too strongly controlled by one religious denomination. That denomination was perceived as dictating every part of Church members' lives, including politics. In fact, such a fear had a basis in fact: When it had the opportunity to do so, the Church did determine most of Utah's governmental policies.

Through the 1870s and 1880s, there had been two political parties in Utah politics, but they were not Republicans and Democrats. Rather, one was the People's Party, which was known as the Mormon political party. Non-Mormons, however, belonged to the Liberal Party, which opposed Church dominance in political affairs. The People's Party usually won elections in the state. This unique party model in Utah symbolized the importance of religion in Utah politics and the continuing Church role in shaping public policy.[1]

Plural marriage had been the stated reason for denying Utah statehood. By the 1890s, polygamy was less of an issue due to the manifesto issued in 1890 by President Wilford Woodruff that withdrew authorization for new plural marriages. However, that proclamation did not entirely allay fears that, with statehood, Utah's government would merely be an appendage of the LDS Church. Moreover, the Church, until recently, had been in an active

---

1. For a discussion of the origin of political parties in Utah, see Frank H. Jonas, "Utah: The Different State," in Frank H. Jonas, ed., *Politics in the American West* (Salt Lake City: University of Utah Press, 1969), 327–79; and Edward Leo Lyman, *Political Deliverance: The Mormon Quest for Utah Statehood* (Urbana: University of Illinois Press, 1986), 150–84.

battle with the U.S. government over plural marriage and the very continuance of the Church as an organization.

Church leaders decided that one way to convince Congress that the Church did not constitute a political threat was to create party divisions within the Church that mimicked the national parties. In other words, Church members would belong to both political parties and would look like people in the rest of the nation. Such a party division would signal that Utah, once admitted into the Union, would function much like any other state and that the Church's political power would be diminished.

The problem for Church leaders was that, once the People's Party was disbanded in 1891, Church members were not inclined to divide equally between the two parties on their own.[2] At that time, most Church members had more favorable attitudes toward the Democratic Party than toward the Republicans. The Republicans had decried the "twin relics of barbarism"—slavery and polygamy—in their first party platform in 1856. Subsequently, Republican presidential administrations typically had been more vigorous enforcers of anti-polygamy legislation than Democratic ones.

By contrast, Democrats favored a more limited federal government role and championed states' rights. Part of this philosophy was driven by southern Democrats' opposition to the federal role in ending slavery during the Civil War and racial discrimination after it. These Democrats concluded that a federal government powerful enough to oppress the Mormons on polygamy also would coerce Southern whites on racial issues.

Therefore, to even out the partisan affiliation of Church members, Church leaders orchestrated a campaign to get more members to become Republicans. Elder Francis Lyman of the Quorum of the Twelve was instructed to visit southern Utah stakes and convey the message that it was all right for a Latter-day Saint to be a Republican.[3] Elder John Henry Smith of the Quorum of the Twelve was allowed to travel around parts of Utah encouraging Church members about to become Republicans. When challenged by other General Authorities in a leadership meeting, Elder Smith explained his position: "As the leanings of the people seemed to be to join the Democrats it seemed absolutely necessary to have someone high in authority who was a Republican to come out and labor for that party."[4]

One method was to buy Utah newspapers in Ogden and Salt Lake and turn their editorial direction toward the Republican Party. Indeed, Elder Smith

2. Edward Leo Lyman, "The Alienation of an Apostle from His Quorum: The Moses Thatcher Case," *Dialogue: A Journal of Mormon Thought* 18 (Summer 1985): 67–91.

3. Lyman, *Political Deliverance*, 166.

4. Ibid., 168.

took charge of one of the newspapers. These newspapers were used to blunt the Democratic Party leanings of prominent Utah newspapers of the day.

Another tactic was door-to-door solicitation for party membership. Elder Smith and local Church leaders who were Republicans were allowed to go from house to house to urge some members to switch sides and become Republicans while Church leaders who were Democrats were urged to be silent.[5] This policy resulted in some odd consequences. When a Church leader came to a house and urged the family to become Republicans, the father declined because he was an ardent Democrat. This leader then went to see the relatives who lived next door, who agreed to make the switch. As a result, one branch of the McKay family, including President David O. McKay, became Republicans, while another branch, including later Utah Democratic Congressman Gunn McKay, remained Democrats.[6]

The switch to the Republican Party was not easy for some members. President McKay related that his father came home from church one Sunday after the Church leader had visited and announced to the family that he was becoming a Republican. President McKay recounted: "I remember how ashamed we children were, because Father and Whiskey Olson were the only two Republicans in Huntsville."[7]

At that time, a few Church leaders played prominent roles in partisan politics. Elder B. H. Roberts of the Seventy was active in the Democratic Party, as was Elder Moses Thatcher of the Quorum of the Twelve. Both ran for elective office as Democrats, although only Roberts won election. (The House of Representatives refused to seat him because he was a polygamist.) Only a few years later, Apostle Reed Smoot, a Republican who was not a polygamist, successfully ran for the Senate and served as U.S. Senator from Utah for thirty years. These two examples reinforced the message that members of the Church, even Church leaders, could differ publicly on politics and still be faithful.

Political Party Diversity

As long as there is a free electoral system and like-minded individuals can form associations to further their political interests, there will be differing political parties. It is the automatic byproduct of freedom of association in a democratic society. Indeed, the presence of more than one political party is a

---

5. Ibid.

6. Jonas, *Politics in the American West*, 329.

7. David O. McKay, quoted in Gregory A. Prince and William Robert Wright, *David O. McKay and the Rise of Modern Mormonism* (Salt Lake City: University of Utah Press, 2005), 334.

sign that people are free to choose sides in public debates and bind themselves together with others to achieve their common goals.

This freedom to choose parties and ideologies is also true within the Church. Despite the common perceptions, abetted by news coverage of Mormons, LDS Church members are not monolithic. Latter-day Saints think differently on a host of doctrinal issues and practices. Church leaders and members often disagree among themselves on the best policies to pursue at any given time. Why should there not also be political differences?

The time is past when Church members are encouraged by Church leaders to join one particular political party, such as the People's Party. In fact, the opposite is true today. When Church leaders recruited some members in Utah communities to become Republicans to attain statehood, they did it to create a two-party system. Indeed, that was the objective. Ever since then, members have belonged to not only both major political parties but also to an array of smaller parties including Libertarian, Constitution, Green, and others.

Historically, Church leaders did not side with one particular political party. Since the 1890s, Church leaders have included Republicans and Democrats. For example, Presidents Wilford Woodruff and Heber J. Grant were Democrats. So were counselors in the First Presidency Charles W. Penrose, Anthony W. Ivins, Hugh B. Brown, Henry D. Moyle, and James E. Faust. On the other hand, Presidents Joseph F. Smith, David O. McKay, and Gordon B. Hinckley openly identified as Republicans.

Members of the Twelve, the Seventy, and the Presiding Bishopric also have taken different sides. When Utah was granted statehood, Elder Brigham Young Jr. was mentioned as a possible Democratic candidate for governor, while Elder Heber J. Grant, also a Democrat, turned down the Democratic gubernatorial nomination.[8] After his release as a counselor in the Presiding Bishopric, Bishop Carl W. Buehner was the Republican candidate for Utah's governor in 1968.

The perception that the Church today is tied to the Republican Party has been reinforced by the fact that Democrats have dwindled in number among the General Authorities. Until 2008, with the passing of President James E. Faust, a Democrat typically was a member of the Quorum of the Twelve or the First Presidency. But as of this writing, that is no longer true. In fact, only two Democrats serve among the Seventy today. All of the members of the Quorum of the Twelve are either Republicans or unaffiliated.[9]

---

8. Lyman, "The Alienation of an Apostle from His Quorum," 67–91.

9. Matt Canham and Thomas Burr, "Top Mormon Church Posts Dominated by Registered Republicans," Salt Lake Tribune, December 6, 2012, http://www.sltrib.com/sltrib/politics/55391586-90/church-lds-republican-mormon.html.csp (accessed March 27, 2014).

Nevertheless, the Church today does not endorse a political party. At times, Church leaders have addressed this issue directly. For example, in 1952, President David O. McKay declared in general conference that the Church was neutral and denounced reports that the General Authorities had decided to support a particular political party.[10] Every election season in the United States, the First Presidency issues a statement reminding members that the Church is neutral. In 2006 and again in successive election years, the First Presidency has added the sentence "Principles compatible with the gospel may be found in the platforms of various political parties."[11] Five years later, the Church reiterated that General Authorities are not allowed to participate in campaigns, including prohibiting them from making financial donations to candidates or parties.[12]

Church members, on the other hand, can and do participate openly in politics, as well as identify with political parties. Today, Church members in the United States are members of various parties, although Republicans predominate. They also can choose among an array of political ideologies, but most consider themselves conservative. A survey of Mormons in the United States conducted by the Pew Research Center found that 74 percent either were Republicans or leaned toward the Republicans, while 17 percent identified with or leaned toward the Democratic Party. Two-thirds called themselves conservatives, while 8 percent were liberal. The others self-identified as moderates. Members who do not live in the West are more likely than westerners to be Democrats and to be liberal.[13] Members who live outside the United States tend to be more politically liberal than those in the United States[14]

---

10. Prince and Wright, *David O. McKay and the Rise of Modern Mormonism,* 335.

11. "First Presidency Letter on Utah Precinct Caucus Meetings," March 10, 2010, http://www.mormonnewsroom.org/article/first-presidency-letter-on-utah-precinct-caucus-meetings (accessed February 12, 2014); and "First Presidency Issues Letter on Utah Precinct Caucus Meetings," February 13, 2012, http://www.mormonnewsroom.org/article/first-presidency-issues-letter-utah-precinct-caucus-meetings (accessed February 12, 2014).

12. "Political Neutrality," at Newsroom: The Official Resource for News Media, Opinion Leaders, and the Public, Church of Jesus Christ of Latter-day Saints, http://www.mormonnewsroom.org/official-statement/political-neutrality (accessed February 12, 2014).

13. "Mormons in America: Certain in Their Beliefs; Uncertain of Their Place in Society," Pew Forum on Religion & Public Life, January 12, 2012, http://www.pewforum.org/Christian/Mormon/mormons-in-america-politics-society-and-morality.aspx?src=prc-section#ideology (accessed February 12, 2014).

14. See Jeffrey C. Fox, *Latter-day Political Views* (Lanham, Md.: Lexington Books, 2006).

Theoretically, that means that nearly one of five people sitting in that Sunday School class or Relief Society meeting is a Democrat and that one individual in three does not consider himself or herself a conservative. Of course, it really is not that way because there are few wards that are exact microcosms of the larger Church. However, it is likely that more political diversity occurs within a ward than many members realize.

Yet despite more diversity being present than one might expect, one of the problems in the Church is the expectation that everyone in a Sunday School class or Relief Society meeting shares the same views. Too often, politics can be discussed openly and conservative politics advocated publicly in many wards, particularly in the Intermountain West, because it is a given for many that the membership is united in certain political views. The idea of pluralism—members belonging to differing political parties and not necessarily sharing the same ideology—may be a foreign concept to some members.

But time is not on the side of these narrow-minded Church members. As the Church's membership expands, such divergence in political parties and views will become more pronounced, not less. Members no longer come from one cultural milieu—the Intermountain West in the United States. Instead, they join from all parts of the United States and all over the world. As they are baptized and confirmed new members of the Church, they bring with them the political preferences they held prior to their baptism. And, since they live in varying cultures, they are affected by those cultures in their politics.

Within the United States, these members could include African American members in large urban areas who view the Democratic Party as the party representing them as a racial group and in their issue priorities, as well as San Francisco Bay Area members who are concerned about the environment and vote Democratic in response. They include Church members who get advanced degrees and acquire a broad understanding of the issues that face the world and seek governmental solutions to problems of global poverty, lack of education, and inadequate health care.

President Benson once asserted that "no true Latter-day Saint can be a Communist or a Socialist because Communist principles run counter to the revealed word of God and to the Constitution of this land which was established by men whom the God of Heaven raised up unto that very purpose."[15] But many European and Latin American members support socialist parties because they help working people like them. Cradle-to-grave socialism not only does not bother them, but helps them to enjoy a higher standard of living in areas such as health, education, and employment than they would

---

15. Quoted in Donald Q. Cannon, ed., *Latter-day Prophets and the United States Constitution* (Provo, Utah: Brigham Young University Religious Studies Center, 1991), 173.

have otherwise. In fact, as one LDS sister in London expressed to me, such governmental policies merely reflect everyone's concern for each other rather than individual selfishness.

Church members come from a variety of backgrounds and live in a wide array of governmental systems. The diversity of political party preferences will become even more apparent as the Church grows. The vast majority of members who are Republicans eventually will be replaced by a greater diversity in political preferences among members. Some members will not see it in their own small Utah, Idaho, or Arizona towns. Still others who live in affluent suburbs of large cities or in similarly homogeneous areas such as South Chicago or the District of Columbia also may not experience much political diversity within their own ward. Nevertheless, they may and, indeed, already do bump up against it when they go on missions or move around the country or the globe.

The challenge for Church members will be handling such diversity within the Church. Let me suggest some ways to do that.

Avoid Rigid Views

Several years ago, a student I will call "Jane" wrote me an email as she was graduating from Brigham Young University. Jane had been in my American government class her first semester. I remembered her as a student who spoke out frequently at the beginning of the semester, but then became quiet. Jane explained in her email why she had done that. Until coming to BYU, she had been home-schooled by her mother, who was extremely politically conservative. Jane expressed her views in class at first because she was confident she knew the answers to questions I raised in discussion. But then she was surprised when others in the class disagreed with her. She had never experienced alternative perspectives before.

Jane was writing to me to describe how much my class and her BYU education had changed her. She wrote that she actually began an "open your mind" program to accept new ideas rather than just holding to her preconceived notions. Through this program, she had become a more tolerant person who accepted that other people really could have different political views than her own.

This experience heartened me as a teacher, but it also reminded me that her initial perspective on politics and government is not unusual. Many Church members hold a myopic view on politics, which is reinforced by their acceptance of the views of writers such as President Benson or Cleon Skousen. Those speeches and writings not only intermingled religion and

politics but implied that others who disagreed with those views were not sufficiently patriotic or faithful in the Church.

One reason people are so rigid in their political views is their association of those views with patriotism. They may define the patriot narrowly as
a person who holds particular political views. Using terminology like "true
patriot" (suggesting that others may not be "true") or associating the term
"patriot" with a particular political perspective such as "Tea Party Patriot"
links patriotism exclusively with specific political stances.

Patriotism, an allegiance to one's nation, is encouraged by Church
leaders. However, patriotism can be an obstacle for a Church that crosses
national borders if members use it to raise barriers against other members.
Elder Charles Didier of the Seventy was asked about the place of national
pride in the gospel and answered that Latter-day Saints should be proud of
their national heritage but warned that, when patriotism "comes out of these
boundaries, it is used more to create differences among people than to bring
them together."[16]

Similarly, Church members need to be careful in defining who is or is not
a faithful member when it comes to politics. Caution should be used in label-
ing others as unfaithful because their views differ from our own. This warning applies both to those on the left (who may view others as un-Christian
because they have contrasting views than them on how to care for the poor)
as well as those on the right (who may be quick to brand those on the left as
"out of harmony with the Brethren").

The liberal soul avoids that narrowness by recognizing that his or her
personal views on politics are not always shared by others, even within the
household of faith. Diversity on politics is a matter of individual background,
values, and choice. The liberal soul realizes that opposing views do not exist
because the other person has chosen evil. They appear because people simply
see the world differently.

Be Willing to Compromise

Compromise seems to be a dirty word today. Candidates rarely get elected because they promise to compromise with other public officials. Once in
office, politicians are encouraged by the extremists in political parties not to
give in to the other side.

There is little incentive for people in public office to compromise today. In
a polarized political atmosphere, compromise can lead to electoral defeat at the

---

16. I Have A Question (department), "What Should Be the Place of National
Feelings among Church Members?" *Ensign*, June 1976, 62.

hands of ideologically extreme party activists. Too often, someone who is willing to compromise is portrayed as a person willing to surrender his or her core beliefs. Compromise can even be portrayed as "making a deal with the devil."

One problem is that politics is often characterized as a debate over hard and fast values. Yet politics is more often about interests than about values. Senator Wallace F. Bennett, a Republican from Utah, once explained that "the most effective legislator is one who always keeps himself free to use his best judgment in doing all he can to see that every bill on which he works contains the best possible and fairest possible balance between the interests of the various entities that will be affected by it."[17]

Often, a political battle is over competing sets of interests. They could be business interests who want to make the largest profit possible versus labor interests who seek the best deal for workers. Or it could be gay rights advocates who want gay families to receive legal recognition and not exist outside the legitimacy of society versus conservative religious organizations who do not want homosexuality to be recognized as a socially acceptable lifestyle.

There are elements of values on both sides that must be addressed. But a failure to understand the other person's interests and concerns results in continued struggle. That continued battle is unproductive and leads to further animosity. Additionally, when one side merely pushes through a victory at the expense of the other, the battle is rarely ended; it merely continues in other forms. On the other hand, a willingness to see the other side's viewpoint could result in a compromise that recognizes each side's concerns.

See Diversity in the Church

Members of the Church do not think alike on politics. However, that may not be apparent since many Church members desire not to discuss politics in Church settings. Or they are fearful of the social consequences if they express their views. Nevertheless, that diversity is almost always there.

As a result, other members do not see that diversity. They use Church settings to express their personal political views, primarily because they feel strongly about those views and they assume that their views are widely shared. Of course, some may not care what effect their statements have on the comfort level of others who disagree. But, probably, most do not realize that others do disagree. For most of these members, it is likely that they would not make offensive comments if they knew that those comments might drive

---

17. I Have A Question (department), Wallace F. Bennett, "What Is the Role of Compromise in Government? Is It a Good Principle Or Does It Inevitably Involve Lowering One's Standards?" *Ensign*, June 1976, 63.

someone from the Church or at least make them feel uncomfortable while there. They likely do not know of the effects because those who disagree do not speak out.

Why do those with differing views tend to say nothing? A German communications scholar, Elizabeth Noelle-Neumann, theorized the existence of a "spiral of silence" on political matters. The theory is that each of us gauges the public opinion of others about politics and adapts our public expressions accordingly. If we feel that others in a group share our views, then we freely express them. If, however, we sense that we are in a minority, then we stay silent. Noelle-Neumann discovered this phenomenon when a student came into her office one morning wearing a button endorsing a political party vying for votes in a current national campaign. However, later in the day she saw the student without the button. She asked why she had removed the button. The student replied that she could not take the hostile comments and stares she received from students who opposed that political party.[18]

A similar situation occurs in LDS Church meetings—in Relief Society, priesthood, Sunday School, and leadership meetings. An individual will make a political comment, typically criticizing or mocking Democrats or liberals or some group that is identified with the left such as gays, environmentalists, minority groups, or the poor. Another individual may chime in to add his or her own derogatory comment. A general discussion may ensue among those who feel the same way.

It is likely that one or more members in the class or meeting will disagree with these views. But he or she remains silent, not wishing to be exposed as differing with the majority and receiving the majority's social disapproval. He or she waits quietly for the discussion to pass. Some members who disagree may even decide not to attend the class in the future because of the political discussion.

Some in the group will be uncomfortable with the discussion, even if they agree with the gist of it, because they do not feel it is appropriate in that setting. Yet they will conclude it is not their place to shift the topic. They, too, will sit silently. The result will be the continuation of the discussion until those talking tire of it and decide to return to the lesson.

I have seen this scenario played out many times, and I have participated silently. At first I, too, would remain quiet and let such discussions pass. I feared not only social disapproval but also creating conflict by opposing others in the class or group. By disagreeing, I felt I would be creating contention and driving away the Spirit. Of course, the reality is that the Spirit had

---

18. Elizabeth Noelle-Neumann, *The Spiral of Silence* (Chicago: University of Chicago Press, 1984).

already left when the political discussion began. But I worried that I could not help guide the discussion back without giving offense.

More recently, I have spoken out on occasion. I have decided that I should do something. I have come to Church to be spiritually enriched, not to be politically indoctrinated. Others have the same objective. It is a shame to waste precious lesson time on political diversions, but such discussions also run the risk of offending and driving away people who come to be spiritually fed. I had that experience one Sunday many years ago when the teacher started her lesson with negative comments about political liberals. A brother I was home teaching looked disgusted and walked out. We are still in the same ward, and I know he has rarely come back to Sunday School since that lesson.

Speaking out does carry risks. It is easy to become the offender along with those who already have offended. Finding the right response, particularly when there are only a few seconds to think of one, is not easy. I have tried to respond in a gentle, respectful way, but still firmly enough that those who started the political discussion understand that it was inappropriate to begin it and that continuation of the discussion would not be useful.

One example was a priesthood meeting where the lesson was about honesty. The teacher decided to focus on dishonest politicians. He said he had in mind a certain senator from Nevada, whom he did not name, but I knew he was talking about Senator Harry Reid. I also knew he would continue down that road if he was not reminded that such remarks had no place in this lesson. I also feared that others would take advantage of that opening to express their gripes about Harry Reid, Democrats, and liberals. So I interrupted him to say that I had a great deal of respect for Harry Reid. There was silence in the room. The teacher made a face-saving joke that he might have been talking about the other senator (a Republican), but then quickly moved back to the lesson.

I had said nothing derogatory about the teacher. I had not chastised him for what he had said. Instead, I remained positive. The incipient political discussion had been nipped in the bud. Others who liked to talk politics remained silent. They realized that the moment for diversion had passed.

What were the consequences of my speaking up? Afterward, the high priest group leader thanked me for stopping the possible discussion. Later, I became friends with that teacher as we served as home teaching companions. I think it also had long-lasting consequences, since subsequent political comments were rare and priesthood meeting political discussions non-existent while I was in that high priests group.

Speaking up in meetings, particularly if done in a courteous and firm way, can have positive consequences for all. It can prevent Church members from saying things that even they might later regret saying in that place and at that time. It allows members of differing political views to feel comfortable coming to Church and joining in classes and meetings.

Some members may feel uneasy playing that role, however. They really may conclude it is not their place. Another option, then, is to go to the organization leader—elders' quorum president, Relief Society president, bishop, etc.—and express concern about the tone of the discussion. Most such leaders will recognize the inherent danger in allowing such a situation to recur. Even if one person expresses discomfort, that usually leads to some action.

A Church leader who sees a potentially offensive discussion begin should gently make comments to lead back to the assigned lesson or, if necessary, remind the teacher and the class that such discussion really is not the objective of the class or quorum and should be avoided. If a teacher persists, it is wise to meet privately with the teacher and enlist his or her support in keeping the lesson on track, avoiding inappropriate discussions, and assuring that every class member feels comfortable participating in the class.

Conclusion

Church leaders, at times, have taken steps to remind members of the existence of political diversity in Church membership. For example, in 1958, Elder Hugh B. Brown, then a member of the Quorum of the Twelve, was encouraged by President McKay to speak at the state Democratic Party convention. In 1998, Elder Marlin K. Jensen, a Democrat, was directed to accept an interview by the *Salt Lake Tribune* to discuss party politics and the need for partisan diversity among Latter-day Saints.[19]

Despite these efforts by Church leaders, individual members sometimes use Church leaders to support their contention that opposing views are antithetical to Church doctrine. In pressing a particular viewpoint, Church members often cite authority—most often a particular General Authority who has expressed that view. A president of the Church, or at least a member of the Quorum of the Twelve, is most frequently quoted since these men are sustained as prophets, seers, and revelators and would be considered the ultimate authority. A friend of mine calls this General Authority chess: "My General Authority trumps your General Authority."

This happens in politics as well. Many right-wing Church members will point to the writings of President Ezra Taft Benson as evidence that particular political views, and those parties and candidates who express such views, enjoy official sanction. Yet those writings have no such official approval. The

---

19. Prince and Wright, *David O. McKay and the Rise of Modern Mormonism*, 336; Dan Harrie, "GOP Dominance Troubles Church," *Salt Lake Tribune*, May 3, 1998, A1.

First Presidency has repeated again and again that the Church does not become involved in political matters, except in rare cases involving a few issues that its authorized spokespersons define as moral and not just political. Nor does the Church endorse candidates or political parties.

Therefore, a Church member should not assume that his or her own party affiliation has the blessing of Church leaders, while another member's party affiliation is opposed by Church leaders. Actually, Church leaders generally recognize the diversity in the Church membership on political matters. They desire that members be civil in expressing their differences. They do not expect members to change their political views to conform to their own political views or to some imaginary Church norm. Nor should members do so.

Moreover, we need to be careful not to consider those who disagree with us as evil or less worthy members of the church. Not only should we be civil and respectful, but we should possess great love toward those with whom we disagree politically. That love should not emanate from some sense of superiority, but rather, as Judge Thomas Griffith has put it, a simple "understanding that they, like us, are children of God for whom the Savior suffered, bled, died, and lives today."[20]

---

20. Thomas Griffith, "A Mormon Approach to Politics," speech at Pi Sigma Alpha banquet, Brigham Young University, April 11, 2008.

GO, AND DO THOU LIKEWISE

When the Prophet Joseph Smith ran for U.S. president in 1844, he proposed a platform that was radical for his day. He recommended that convicts be released from prisons and be told to "go thy way, and sin no more." He suggested that law breakers be given work so they could "be taught more wisdom and more virtue, and become more enlightened. Rigor and seclusion will never do as much to reform the propensities of men as reason and friendship." He also wanted Congress to free the slaves by buying them from their owners, using money raised from the sale of public lands. He urged the government to "break off the shackles from the poor black man, and hire him to labor like other human beings."[1]

Joseph Smith was a liberal soul of his day, particularly in the sense that he understood that we are all changed for the better by individual, group, and societal action. And that societal action included a role for government that was larger than simply property rights. It is no coincidence that, through running for president, he wanted to be part of government in order to accomplish those goals. The Prophet Joseph understood that the way that government treats its citizens impacts the extent to which each individual can fulfill his or her mission on this earth. To him, government was not just potentially negative, as is the view of many today, but also potentially positive. His approach was not one of getting government out of the way or getting it "off our backs," which is the objective of many people today. Rather, Joseph appreciated that government could be a positive tool for improving society.

The liberal soul today similarly wants to help all secure the blessings of prosperity. The liberal soul sees all as equal brothers and sisters and respects them regardless of earthly differences. The liberal soul is open to new ideas. He or she celebrates progress and therefore is forward- and future-thinking rather than preferring the nostalgia of a supposedly better past.

The liberal soul understands that society uses government to accomplish certain collective ends. Therefore, liberal souls do not discount the government's

---

1. *The Prophet Joseph Smith's Views on the Powers and Policy of the Government of the United States* (Salt Lake City: Jos. Hyrum Parry & Co., 1886), 16–17.

role as a means for improving the society as a whole, as well as the lives of individuals. At the same time, liberal souls know that government is only one means for bettering society. Individual and group actions are important in fulfilling the liberal soul's aims as well.

This book is not designed to create guilt in a person who wishes to be a liberal soul but is not. Perhaps all of us fall in that category because, as Paul says, we all "come short of the glory of God" (Rom. 3:23). Rather, it is a call for all of us to be better people and a better society, and to understand that we can work singly and collectively (including through our government) to achieve that end.

This book also does not intend to dictate one acceptable application of the gospel of Jesus Christ to society and government. The marriage of LDS faith and right-wing or libertarian politics is not the sole perspective for understanding the relationship between the gospel and the role of government. The liberal soul recognizes that Church doctrine is remarkably spare on the subject of support for specific government models, not to mention an approach to specific public policies or processes. There are multiple interpretations of the gospel's intersection with government, not just one. This book's interpretation is only one.

Nevertheless, it is important that, whatever our views, our approach to politics and policymaking be driven primarily by the gospel and not the other way around. It is too easy to overlay our political views onto the gospel rather than to apply the gospel to politics. Indeed, it is tempting to make the political cause the most important element of one's faith. When that happens, extremism follows. The outcome is a gospel suited for political, not spiritual, conversion.

BYU Religion Professor Stephen Robinson explained the dangers of reversing that approach. "On a strait and narrow path, it doesn't matter whether we fall off to the right or to the left, we are in trouble either way. It doesn't matter whether we are 'liberals' or 'conservatives,' whether we believe 'too little' or 'too much.'" He warns that it requires "discipline to embrace as gospel and to teach as gospel exactly what the Lord has revealed, no more and no less, and to avoid revising the gospel to suit ourselves."[2]

Make the Difference

At the same time, we should not be afraid to go forward and be "anxiously engaged in a good cause" (D&C 58:27). Participating in making our community better is one way we can be so engaged. President Ezra Taft Benson admonished members to do more than wait for others to act: "We

---

2. Stephen E. Robinson, "Enduring to the End," *Ensign*, October 1993, 12.

must become involved in civic affairs. As citizens of this republic, we cannot do our duty and be idle spectators."[3]

We live in a spectator society. It is easy to sit on a couch in a family room and watch things happen—revolutions that overthrow governments, protests against unpopular policies, activists in the community who make a difference in small and large ways, and elections that change public policy direction on various governmental levels. We can watch all of these events and not become involved ourselves.

I was on a subway train in Boston one evening. It happened to be primary election day in Massachusetts, and I could overhear the conversation of a group of college students about the candidates competing in the election for their party's presidential nomination. All of them expressed strong support for one candidate. Then one of them asked the others who had actually voted that day. None of them had. They were spectators. They were interested in what they were watching. They had even taken sides. But that had not propelled them to do more than just spectate.

Too many people do too much spectating. They are like football players who sit in the bleachers and complain about the game. While spectators cannot join a football game, they can go out on the field of government. Yet too often they refuse to do so in order to change the outcome. They grumble about how bad government is. They complain about policies they do not like, decisions they disagree with, or people they believe should not be in public office. Yet they fail to make the connection between their own involvement and the actual outcome of these decisions and events. They do not understand that they, too, can make a difference, and that even their effort to do so is important in channeling their frustration, giving them experience on how to make a difference, and setting a positive example for others.

The liberal soul understands his or her role in bringing about a Zion society, but also views all three levels of involvement—individual, group, and societal—as instrumental as well. Since government is ordained of God for the benefit of man, it, too, is a powerful force in achieving the type of society where all are benefited. Positive government action cannot be put aside as outside of the "proper role of government."

I have faith that our Heavenly Father will assist us in our efforts to become liberal souls. He will do so because it is our purpose on earth to become more like Christ, who was the ultimate liberal soul on this earth. After all, what is a Zion society? Actually, it is a group of liberal souls working together to bring about the better world we can achieve.

---

3. Ezra Taft Benson, *The Constitution—A Heavenly Banner*, (Salt Lake City: Deseret Book, 2008).

The Liberal Soul Shall Be "Made Fat"

The blessings of the Lord will come to those who are liberal in their approach to life and to others (Prov. 11:25). They shall be "made fat" in the sense that, by seeing the world in a positive light, they will find joy and hope rather than evil and degradation. They will look for the good in others rather than be suspicious or cynical. They will desire to give to others rather than hoard. They will extend mercy rather than insist exclusively on justice. They will desire to help others individually, but also understand that building a better world involves the efforts of groups of people as well as even whole societies. They will view government as a tool to achieve positive ends in lifting and serving and building rather than perceiving it as inherently untrustworthy and evil.

We should all be liberal souls. That should be our goal. It is, after all, why we are here.

INDEX

Also available from
GREG KOFFORD BOOKS

Common Ground—Different Opinions:
Latter-day Saints and Contemporary Issues

Edited by Justin F. White
and James E. Faulconer

Paperback, ISBN: 978-1-58958-573-7

There are many hotly debated issues about which many people disagree, and where common ground is hard to find. From evolution to environmentalism, war and peace to political partisanship, stem cell research to same-sex marriage, how we think about controversial issues affects how we interact as Latter-day Saints.

In this volume various Latter-day Saint authors address these and other issues from differing points of view. Though they differ on these tough questions, they have all found common ground in the gospel of Jesus Christ and the latter-day restoration. Their insights offer diverse points of view while demonstrating we can still love those with whom we disagree.

Praise for *Common Ground—Different Opinions*:

"[This book] provide models of faithful and diverse Latter-day Saints who remain united in the body of Christ. This collection clearly demonstrates that a variety of perspectives on a number of sensitive issues do in fact exist in the Church. . . . [T]he collection is successful in any case where it manages to give readers pause with regard to an issue they've been fond of debating, or convinces them to approach such conversations with greater charity and much more patience. It served as just such a reminder and encouragement to me, and for that reason above all, I recommend this book." — Blair Hodges, Maxwell Institute

WOMEN AT CHURCH

Women at Church: Magnifying LDS Women's Local Impact

Neylan McBaine

Paperback, ISBN: 978-1-58958-688-8

Women at Church is a practical and faithful guide to improving the way men and women work together at church. Looking at current administrative and cultural practices, the author explains why some women struggle with the gendered divisions of labor. She then examines ample real-life examples that are currently happening in local settings around the country that expand and reimagine gendered practices. Readers will understand how to evaluate possible pain points in current practices and propose solutions that continue to uphold all mandated church policies. Readers will be equipped with the tools they need to have respectful, empathetic and productive conversations about gendered practices in Church administration and culture.

Praise for *Women at Church*:

"Such a timely, faithful, and practical book! I suggest ordering this book in bulk to give to your bishopric, stake presidency, and all your local leadership to start a conversation on changing Church culture for women by letting our doctrine suggest creative local adaptations—Neylan McBaine shows the way!" — Valerie Hudson Cassler, author of *Women in Eternity, Women of Zion*

"A pivotal work replete with wisdom and insight. Neylan McBaine deftly outlines a workable programme for facilitating movement in the direction of the 'privileges and powers' promised the nascent Female Relief Society of Nauvoo." — Fiona Givens, co-author of *The God Who Weeps: How Mormonism Makes Sense of Life*

"In her timely and brilliant findings, Neylan McBaine issues a gracious invitation to rethink our assumptions about women's public Church service. Well researched, authentic, and respectful of the current Church administrative structure, McBaine shares exciting and practical ideas that address diverse needs and involve all members in the meaningful work of the Church." — Camille Fronk Olson, author of *Women of the Old Testament* and *Women of the New Testament*

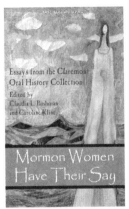

Essays from the Claremont
Oral History Collection
Edited by
Claudia L. Bushman
and Caroline Kline

Mormon Women
Have Their Say

Mormon Women Have Their Say: Essays from the Claremont Oral History Collection

Edited by Claudia L. Bushman and Caroline Kline

Paperback, ISBN: 978-1-58958-494-5

The Claremont Women's Oral History Project has collected hundreds of interviews with Mormon women of various ages, experiences, and levels of activity. These interviews record the experiences of these women in their homes and family life, their church life, and their work life, in their roles as homemakers, students, missionaries, career women, single women, converts, and disaffected members. Their stories feed into and illuminate the broader narrative of LDS history and belief, filling in a large gap in Mormon history that has often neglected the lived experiences of women. This project preserves and perpetuates their voices and memories, allowing them to say share what has too often been left unspoken. The silent majority speaks in these records.

This volume is the first to explore the riches of the collection in print. A group of young scholars and others have used the interviews to better understand what Mormonism means to these women and what women mean for Mormonism. They explore those interviews through the lenses of history, doctrine, mythology, feminist theory, personal experience, and current events to help us understand what these women have to say about their own faith and lives.

Praise for *Mormon Women Have Their Say*:

"Using a variety of analytical techniques and their own savvy, the authors connect ordinary lives with enduring themes in Latter-day Saint faith and history." --Laurel Thatcher Ulrich, author of *Well-Behaved Women Seldom Make History*

"Essential. . . . In these pages, Mormon women will find *ourselves*." --Joanna Brooks, author of *The Book of Mormon Girl: A Memoir of an American Faith*

"The varieties of women's responses to the major issues in their lives will provide many surprises for the reader, who will be struck by how many different ways there are to be a thoughtful and faithful Latter-day Saint woman." --Armand Mauss, author of *All Abraham's Children: Changing Mormon Conceptions of Race and Lineage*

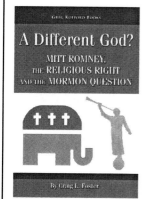

A Different God?
Mitt Romney the Religious Right and the Mormon Question

Craig L. Foster

Paperback, ISBN: 978-1-58958-117-3

In the contested terrain of American politics, nowhere is the conflict more intense, even brutal, than in the territory of public life also claimed by religion. Mitt Romney's 2007–08 presidential campaign is a textbook example.

Religious historian (and ardent Republican) Craig L. Foster revisits that campaign with an astute focus on the never-quite-contained hostility that Romney triggered among America's religious right. Although few political campaign are known for their kindness, the back-stabbing, mean-spirited attacks, eruptions of irrationalism, and downright lies exploded into one of the meanest chapters of recent American political history.

Foster readjusts rosy views of America as the tolerant, pluralistic society against the context of its lengthy, colorful, and bruising history of religious discrimination and oppression against many religious groups, among them Mormonism. Mormons are now respected and admired--although the image hasn't tilted enough to work for Romney instead of against him. Their turbulent past of suspicion, marginalization, physical violence, and being deprived of voting rights has sometimes made them, in turn, suspicious, hostile, and politically naive. How much of this pattern of mutual name-calling stems from theology and how much from theocratic ideals?

Foster appraises Romney's success and strengths—and also places where he stumbled, analyzing an intriguing pattern of "what-ifs?" of policy, personality, and positioning. But perhaps even more intriguing is the anti-Romney campaign launched by a divided and fragmenting religious right who pulled together in a rare show of unity to chill a Mormon's presidential aspirations. What does Romney's campaign and the resistance of the religious right mean for America in the twenty-first century?

In this meticulously researched, comprehensively documented, and passionately argued analysis of a still-ongoing campaign, Craig Foster poses questions that go beyond both Romney and the religious right to engage the soul of American politics.

Re-reading Job: Understanding the Ancient World's Greatest Poem

Michael Austin

Paperback, ISBN: 978-1-58958-667-3

Job is perhaps the most difficult to understand of all books in the Bible. While a cursory reading of the text seems to relay a simple story of a righteous man whose love for God was tested through life's most difficult of challenges and rewarded for his faith through those trials, a closer reading of Job presents something far more complex and challenging. The majority of the text is a work of poetry that authors and artists through the centuries have recognized as being one of--if not the--greatest poem of the ancient world.

In *Re-reading Job: Understanding the Ancient World's Greatest Poem*, author Michael Austin shows how most readers have largely misunderstood this important work of scripture and provides insights that enable us to re-read Job in a drastically new way. In doing so, he shows that the story of Job is far more than that simple story of faith, trials, and blessings that we have all come to know, but is instead a subversive and complex work of scripture meant to inspire readers to rethink all that they thought they knew about God.

Praise for *Re-reading Job*:

"In this remarkable book, Michael Austin employs his considerable skills as a commentator to shed light on the most challenging text in the entire Hebrew Bible. Without question, readers will gain a deeper appreciation for this extraordinary ancient work through Austin's learned analysis. Rereading Job signifies that Latter-day Saints are entering a new age of mature biblical scholarship. It is an exciting time, and a thrilling work." — David Bokovoy, author, *Authoring the Old Testament*

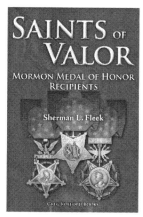

Saints of Valor: Mormon Medal of Honor Recipients

Sherman L. Fleek

Hardcover, ISBN: 978-1-58958-171-5

Since 1861 when the US Congress approved the concept of a Medal of Honor for combat valor, 3,457 individuals have received this highest military decoration that the nation can bestow. Nine of those have been Latter-day Saints. The military and personal stories of these LDS recipients are compelling, inspiring, and tragic. The men who appear in this book are tied by two common threads: the Medal of Honor and their Mormon heritage.

The purpose of this book is to highlight the valor of a special class of LDS servicemen who served and sacrificed "above and beyond the call of duty." Four of these nine Mormons gave their "last full measure" for their country, never seeing the high award they richly deserved. All four branches of the service are represented: five were Army (one was a pilot with the Army Air Forces during WWII), two Navy, and one each of the Marine Corps and Air Force. Four were military professionals who made the service their careers; five were not career-minded; three died at an early age and never married. This book captures these harrowing historical narratives from personal accounts.

War & Peace in Our Time: Mormon Perspectives

Edited by Patrick Q. Mason, J. David Pulsipher, and Richard L. Bushman

Paperback, ISBN: 978-1-58958-099-2

"This provocative and thoughtful book is sure both to infuriate and to delight. . . . The essays demonstrate that exegesis of distinctly Latter-day Saint scriptures can yield a wealth of disputation, the equal of any rabbinical quarrel or Jesuitical casuistry. This volume provides a fitting springboard for robust and lively debates within the Mormon scholarly and lay community on how to think about the pressing issues of war and peace." - ROBERT S. WOOD, Dean Emeritus, Center for Naval Warfare Studies, Chester W. Nimitz Chair Emeritus, U.S. Naval War College

"This is an extraordinary collection of essays on a topic of extraordinary importance. . . .Whatever your current opinion on the topic, this book will challenge you to reflect more deeply and thoroughly on what it means to be a disciple of Christ, the Prince of Peace, in an era of massive military budgets, lethal technologies, and widespread war." - GRANT HARDY, Professor of History and Religious Studies, University of North Carolina, Asheville, Author, *Understanding the Book of Mormon: A Reader's Guide*

"Mormons take their morality seriously. They are also patriotic. Tragically, the second trait can undermine the first. When calls for war are on the horizon, it is possible for well-intended Saints to be too sure of our selective application of scripture to contemporary matters of life and death, too sure that we can overcome evil by force, that we can control the results of military conflict, that war is the only option for patriots. Yet pacifism has its own critics. This collection of differing views by thoughtful scholars comprises a debate. Reading it may save us in the future from enacting more harm than good in the name of God, country, or presumption." - PHILIP BARLOW, Arrington Chair of Mormon History and Culture, Utah State University, Author, *Mormons and the Bible: The Place of the Latter-day Saints in American Religion*

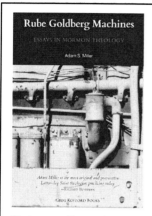

Rube Goldberg Machines:
Essays in Mormon Theology

Adam S. Miller

Paperback, ISBN: 978-1-58958-193-7

"Adam Miller is the most original and provocative Latter-day Saint theologian practicing today."

—Richard Bushman, author of *Joseph Smith: Rough Stone Rolling*

"As a stylist, Miller gives Nietzsche a run for his money. As a believer, Miller is as submissive as Augustine hearing a child's voice in the garden. Miller is a theologian of the ordinary, thinking about our ordinary beliefs in very non-ordinary ways while never insisting that the ordinary become extra-ordinary."

—James Faulconer, Richard L. Evans Chair of Religious Understanding,Brigham Young University

"Miller's language is both recognizably Mormon and startlingly original.... The whole is an essay worthy of the name, inviting the reader to try ideas, following the philosopher pilgrim's intellectual progress through tangled brambles and into broad fields, fruitful orchards, and perhaps a sacred grove or two."

—Kristine Haglund, editor of *Dialogue: A Journal of Mormon Thought*

"Miller's Rube Goldberg theology is nothing like anything done in the Mormon tradition before."

—Blake Ostler, author of the EXPLORING MORMON THOUGHT series

"The value of Miller's writings is in the modesty he both exhibits and projects onto the theological enterprise, even while showing its joyfully disruptive potential. Conventional Mormon minds may not resonate with every line of poetry and provocation—but Miller surely afflicts the comfortable, which is the theologian's highest end."

—Terryl Givens, author of *By the Hand of Mormon: The American Scripture that Launched a New World Religion*

Dead Wood and Rushing Water: Essays on Mormon Faith, Culture, and Family

Boyd Jay Petersen

Paperback, ISBN: 978-1-58958-658-1

For over a decade, Boyd Petersen has been an active voice in Mormon studies and thought. In essays that steer a course between apologetics and criticism, striving for the balance of what Eugene England once called the "radical middle," he explores various aspects of Mormon life and culture—from the Dream Mine near Salem, Utah, to the challenges that Latter-day Saints of the millennial generation face today.

Praise for *Dead Wood and Rushing Water*:

"*Dead Wood and Rushing Water* gives us a reflective, striving, wise soul ruminating on his world. In the tradition of Eugene England, Petersen examines everything in his Mormon life from the gold plates to missions to dream mines to doubt and on to Glenn Beck, Hugh Nibley, and gender. It is a book I had trouble putting down." — Richard L. Bushman, author of *Joseph Smith: Rough Stone Rolling*

"Boyd Petersen is correct when he says that Mormons have a deep hunger for personal stories—at least when they are as thoughtful and well-crafted as the ones he shares in this collection." — Jana Riess, author of *The Twible* and *Flunking Sainthood*

"Boyd Petersen invites us all to ponder anew the verities we hold, sharing in his humility, tentativeness, and cheerful confidence that our paths will converge in the end." — Terryl. L. Givens, author of *People of Paradox: A History of Mormon Culture*

Hugh Nibley:
A Consecrated Life

Boyd Jay Petersen

Hardcover, ISBN: 978-1-58958-019-0

Winner of the Mormon History Association's Best Biography Award

As one of the LDS Church's most widely recognized scholars, Hugh Nibley is both an icon and an enigma. Through complete access to Nibley's correspondence, journals, notes, and papers, Petersen has painted a portrait that reveals the man behind the legend.

Starting with a foreword written by Zina Nibley Petersen and finishing with appendices that include some of the best of Nibley's personal correspondence, the biography reveals aspects of the tapestry of the life of one who has truly consecrated his life to the service of the Lord.

Praise for *A Consecrated Life*:

"Hugh Nibley is generally touted as one of Mormonism's greatest minds and perhaps its most prolific scholarly apologist. Just as hefty as some of Nibley's largest tomes, this authorized biography is delightfully accessible and full of the scholar's delicious wordplay and wit, not to mention some astonishing war stories and insights into Nibley's phenomenal acquisition of languages. Introduced by a personable foreword from the author's wife (who is Nibley's daughter), the book is written with enthusiasm, respect and insight. . . . On the whole, Petersen is a careful scholar who provides helpful historical context. . . . This project is far from hagiography. It fills an important gap in LDS history and will appeal to a wide Mormon audience."
  —Publishers Weekly

"Well written and thoroughly researched, Petersen's biography is a must-have for anyone struggling to reconcile faith and reason."
  —Greg Taggart, Association for Mormon Letters

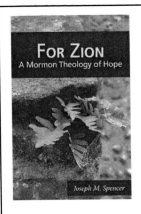

For Zion:
A Mormon Theology of Hope

Joseph M. Spencer

Paperback, ISBN: 978-1-58958-568-3

What is hope? What is Zion? And what does it mean to hope for Zion? In this insightful book, Joseph Spencer explores these questions through the scriptures of two continents separated by nearly two millennia. In the first half, Spencer engages in a rich study of Paul's letter to the Roman to better understand how the apostle understood hope and what it means to have it. In the second half of the book, Spencer jumps to the early years of the Restoration and the various revelations on consecration to understand how Latter-day Saints are expected to strive for Zion. Between these halves is an interlude examining the hoped-for Zion that both thrived in the Book of Mormon and was hoped to be established again.

Praise for *For Zion*:

"Joseph Spencer is one of the most astute readers of sacred texts working in Mormon Studies. Blending theological savvy, historical grounding, and sensitive readings of scripture, he has produced an original and compelling case for consecration and the life of discipleship." — Terryl Givens, author, *Wrestling the Angel: The Foundations of Mormon Thought*

"*For Zion: A Mormon Theology of Hope* is more than a theological reflection. It also consists of able textual exegesis, historical contextualization, and philosophic exploration. Spencer's careful readings of Paul's focus on hope in Romans and on Joseph Smith's development of consecration in his early revelations, linking them as he does with the Book of Mormon, have provided an intriguing, intertextual avenue for understanding what true stewardship should be for us—now and in the future. As such he has set a new benchmark for solid, innovative Latter-day Saint scholarship that is at once provocative and challenging." — Eric D. Huntsman, author, *The Miracles of Jesus*

CPSIA information can be obtained at www.ICGtesting.com
Printed in the USA
BVOW02s0021240316

441446BV00012B/231/P